An Introduction to the
FAMILY AND MEDICAL LEAVE ACT
for Public Employers

DIANE M. JUFFRAS

The School of Government at the University of North Carolina at Chapel Hill works to improve the lives of North Carolinians by engaging in practical scholarship that helps public officials and citizens understand and improve state and local government. Established in 1931 as the Institute of Government, the School provides educational, advisory, and research services for state and local governments. The School of Government is also home to a nationally ranked Master of Public Administration program, the North Carolina Judicial College, and specialized centers focused on community and economic development, information technology, and environmental finance.

As the largest university-based local government training, advisory, and research organization in the United States, the School of Government offers up to 200 courses, webinars, and specialized conferences for more than 12,000 public officials each year. In addition, faculty members annually publish approximately 50 books, manuals, reports, articles, bulletins, and other print and online content related to state and local government. The School also produces the *Daily Bulletin Online* each day the General Assembly is in session, reporting on activities for members of the legislature and others who need to follow the course of legislation.

Operating support for the School of Government's programs and activities comes from many sources, including state appropriations, local government membership dues, private contributions, publication sales, course fees, and service contracts.

Visit sog.unc.edu or call 919.966.5381 for more information on the School's courses, publications, programs, and services.

Aimee N. Wall, DEAN
Jeffrey B. Welty, SENIOR ASSOCIATE DEAN FOR FACULTY AFFAIRS
Anita R. Brown-Graham, ASSOCIATE DEAN FOR STRATEGIC INITIATIVES
Willow S. Jacobson, ASSOCIATE DEAN FOR GRADUATE STUDIES
Kara A. Millonzi, ASSOCIATE DEAN FOR RESEARCH AND INNOVATION
Lauren G. Partin, SENIOR ASSOCIATE DEAN FOR ADMINISTRATION
Sonja Matanovic, ASSOCIATE DEAN FOR STRATEGIC COMMUNICATIONS
Jen Willis, ASSOCIATE DEAN FOR ADVANCEMENT AND PARTNERSHIPS

FACULTY

Whitney Afonso	Kimalee Cottrell Dickerson	Adam Lovelady	Meredith Smith
Gregory S. Allison	Phil Dixon, Jr.	James M. Markham	Michael Smith
Lydian Altman	Belal Elrahal	Christopher B. McLaughlin	Daniel Spiegel
Rebecca Badgett	Rebecca L. Fisher-Gabbard	Jill D. Moore	Carl W. Stenberg III
Maureen Berner	Jacquelyn Greene	Jonathan Q. Morgan	John B. Stephens
Kirk Boone	Timothy Heinle	Ricardo S. Morse	Elliot Stoller
Mark F. Botts	Margaret F. Henderson	C. Tyler Mulligan	Charles Szypszak
Brittany LaDawn Bromell	Cheryl Daniels Howell	Kimberly L. Nelson	Shannon H. Tufts
Melanie Y. Crenshaw	Joseph L. Hyde	Kristi A. Nickodem	Emily Turner
Crista M. Cuccaro	James L. Joyce	Obed Pasha	Amy Wade
Leisha DeHart-Davis	Robert P. Joyce	William C. Rivenbark	Richard B. Whisnant
Shea Riggsbee Denning	Diane M. Juffras	John Rubin	Teshanee T. Williams
Sara DePasquale	Kirsten Leloudis	Jessica Smith	Kristina M. Wilson

Cover design by Kit Sweeney
Text design and composition by Kit Sweeney

Cover illustration based on art by ngupakarti–stock.adobe.com; Simple Line–stock.adobe.com; Ali–stock.adobe.com

Printed in the United States of America
28 27 26 25 24   1 2 3 4 5
ISBN 978-1-64238-101-6

Summary Contents

Contents

Chapter 3

Measuring FMLA Leave 33

Chapter 4

Compensation and Benefits During FMLA Leave 45

Chapter 5

How FMLA Leave Gets Started and How It Is Administered ... 57

Chapter 6

The Return to Work After FMLA Leave

Chapter 7

Limitations on an Employee's Right to Reinstatement: Termination During and at the Conclusion of FMLA Leave

Chapter 8

Denying Reinstatement to Key Employees

Chapter 9
Military FMLA: Qualifying Exigency Leave and Military Caregiver Leave

APPENDIXES

Appendix A
United States Department of Labor Family and Medical Leave Act Forms

Appendix B

A Comprehensive Discussion of Intermittent and Reduced Schedule FMLA Leave

Appendix C

The Difference Between a Serious Health Condition Under the FMLA and a Disability Under the Americans with Disabilities Act

Chapter 1

Introduction

In 2023, the federal Family and Medical Leave Act of 1993 (FMLA) turned thirty years old. The FMLA has been amended several times since 1993, but its fundamental premise and the fundamental rules governing its use have remained the same. Thirty years, however, have given us numerous cases interpreting the nuances of the act—from federal district courts (trial courts) and courts of appeals—as well as a collection of opinion letters from the U.S. Department of Labor (DOL), the agency charged with implementation and enforcement of the FMLA. The year 2024 also marks my twenty-third anniversary with the University of North Carolina at Chapel Hill School of Government. During that time, I have worked through some thorny FMLA issues with North Carolina local governments, community colleges, and state agencies. Those discussions inform this book throughout.

While this book explains the basic framework of the FMLA, it also discusses the more difficult problems it presents to North Carolina public employers. Some are issues that have arisen repeatedly over time, while others reflect questions made newly urgent by the increasing pace of workplace change.

Many people, employers and employees alike, find the FMLA frustrating. To understand one section, you must cross-reference and understand another, and sometimes yet another. The choices Congress made do not always seem logical. To employers, the FMLA's requirements seem overly generous, slanted in favor of employees to the detriment of the organizations for which they work. To employees, the FMLA never seems to go far enough to meet their needs. There is no surprise in that because the FMLA is a balancing act—a tightrope, if you will—that provides job security in those situations for which most employees need time off at some point in their careers, while limiting the amount of time that an employer must operate short-staffed. This is, indeed, what the very first section of the FMLA says in subsection (b):

> It is the purpose of this Act—
> (1) to balance the demands of the workplace with the needs of families, to promote the stability and economic security of families, and to promote national interests in preserving family integrity;

(2) to entitle employees to take reasonable leave for medical reasons, for the birth or adoption of a child, and for the care of a child, spouse, or parent who has a serious health condition; [and]

(3) to accomplish the purposes described in paragraphs (1) and (2) in a manner that accommodates the legitimate interests of employers . . . .[1]

Employers and employees who keep these purposes in mind may find it easier to navigate the FMLA.

Overview of the FMLA

The best summary of the FMLA's provisions is found in the first section of the U.S. DOL's FMLA regulations. It is set forth below with minor editing and formatting to make for easier reading.

(a) The Family and Medical Leave Act of 1993 . . . allows *eligible employees* of a *covered employer* to take *job-protected, unpaid leave,* or to substitute appropriate paid leave if the employee has earned or accrued it, *for up to a total of 12 workweeks in any 12 months* because of

[1] the *birth of a child* and to care for the newborn child, because of the *placement of a child* with the employee for adoption or foster care,

[2] because the employee is needed to care for a family member (child, spouse, or parent) with a serious health condition,

[3] because the *employee's own serious health* condition makes the employee unable to perform the functions of his or her job, or

[4] because of any *qualifying exigency* arising out of the fact that the employee's spouse, son, daughter, or parent is a *military member* on active duty or call to covered active duty status . . . .

[5] In addition, the employee may take [such leave for] up to a total of 26 workweeks in a single 12-month period to *care for a covered servicemember with a serious injury or illness.* In certain cases, FMLA leave may be taken on an intermittent basis rather than all at once, or the employee may work a part-time schedule.

(b) An employee on FMLA leave is also entitled to have health benefits maintained while on leave as if the employee had continued to work instead of taking the leave. If an employee was paying all or part of the premium payments prior to leave, the employee would continue to pay his or her share during the leave period. The employer may recover its share only if the employee does not return to work for a reason other than the serious health condition of the employee or the employee's

---

1. 29 U.S.C. § 2601(b).

covered family member, the serious injury or illness of a covered ser-vicemember, or another reason beyond the employee's control.

(c) *An employee generally has a right to return to the same position or an equivalent position* with equivalent pay, benefits, and working conditions at the conclusion of the leave. The taking of FMLA leave cannot result in the loss of any benefit that accrued prior to the start of the leave.

(d) The employer generally has a right to advance notice from the employee. In addition, the employer may require an employee to submit certification to substantiate that the leave is due to the serious health condition of the employee or the employee's covered family member, due to the serious injury or illness of a covered servicemember, or because of a qualifying exigency. Failure to comply with these requirements may result in a delay in the start of FMLA leave. Pursuant to a uniformly applied policy, the employer may also require that an employee present a certification of fitness to return to work when the absence was caused by the employee's serious health condition. The employer may delay restoring the employee to employment without such certificate relating to the health condition which caused the employee's absence.[2]

This book will refer to leave taken for reasons 1–3 (birth or placement of a child, family member's health condition, employee's health condition) as *FMLA leave* or *original FMLA leave* and leave taken for reasons 4–5 (qualified exigency leave and need to care for an ill or injured military servicemember) as *military FMLA leave*. Military FMLA leave is discussed separately from original FMLA leave in Chapter 9.

Administration and Enforcement of the FMLA

Administration

The FMLA gives the United States Department of Labor the authority to administer and enforce the FMLA. To that end, DOL issued initial regulations to implement the FMLA in 1993 and 1995. It subsequently made substantive and organizational changes to the regulations in 2008 based on DOL's and the public's experiences with the FMLA since its inception. At the same time, it incorporated new rules applicable to military FMLA leave after Congress amended the FMLA to add both qualified exigency leave and military caregiver leave, issuing a final set of military FMLA regulations in 2013. In 2015, it amended the definition of the term *spouse* in light of the U.S. Supreme Court's recognition of same-sex marriage in the case

---

2. 29 C.F.R. § 825.100 (emphasis added) (citations omitted) (numbers in paragraph (a) added).

Obergefell v. Hodges.[3] Congress amended the FMLA in March 2020 in the Families First Coronavirus Response Act, at the outset of the COVID 19 pandemic, and DOL followed the next month with regulations. These provisions and regulations were time-limited and have expired, so they are not discussed in this book.

Enforcement

DOL's Wage and Hour Division enforces the FMLA. It does so primarily through the investigation of complaints filed by individual employees. If Wage and Hour Division investigators find that an employer has violated the FMLA, the matter is usually settled through an agreement by the employer to change its practices and to pay a penalty. If the employer contests the finding of a violation, DOL may go to federal district court to compel the employer to comply.

In addition to DOL's enforcement actions, employees may bring a lawsuit against their employer for FMLA violations. In general, violations of the FMLA involve

- interfering with, restraining, or denying the exercise of (or attempts to exercise) any rights provided by the FMLA (an "interference" claim), or
- discharging or in any other way discriminating against any person (whether or not an employee) for opposing or complaining about any unlawful practice under the FMLA (a "retaliation" claim).[4]

Interference would include not only refusing to authorize FMLA leave but also discouraging an employee from using FMLA leave.[5] To prevail on an interference claim, an employee must show that they suffered a loss of some kind as a result of the interference.[6] Retaliation would include using the taking of FMLA leave as a negative factor in employment actions, such as dismissal or lesser disciplinary actions, as well as in decisions about hiring and promotions. Retaliation would also include counting FMLA leave as an absence under a no-fault attendance policy.[7]

Claims of both interference and retaliation may be proven by direct evidence, but employees more frequently try to prove their cases using indirect evidence through the *McDonnell Douglas* burden-shifting framework used in Title VII discrimination cases. This means that once an employee has established a prima facie case of either interference or retaliation, the burden shifts to the employer to provide a legitimate, nonretaliatory reason for the adverse action. Once the employer

---

3. *See generally* Obergefell v. Hodges, 576 U.S. 644 (2015).
4. 29 U.S.C. § 2615(a)(1); 29 C.F.R. § 825.220(a)(1)–(2).
5. 29 C.F.R. § 825.220(b).
6. *See* Hannah P. v. Haines, 80 F.4th 236, 244 (4th Cir. 2023); Ragsdale v. Wolverine World Wide, Inc., 535 U.S. 81, 82, 89 (2002) (U.S. DOL regulation was inconsistent with FMLA and exceeded DOL authority where it provided that employer's failure to inform employee that twelve weeks of such absence would count against her twelve-week FMLA leave entitled employee to additional twelve weeks of FMLA leave following a thirty-week leave of absence).
7. 29 C.F.R. § 825.220(c). *See* 29 U.S.C. § 2615(a)(2).

has done so, the burden shifts back to the employee to show that the employer's proffered reason is merely a pretext.[8]

In discussing FMLA cases, this book will refer to interference and retaliation claims. Understanding the difference, however, is not necessary for a working understanding of the practical aspects of the FMLA on which the book focuses.

Overview of the Book

This book is divided into nine chapters (including this one) and has three appendixes.

Chapter 2 addresses the most basic questions about the FMLA: who is covered by this statute and who is entitled to leave. These questions are more complicated than they might seem. All public employers are covered by the FMLA, but not all employees of public employers are eligible for FMLA leave. Chapter 2 also looks closely at the terms *serious health condition, spouse, child*, and *parent*—all of which have precise meanings defined in the text of the FMLA. These seemingly simple concepts are quite complex. A serious health condition, for example, is one that makes an employee unable to perform their job duties for a period of at least three days and requires a visit and supervision by a health care provider. Many common conditions that may keep an employee out of work for three or more days do not require medical assessment or treatment, and so do not bring FMLA leave into play because they do not qualify as serious health conditions. *Serious health condition* should not be confused with *disability*, which is a term of art with a very different meaning under the Americans with Disabilities Act (ADA). In some cases, however, a serious health condition may also constitute a disability under the ADA.

One might be forgiven for thinking that *parent* and *child*, at least, have commonly understood meanings. But when it drafted the FMLA, Congress realized that family relationships now take many different shapes. It chose to allow FMLA leave to be taken for relationships akin to that of a parent—people standing *in loco parentis* to a child—but not for grandparents, grandchildren, or siblings, although most Americans would consider them to be immediate and close family members. And while the FMLA allows leave to care for a minor child with a serious

---

8. For retaliation cases, see *Sawyer v. Tidelands Health ASC, LLC*, 2023 WL 4026089, at *6–7 (4th Cir. 2023) (finding that employer's proffered reason for terminating employee was not pretextual); *Sharif v. United Airlines, Inc.*, 841 F.3d 199, 203 (4th Cir. 2016) (same); and *Adams v. Anne Arundel County Public Schools*, 789 F.3d 422, 429 (4th Cir. 2015) (school board did not take any adverse action against principal). For interference cases, see *Hannah P* at 246 (employee's nonselection for permanent position was not caused by employer's failure to notify employee of right to take FMLA leave but because of legitimate, nondiscriminatory reason); *Roberts v. Gestamp West Virginia, LLC*, 45 F.4th 726, 732 (4th Cir. 2022) (affirming grant of summary judgment in favor of employer where employee did not follow employer's FMLA-notice policy); and *Fry v. Rand Construction Corporation*, 964 F.3d 239, 246 (4th Cir. 2020) (employee failed to present sufficient evidence to find that employer's justification for the termination was false and merely a pretext for retaliation).

health condition, that right does not extend to caring for adult children except in certain situations.

Chapter 2 also discusses what it means to "care for" a family member. Like so many other terms used in the FMLA, "to care for" has a particular meaning and is more expansive than most people realize. Caring for a spouse, parent, or child can mean helping to feed and bathe the family member, of course, but it can also mean simply being present and providing psychological comfort, even while the family member is taking a trip.

Chapter 3 discusses the options for measuring the twelve-week FMLA entitlement (the "FMLA year") and the ways to measure individual instances of leave. FMLA leave does not have to be for a consecutive twelve-week period or in any solid block of time. It is only to be granted for the actual amount of time off from work for which the employee has a documented need. Some medical conditions are chronic or episodic and neither interfere with an employee's ability to work continuously nor require the care of a family member all the time. Treatments for some conditions occur periodically (chemotherapy, for example). Because of this, FMLA leave may be taken on an intermittent basis or on a reduced leave schedule. When, for example, is it appropriate to record FMLA leave in hours rather than in weeks? How do you measure FMLA-leave increments for employees who work a fluctuating schedule? Does a paid holiday that occurs while an employee is on FMLA leave count against the leave entitlement? Many issues lurk behind the simple statement that an employee is entitled to a total of twelve weeks of job-protected leave each year.

Chapter 4 covers the ways to handle compensation and benefits during FMLA leave. FMLA leave is unpaid leave, but an employee's accrued paid leave may be used simultaneously with FMLA leave (thus turning FMLA leave into paid leave). Chapter 4 considers the various permutations of substituting paid leave for unpaid leave, including accrued sick leave, vacation and personal leave, and accrued "comp time" (compensatory time off under the Fair Labor Standards Act). It also discusses the rules governing the running of FMLA leave alongside workers' compensation leave and the payment of short-term disability benefits.

Chapter 4 also looks at the treatment of employee benefits during FMLA leave. FMLA leave, unlike other unpaid leaves of absence, requires employers to continue making their contributions toward the cost of the employee's health insurance premium. Employees must also continue to make their premium contributions. This is not complicated when an employee uses accrued paid leave at the same time as FMLA leave. But sometimes employees have no accrued paid leave available. The regulations spell out how to assess employees on FMLA leave for their contributions, how employers may discontinue employees' health insurance when they fail to make their contributions while on leave, and when an employer's obligation to contribute its share of premium contributions ceases. Employers need a working knowledge of these rules, both to explain to employees the consequences of failing to pay their share of premiums in a timely manner and to take action to protect their own financial interests when warranted.

Chapter 5 could be called the "FMLA paperwork" chapter, since that is how many people refer to the notices employers must give employees about their opportunity to take FMLA leave and their rights and responsibilities while on FMLA leave. These notices must be given at specific times and in a specific order: the Notice of Eligibility, the Notice of Rights and Responsibilities, and the Designation Notice. The content and timing of these notices, as well as the reasons for them, are discussed in this chapter. These are employer responsibilities, but Chapter 5 begins by looking at the employee's responsibility to give the employer notice of the need for FMLA leave. Does an employee have to say, "I want to take FMLA leave"? The answer to that question is no. How, then, is an employer to know that an employee needs FMLA leave?

An employee's obligations extend beyond giving the initial notice. When an employee requests leave for their own serious health condition or that of a family member, the employer has the right to know a serious health condition actually exists. An employer therefore has the option to request a medical certification from the employee or family member's health care provider. Chapter 5 details what information may and may not be asked on a medical certification, what follow-up information the employer may require, and timelines the employee must meet. Chapter 5 also discusses how to protect the confidentiality of an employee's FMLA medical information.

In Chapter 6, the book reaches the conclusion of FMLA leave: an employee's return to work to the same or an equivalent position. Part of that is clear—the same position is the one that the employee held before going on FMLA leave—but what makes a different position an *equivalent* position is less obvious. Chapter 6 discusses the regulations and interpretive case law from the courts that expand on the meaning of this requirement. The chapter also addresses whether an employer can impose any prerequisites on an employee's return to work, such as licensures or fitness-for-duty certifications. Employers often ask what happens if they are forced to make a reduction-in-force or reorganization while an employee is on FMLA leave. Does FMLA leave protect an employee from layoffs? The chapter considers this issue before concluding with a look at an employer's responsibilities when an employee is unable to return to work after the conclusion of twelve weeks of leave.

Chapter 7 considers instances where an employer may refuse to reinstate an employee and may even dismiss an employee during FMLA leave. It sometimes surprises both employers and employees to learn that the FMLA is not a shield against an employee's performance issues or misconduct. If discipline or discharge was in the works before an employee began FMLA leave, the process may continue. If an employee would have been disciplined or discharged for the same reasons when not on FMLA leave, the employer may take action against the employee *during FMLA leave.* This is also true when the employer discovers a previous performance or conduct issue only after the employee has begun leave. Chapter 7 also discusses the measures an employer may take when an employee on FMLA leave fails to follow the employer's absence policies or when an employer suspects that an employee is using FMLA leave fraudulently.

Chapter 8 discusses employer options in the case of FMLA leave taken by a "key employee"—that is, an employee whose salary is within the highest 10 percent of all the employer's employees. Under the key-employee exception, an employer does not have to reinstate a key employee when reinstatement will cause "substantial and grievous economic injury" to the organization. It does not mean, however, that a key employee may be denied FMLA leave. "Substantial and grievous economic injury" is a high standard to meet, so this exception is one that many employers will not be able to use. Even when an employer can meet the grievous-harm standard, it must be sure to carefully follow the rules governing identification and notification of the key employee.

Chapter 9 is devoted to the rules applicable to military FMLA leave. There are two forms of military FMLA leave: qualified exigency leave and military caregiver leave. Both draw on original FMLA leave but also differ from it in some crucial respects. Qualified exigency leave is available to an employee whose spouse, child, or parent is a member of the armed forces or reserves and who is being either deployed to a foreign country or called to active duty in support of a contingency operation. Military caregiver leave is available to an employee whose spouse, child, parent, or next of kin is a military member or veteran who has been injured or has suffered an illness in the line of duty. Qualified exigency leave is another reason for which an employee may take the annual twelve-week entitlement to FMLA leave. It is not an additional entitlement. Military caregiver leave, on the other hand, is an additional entitlement of job-protected leave. Eligible employees may take up to twenty-six weeks of military caregiver leave, which is measured separately from original FMLA's twelve-week "FMLA year." To say that this is confusing to apply is probably an understatement. Chapter 9 discusses the family definitions applicable to military FMLA leave, the definitions related to the kinds of applicable military service, the meaning of *serious illness or injury* for the purposes of military caregiver leave, how to measure both qualified exigency and military caregiver leave, and how to coordinate them with original FMLA leave.

Appendix A collects all of the U.S. DOL's forms for both original and military FMLA leave. Appendix B is a comprehensive discussion of reduced schedule and intermittent FMLA leave. Reduced schedule and intermittent FMLA leave are discussed throughout this book as each chapter's subject matter affects them. But readers may find helpful a unified discussion of reduced schedule and intermittent FMLA leave that gathers in one place the material covered here and there throughout the book. Appendix C contains a brief discussion of the difference between the FMLA and the ADA.

Chapter 2

The FMLA Entitlement: Who Gets to Take FMLA Leave and for Which Reasons

This chapter defines the basic benefits to which certain employees are entitled under the FMLA. Those benefits start with the right of an eligible employee to take up to twelve weeks of leave each year when the employee is unable to work because of their own serious health condition, because the employee is needed to care for a family member with a serious health condition, or because a new child has joined the employee's family. Employees are entitled to FMLA leave only if they work for an employer covered by the act and they have worked for that employer for a specified minimum amount of time. And not every health issue qualifies as a serious health condition, nor may an employee take FMLA leave to care for every relative. This chapter looks first at which employers are covered by the FMLA, and second, at the length-of-service requirements employees must meet to be eligible for FMLA leave. It then discusses the meaning of the term *serious health condition*, a mastery of which is necessary to administer the FMLA correctly. Finally, the chapter considers how the FMLA defines the terms *spouse, son, daughter*, and *parent*, which are the only familial relationships for which FMLA leave is allowed.

Covered Employers and Eligible Employees

In the private sector, the FMLA applies to any employer who has fifty or more employees.[1] In contrast, the FMLA applies to *all* public employers, regardless of

---

1. 29 U.S.C. § 2611(4)(A)(i).

size.[2] But not all employees who work for a covered employer are automatically eligible for FMLA leave. To be eligible for FMLA leave, an employee must

- have a total of at least twelve months of service with the employer, although the twelve months need not be consecutive;
- have worked at least 1,250 hours during the last twelve (consecutive) months; and
- work at a worksite that has at least fifty employees within a seventy-five-mile radius.[3]

This means that some North Carolina local government employers will be covered by the FMLA but will not have any employees eligible for FMLA leave. That is, those with fewer than fifty employees will be covered employers, but none of the employees in a unit of local government that has fewer than fifty employees will be eligible to take FMLA leave. Nevertheless, even employers with fewer than fifty employees and no eligible employees must comply with the U.S. Department of Labor (DOL) regulation that requires every covered employer to post and keep posted on its premises, in conspicuous places where employees are employed, *whether or not it has any "eligible" employees,* "a notice explaining the Act's provisions and providing information concerning the procedures for filing complaints of violations of the Act with the Wage and Hour Division."[4]

There is a model notice published by DOL that includes information about eligibility requirements, but the eligibility information is buried in the middle of a dense document.[5] Employers with fewer than fifty employees should consider highlighting information about eligibility in an adjacent posting so that employees do not form the mistaken impression that they are entitled to leave under the FMLA.

Note that a local government employer with fewer than fifty employees may choose voluntarily to *adopt* a policy extending leave to its employees under the same terms as provided by the FMLA. This will be a local policy, however, and will not be subject to the oversight or enforcement of DOL.

---

2. *Id.* § 2611(4)(A)(iii) (cross-referencing *id.* § 203(x)). *See* 29 C.F.R. § 825.104(a).

3. 29 C.F.R. § 825.111.

4. *Id.* § 825.300(a)(1)–(2).

5. The model notice may be found at *Family and Medical Leave Act (FMLA) Poster,* U.S. Dept. of Labor, https://www.dol.gov/sites/dolgov/files/WHD/legacy/files/fmlaen.pdf (revised Apr. 2023).

Reasons for Which FMLA Leave Must Be Granted

Employers are sometimes confronted by a dizzying array of FMLA requests. One employee wants FMLA leave to help a daughter who is having a baby. Another employee wants FMLA leave to care for a beloved aunt who is terminally ill. A third employee wants FMLA leave for cosmetic surgery. An employee's right to FMLA leave is not automatic, however. Only certain circumstances give rise to a right to FMLA leave and its corresponding guarantees of job protection and continued health insurance coverage. Here are the four reasons for which FMLA leave must be granted:

1. the birth of a child;
2. the adoption of a child or placement of a child with the employee for foster care;
3. the employee's own serious health condition, when the condition makes the employee unable to perform the job; and
4. the serious health condition of an employee's spouse, child, or parent, when the employee is needed to help care for that person.[6]

The first two reasons, involving the addition of a child to an employee's family, are relatively straightforward. Both parents are entitled to twelve weeks of FMLA leave following the birth or adoption of a healthy child or placement of a healthy child for foster care unless they work for the same employer. The FMLA regulations expressly recognize this reason for leave as one provided so that the parents and child may bond.[7] This form of FMLA leave is separate from FMLA leave taken to care for the serious health condition of an employee's child. FMLA leave for the birth, adoption, or foster care placement of a child is discussed in the next part of this section.

The second two qualifying reasons for leave are more complex due to the FMLA's definitions of a serious health condition and of the relationships of spouse, child, and parent. The remainder of the chapter is devoted to a discussion of those terms as they apply to FMLA leave.

Birth, Adoption, or Foster Care Placement

The basic rules governing FMLA leave for the birth or adoption of an employee's child, or the foster care placement of a child with an employee, are as follows. First, if the parents work for different employers, each parent is entitled to twelve weeks of leave to bond with the child. The leave may be taken at any time within the twelve-month period following the date of birth or the date of placement of a child with the employee.[8] The leave must be taken in a continuous block of time

---

6. 29 C.F.R. § 825.112. Two additional reasons, leave to deal with military exigencies and military caregiver leave, are discussed separately in Chapter 9, *Military FMLA*.

7. 29 C.F.R. § 825.120(a)(2).

8. *Id.* §§ 825.120(a)(2), .121(a)(2).

unless the employer agrees to allow the employee to take leave on an intermittent or reduced schedule, in which case the leave must still be completed within the twelve-month period following the child's birth or placement with the employee. When an employer agrees to either an intermittent or reduced schedule leave, it has the right to transfer the employee to another position or to modify the employee's position to better accommodate workplace needs while the employee is on the leave. At the end of the leave, the employer must return the employee to the same or an equivalent position.[9]

Sometimes, however, both parents work for the same employer. That is not uncommon in North Carolina local government. What happens then? Do the new parents each get twelve weeks of FMLA leave, for a total of twenty-four weeks of bonding time? Consider the following scenario:

> *Kathy and Ron, a married couple, both work for Paradise County. Kathy becomes pregnant. Her pregnancy is uneventful and the baby arrives on her due date, August 15. The prospective parents had initially planned to take their FMLA leave at the same time, imagining a blissful twelve weeks in which the three of them, Mom, Dad and Baby, would be home together. But after exploring the costs of daycare, they decide to take their FMLA leave sequentially to save money: Kathy for the first twelve weeks, Ron for the second twelve weeks. When they go to HR six weeks before the baby's due date to formalize their plans, they are crushed to learn that the FMLA allows married couples working for the same employer to take only a combined twelve weeks of leave for the birth of a child. They reluctantly decide to have Kathy take eight weeks of FMLA leave and for Ron to follow with four weeks of FMLA leave.*

That's right. When a married couple, opposite-sex or same-sex, has a baby, each parent is entitled to twelve weeks of FMLA leave to bond with the baby if the parents work for different employers. But if both parents work for the same city, county, or state agency, they are only entitled to twelve weeks between them. This is true even if the parents work in different departments within the same unit of government. The same rule applies to married couples adopting a child or becoming foster parents. When parents working for the same employer split the twelve weeks between them, each parent retains the balance of that parent's *individual* twelve-week annual allotment of FMLA leave to use for other purposes.[10] So in the scenario above, Kathy will still have four weeks of FMLA leave and Ron will have eight weeks of FMLA leave, which each may use for their own or a family member's serious health condition.

---

9. *See id.* § 825.120(b), .212(b).
10. *See id.* § 825.120(a)(3).

What if Kathy and Ron were an unmarried couple, living together and having a baby? The answer in this case, as illogical and as unfair as it may seem, is that even though they work for the same employer, each would get twelve weeks of FMLA leave for the birth of their child. This result turns on the language used in the statute and the regulations. The text of the FMLA says,

> In any case in which a *husband and wife* entitled to leave under subsection (a) [that is, for the birth, adoption, or foster care placement of a child] are employed by the same employer, the aggregate number of workweeks of leave to which both may be entitled may be limited to 12 workweeks during any 12-month period . . . .[11]

The FMLA regulations explain,

> *Spouses* who are eligible for FMLA leave and are employed by the same covered employer may be limited to a combined total of 12 weeks of leave during any 12-month period if the leave is taken for birth of the employee's son or daughter or to care for the child after birth, for placement of a son or daughter with the employee for adoption or foster care or to care for the child after placement . . . .[12]

The regulations define *spouse* as

> the other person with whom an individual entered into marriage as defined or recognized under state law for purposes of marriage in the State in which the marriage was entered into . . . . This definition includes an individual in a same-sex or common law marriage . . . .[13]

All fifty states recognize same-sex marriage, but some states—including North Carolina—do not recognize common-law marriage. This means that Kathy and Ron would be entitled to double the amount of FMLA leave to bond with their child (a total of twenty-four weeks) if they were not married than they would be as a married couple.

This limitation on parents who work for the same employer does not apply when a baby or a newly adopted or newly placed child has a serious health condition. In that situation, *each* parent is entitled to a full twelve weeks of FMLA to care for the child, regardless of their marital status or of whether they work for the same employer—unless, of course, either parent has already used some of that twelve-week entitlement for other qualifying reasons during that FMLA year.[14]

---

11. 29 U.S.C. § 2612(f)(1)(A) (emphasis added).
12. 29 C.F.R. § 825.120(a)(3) (emphasis added).
13. *Id.* § 825.102 (s.v. "spouse").
14. *See id.* §§ 825.120(a)(6), .121(a)(4).

Circumstances Preceding Birth or Placement of a Child

While the leave afforded biological, adoptive, and foster parents for bonding is the same, there are some differences in the use of FMLA for circumstances that precede the arrival of the child. For example, the regulations expressly allow pregnant women to use FMLA leave for prenatal check-ups and in circumstances where they are unable to work because of their pregnancy. Some conditions that occur during pregnancy, such as those necessitating bedrest, will likely qualify for FMLA leave. If the pregnant woman is hospitalized, she will qualify because inpatient care automatically satisfies the definition of a serious health condition. Bed rest at home will be a period of incapacity that typically lasts more than three days. In addition, an inability to work due to a pregnancy-related condition that neither requires inpatient hospital care nor lasts more than three days may still qualify for FMLA leave.[15] Morning sickness, for example, even if it passes after a short time, still qualifies the pregnant woman for FMLA leave while the morning sickness is present. This is the most frequently occurring condition to which this rule applies. A pregnant woman's spouse is also entitled to FMLA leave, when needed, to assist in prenatal care or to care for her during a period of pregnancy-related incapacity, even when that incapacity lasts fewer than three days.[16]

Employees who are adopting or becoming foster parents may also need leave before the arrival of the child. FMLA leave is available for any reason related to completing the adoption or foster placement of the child, including for events that occur before the child's placement. Examples from the FMLA regulations include required counseling sessions, court appearances, and consultations with attorneys or with the health care providers representing the birth parent. They also include the need for the prospective parents to undergo a medical examination. As with leave for pregnancy-related conditions, an absence of more than three days is not required. FMLA leave must also be granted for an employee to travel to another country to complete an adoption.[17]

Exception: FMLA Leave Not Authorized for Birth or Placement of a Grandchild

Employees who are becoming grandparents are not eligible for FMLA leave for the birth of a grandchild or for the placement of a child with the employee's adult child for adoption or foster care. If the new grandchild has a serious health condition, the grandparent employee will not be entitled to FMLA to help care for the child unless the grandparent employee is acting *in loco parentis*, in the place of the parents, as discussed below. If, however, the employee's child (the new parent) has a serious health condition following the birth and is incapable of self-care, the employee may be eligible for FMLA leave on those grounds, as discussed below.

---

15. *See* 29 C.F.R. § 825.120(a)(4). While an employer cannot ask for a medical certification for the birth of a child, it may (but does not have to) ask for certification of pregnancy-related illnesses. See Chapter 5, pages 68–69.

16. 29 C.F.R. § 825.120(a)(5).

17. 29 C.F.R. § 825.121(a)(1).

Serious Health Conditions

The purpose of the FMLA is to give employees a reasonable but limited amount of time in which to take care of their own or family members' health issues without losing their jobs.[18] In addition to the birth, adoption, or foster care placement of a child, the two other circumstances that qualify for FMLA leave are where (1) the employee has a serious health condition that makes the employee unable to perform their job, or (2) the employee needs to care for a spouse, child, or parent with a serious health condition. What is a serious health condition?

Definition

The FMLA's definition of a serious health condition is a complicated one. *Serious health condition* means an illness, injury, or impairment, or a physical or mental condition that involves

1. any period of incapacity requiring *an absence from work of more than three full, consecutive calendar days* that also involves one in-person visit to a health care provider within the first seven days of illness and either a second visit within the first thirty days or continuing treatment (such as treatment with prescription drugs) under the supervision of a health care provider;
2. any period of incapacity or treatment connected with inpatient care;
3. any period of incapacity due to pregnancy;
4. any period of incapacity or treatment due to a *chronic health condition*;
5. any period of incapacity that is long-term or permanent due to a condition for which treatment may not be effective (e.g., cancer, AIDS); or
6. any absence to receive (and recover from) multiple treatments for a condition that would likely result in a period of incapacity for more than three consecutive days if left untreated (e.g., physical therapy, chemotherapy, dialysis).[19]

Of course, the mere existence of a serious health condition is not enough to entitle an employee to FMLA leave. The employee must be unable to work because of it,

---

18. This is very different from the federal Americans with Disabilities Act (ADA). The ADA has an entirely different purpose. The ADA is an antidiscrimination statute. It prohibits employers from discriminating on the basis of disability against a qualified individual in hiring, promotion, discharge, and all other terms and conditions of employment. The FMLA's focus is separating short-term illnesses that keep an employee out of work for only a few days (and which can usually be handled using sick leave) from those whose effects are longer lasting and require care supervised by a health care provider. Like the FMLA, the ADA offers protections to employees with medical conditions that leave them unable to work for longer periods than just a few days. But the focus of the ADA is on the effort to find ways to restructure work or provide assistive devices to accommodate employees' medical conditions. See Appendix C for further discussion.

19. *See* 29 C.F.R. §§ 825.113–.115. The definition of *serious illness or injury* for the purposes of military caregiver leave is like that of *serious health condition*, but the two are not identical. *See id.* § 825.127. Military caregiver leave is discussed in Chapter 9.

or the family member must be unable to attend school or perform daily activities because of it, before FMLA is available.[20]

The first one of these elements of the definition of *serious health condition* is the only one that requires a specific period of incapacity—namely, an incapacity that lasts more than three full, consecutive calendar days. This first element also requires a visit to a health care provider within the first seven days of illness *and* either a second provider visit or a continuing regimen of treatment supervised by the provider. For convenience's sake, let's call this the "continuing-treatment" serious health condition or "continuing-treatment" definition. The continuing-treatment definition covers many acute illnesses and infections as well as medical procedures that require prolonged recovery but generally result in the employee returning to work at the conclusion of leave.

In comparison, the other five elements of the definition of a serious health condition, whether related to inpatient care, pregnancy, chronic health conditions, incurable conditions, or their treatments, are defined in terms of *"any* period of incapacity" or *"any* absence." In the second element, *inpatient care* refers to a hospital admission of more than twenty-four hours along with any associated recovery period.[21] This form of serious health condition may be long or quite short. Elements three through six generally cover conditions that are not acute but are instead episodic or require treatments that are episodic. The conditions that fall into this category are numerous. They range from the severe morning sickness that may accompany pregnancy to chemotherapy and dialysis for cancer and kidney disease, to name just a few. For conditions such as these, the FMLA makes a provision for intermittent (recurring) job-protected leave and reduced schedule job-protected leave, the details of which are discussed in Appendix B.

Chronic Health Conditions

As mentioned earlier, a period of incapacity that is due to a chronic health condition also qualifies as an FMLA serious health condition, even if it lasts fewer than three days. The regulations define a chronic health condition as one that continues over an extended period, causing episodic rather than continuing periods of incapacity, and requires treatment by a health care provider *at least twice a year.*[22] Chronic episodic conditions may require leave of periods of as little as an hour over several weeks rather than for a continuous period of time. Examples

---

20. *See* 29 C.F.R. §§ 825.112(a)(4), .113(b).

21. *See* Bonkowski v. Oberg Indus., Inc., 787 F.3d 190 (3d Cir. 2015) (employee who arrived at hospital just before midnight, was admitted just after midnight, and discharged later that day did not undergo the "overnight stay" required to establish a qualifying serious health condition because the visit began with his admission and not his arrival); *see also* Isley v. Aker Phila. Shipyard, Inc., 275 F. Supp. 3d 620, 633–34 (E.D. Pa. 2017) (emergency-room visit that did not result in hospital admission was not inpatient care, and condition that led to the visit was not serious health condition where there was no follow-up treatment or visit to a provider).

22. 29 C.F.R. § 825.115(c).

of chronic conditions include asthma, diabetes, and migraine headaches. Not all instances of a chronic condition will qualify as serious health conditions, however, so employers must apply the FMLA's definitions to the medical facts given by the employee's health care provider. For example, it may be that an employee who has been diagnosed with a condition in the past is not being treated for the condition twice a year at the present time. In *Justice v. Renasant Bank*, for example, the court found that an employee's migraines were not a chronic serious health condition because she had not visited a health care provider for treatment twice a year. All the employee could show was that she had been treated approximately 3–5 times over the five-year period before she sought FMLA leave.[23]

The same is true for the fifth element of the definition, a serious health condition caused by a period of incapacity due to a permanent or long-term condition for which there is no effective treatment. In that case, the employee or family member must be under the continuing supervision of a health care provider but need not be receiving active treatment. Examples of this kind of condition include Alzheimer's Disease, a severe stroke, HIV/AIDS, or the terminal stages of cancer.[24] As with chronic serious health conditions, these permanent, long-term health conditions do not qualify as serious health conditions for FMLA purposes in the absence of visits to a health care provider. In *Jallow v. Kraft Foods Global, Inc.*, for example, an employee's HIV status did not entitle him to FMLA leave because he could not show that he was unable to perform his job duties and that he was under the continuing supervision of a health care provider.[25]

Mental Health Conditions

Mental health conditions such as depression, anxiety, bipolar disorder, obsessive-compulsive disorder, and schizophrenia are chronic conditions that may incapacitate a person for a continuous period longer than three consecutive days or on an intermittent basis for shorter periods of time. Mental health conditions like treatment for substance abuse may require an overnight stay in a hospital or a longer stay in a residential medical facility. They are serious health conditions entitling an employee to FMLA leave when (1) the patient sees a health care provider once and continues under a regimen of treatment supervised by the provider, (2) the patient sees the health care provider twice within thirty days, or (3) the episodic nature of the patient's incapacity requires visits to a health care provider at least two times per year. For FMLA leave to be available for mental health conditions, as with physical ailments, the employee must be unable to perform one or more of their job functions due to the condition, or a family member must need either physical assistance or psychological comfort care due to the condition.

---

23. Justice v. Renasant Bank, No. 1:15-CV-00136-NBB-DAS, 2016 WL 6635638 (N.D. Miss. Nov. 8, 2016).

24. 29 C.F.R. § 825.115(d).

25. Jallow v. Kraft Foods Glob., Inc., No. 15-cv-249-wmc, 2016 WL 3893181 (W.D. Wis. July 14, 2016).

Related Multiple Health Conditions

People sometimes have two or more medical conditions that become symptomatic at the same time and combine to make them unable to perform their job duties. These health conditions may together qualify as a serious health condition for FMLA purposes, even if the conditions are different and seemingly unrelated. Consider the case *Price v. City of Fort Wayne* from the federal Seventh Circuit Court of Appeals. The plaintiff had been diagnosed with high blood pressure, hyperthyroidism, back pain, severe headaches, sinusitis, an infected cyst, a sore and swelling throat, cough, and feelings of stress and depression. The court found that this "assemblage of diagnoses" could rise to the level of a serious health condition. Whether or not they did in a particular case, it said, was a question of fact.[26]

Conditions Unlikely to Qualify as Serious Health Conditions

Colds, Flu, and Stomach Viruses

The FMLA regulations say that colds, stomach viruses, the flu, and similar conditions do not qualify as serious health conditions unless they require inpatient care or continuing treatment by a health care provider.[27] Taking over-the-counter medications such as aspirin, antihistamines, or salves, being on bedrest, drinking fluids, exercising, or engaging in other similar activities that an employee can begin without a visit to a health care provider do not constitute a regimen of continuing treatment for FMLA purposes.[28] An example of continuing treatment is a course of prescription medication, like an antibiotic, or a therapy requiring special equipment such as the delivery of oxygen. Examinations to determine *whether a serious health condition exists* and evaluations of the condition do constitute "treatment,"[29] but treatment does not include *routine* physical examinations, eye examinations, or dental examinations.[30] Nor does *serious health condition* include

---

26. Price v. City of Fort Wayne, 117 F.3d 1022, 1023 (7th Cir. 1997). *Cf.* Hayduk v. City of Johnstown, 580 F. Supp. 2d 429, 467 (W.D. Pa. 2008) (citing *Price* but finding that this plaintiff's many health conditions occurred over time and did not render him unable to perform his job duties); Ozolins v. Northwood-Kensett Cmty. Sch. Dist., 40 F. Supp. 2d 1055, 1065 (N.D. Iowa 1999) (employee's mother suffered a serious health condition from a fall combined with already-existing serious chronic health issues).

27. 29 C.F.R. § 825.113(d). *See* Beaver v. RGIS Inventory Specialists, Inc., 144 F. App'x 452, 456 (6th Cir.2005) (sore throat, sinusitis, bronchitis, and ear infections are routine, short-term illnesses not covered by the FMLA); Easter v. Asurion Ins. Servs., 96 F. Supp. 3d 789, 798 (M.D. Tenn. 2015) (same); *cf.* Miller v. AT & T Corp., 250 F.3d 820, 830–31 (4th Cir. 2001) (employee had a serious health condition where her flu symptoms did not improve and second visit to the doctor involved an exam and blood test to evaluate her condition).

28. 29 C.F.R. § 825.113(c). *See, e.g.*, Johnson v. Wheeling Mach. Prods., 779 F.3d 514, 519–21 (8th Cir. 2015) (instruction to exercise more was not a regimen of continuing care).

29. Krenzke v. Alexandria Motor Cars, Inc., 289 F. App'x 629, 634 (4th Cir. 2008) (plaintiff satisfied requirements for serious health condition where, during multiple appointments, doctor conducted a regimen of tests to evaluate her condition, prescribed medications to alleviate symptoms, and referred plaintiff to a cardiologist and pulmonary specialist for further testing).

30. 29 C.F.R. § 825.113(c).

outpatient procedures like needle biopsies. Although needle biopsies may involve a follow-up visit with a provider, they qualify as serious health conditions only if the employee is, in fact, incapacitated and unable to work for more than three consecutive workdays.[31]

Even though the FMLA regulations say that ordinary illnesses like colds, flu, and stomach viruses do not generally meet the criteria for a serious health condition, complications of what are otherwise ordinary illnesses can satisfy the definition.

Consider what happened in the Fourth Circuit case *Miller v. AT&T Corp.* The plaintiff in that case was an employee with attendance issues that culminated in a final letter of warning and a last-chance agreement. When she came down with the flu, she was forced to take additional time off. The plaintiff's bout with flu left her severely dehydrated and when she visited a doctor, he administered intravenous fluid and did a blood test that showed that her white blood cell and platelet counts were significantly lower than normal. She was directed to return for a second visit with the doctor two days later, when the doctor conducted another blood test, which showed that her counts were still low. The doctor consulted a blood specialist and told the plaintiff to return in two weeks, by which time her blood counts had returned to normal. The plaintiff was absent from work for six days, after which she felt well enough to return to work despite her abnormal blood counts. She asked that the six days during which she was too ill to work to be designated as FMLA leave, but AT&T refused, saying that the flu was not usually considered a serious health condition and that she had not demonstrated that she received medical treatment on two or more occasions. The plaintiff was then terminated for excessive absenteeism. Had her last absence been designated as FMLA leave, it could not have been counted against her.[32]

The Fourth Circuit Court of Appeals held that although the FMLA regulations provide that flu does not "ordinarily" qualify as a serious health condition, that did not mean that the flu could *never* form the basis for FMLA leave. It rejected the employer's argument that the employee's second doctor's visit did not count as treatment because it was an evaluation of the plaintiff's continuing low blood cell count, noting that the regulations define *treatment* to include "examinations to determine if a serious health condition exists and evaluations of the condition." The doctor's administration of a second blood test and his consultation with a hematologist therefore counted as treatment, and her condition met the definition of serious health condition.[33]

---

31. *See, e.g.,* Morris v. Family Dollar Stores of Ohio, Inc., 320 F. App'x 330, 337–38 (6th Cir. 2009); *cf.* Marchisheck v. San Mateo County, 199 F.3d 1068, 1075 (9th Cir. 1999) (drug-counseling session did not constitute continuing treatment).

32. Miller v. AT&T Corp., 250 F.3d 820 (4th Cir. 2001).

33. *Miller,* 250 F.3d at 830–31 (quoting 29 C.F.R. § 825.113(c)).

COVID-19 and Long COVID

COVID-19 resembles seasonal flu in that for most people, even where its symptoms prevent an employee from working, the employee rarely sees a physician once, much less twice. As most people in the workforce do not qualify for Paxlovid or one of the other treatments prescribed to reduce the severity of COVID-19 infection, employees are unlikely to meet the alternative requirement for a serious health condition, namely, that they be on a course of continuing-treatment regimen under the supervision of their provider. Nevertheless, as with seasonal flu, some employees will experience COVID-19 illness that does meet the FMLA standard for a serious health condition.

The self-isolation recommendations of the Centers for Disease Control and Prevention have engendered confusion among both employees and employers about the availability of FMLA leave for exposure to COVID-19. As of this writing, the CDC no longer recommends isolation for those *exposed* to others with COVID-19. Instead, the CDC recommends that those who have been exposed wear a mask in public. Exposure does not, therefore, make an employee unable to perform their job duties. Even if it did, exposure alone does not satisfy the requirements of a serious health condition.[34] Consider *Mays v. RHA Health Services, LLC*, a federal district court case from Tennessee. Asia Mays, the plaintiff-employee, was twice exposed to COVID-19 in the course of her work, was tested for COVID-19 twice by her doctor and was twice advised to quarantine at home. In the lawsuit challenging her termination, she claimed that the in-person testing by her doctor and his advice to quarantine met the requirements for a serious health condition: her visit to the doctor was for the purpose of diagnosis and his advice to quarantine constituted a regimen of continuing care. Although the court ultimately denied the employer's motion to dismiss the case, it noted that quarantining, without more, does not constitute a regimen of continuing care because quarantining, like taking pain relievers and drinking plenty of fluids, is an activity that employees can initiate themselves without visiting a health care provider.[35]

Long COVID may qualify as a serious health condition under the FMLA. *Long COVID* refers to a conglomeration of symptoms that some people who have been infected with COVID-19 continue to suffer in the months and years following their infection. Long COVID is sometimes referred to as post-COVID syndrome or as PASC (post-acute sequelae of SARS CoV-2 infection). People suffering from long COVID are sometimes referred to as "long-haulers." Symptoms of long COVID include tiredness or fatigue that interferes with daily life, fever, muscle pain,

---

34. *See. e.g.*, Outlaw v. Prattville Health & Rehab., LLC, No. 2:22-CV-31-WKW, 2022 WL 1491666, at *2 (M.D. Ala. May 11, 2022) (granting motion to dismiss FMLA interference and retaliation claims).

35. Mays v. RHA Health Servs., LLC, 2021 WL 3909674 (W.D. Tenn.) at *3. *See also* Anzalone v. United Bank, 2021 WL 4759633 at **4–5 (S.D. Ala. 2021) (denying employer's motion to dismiss but noting that without more a doctor's advising an employee to quarantine does not satisfy the continuing treatment requirement for a serious health condition).

respiratory and heart symptoms, neurological symptoms, and digestive symptoms.[36] The Equal Employment Opportunity Commission has recognized long COVID as a condition that may qualify as disability under the Americans with Disabilities Act (ADA).[37] As with all medical conditions, long COVID can be a qualifying reason for FMLA leave if the definition of a serious health condition is met.

Substance Abuse

Incapacity caused by substance abuse does not qualify for FMLA leave, although FMLA leave is available for the *treatment* of drug and alcohol abuse. As the regulations explain,

> [s]ubstance abuse may be a serious health condition if the conditions of §§ 825.113 [Serious Health Condition] through 825.115 [Continuing Treatment] are met. However, FMLA leave may only be taken for treatment for substance abuse by a health care provider or by a provider of health care services on referral by a health care provider. On the other hand, absence because of the employee's use of the substance, rather than for treatment, does not qualify for FMLA leave.[38]

The regulation makes two important points. First, when FMLA leave is taken for substance abuse treatment, the treatment must be provided by a health care provider. Self-help and non-health care interventions do not qualify for FMLA leave. Second, employees who are absent because they are hungover or high cannot claim FMLA leave to cover their absences because they are not serious health conditions even if their recovery period lasts three or more days.

Note that while an employer cannot take disciplinary action or dismiss an employee for taking FMLA leave for substance abuse treatment, it can do so

---

36. For more on long COVID, see generally Ctrs. for Disease Control & Prevention, *Long Covid or Post-Covid Conditions*, CDC.GOV (Mar. 14, 2024), https://www.cdc.gov/coronavirus/ 2019-ncov/long-term-effects/index.html, and Nat'l Insts. of Health, *Long Covid*, NIH.GOV (Sept. 28, 2023), https://covid19.nih.gov/covid-19-topics/long-covid.

37. *What You Should Know About COVID-19 and the ADA, the Rehabilitation Act, and Other EEO Laws* § N, U.S. EQUAL EMP. OPPORTUNITY COMM'N (May 15, 2023) https://www .eeoc.gov/wysk/what-you-should-know-about-covid-19-and-ada-rehabilitation-act-and-other -eeo-laws#N. *See also* U.S. Dep't of Health & Hum. Servs. & U.S. Dep't of Just., *Guidance on "Long COVID" as a Disability Under the ADA, Section 504, and Section 1557*, HHS.GOV (July 26, 2012), https://www.hhs.gov/civil-rights/for-providers/civil-rights-covid19/guidance -long-covid-disability/index.html.

38. 29 C.F.R. § 825.119(a). *Cf.* Ames v. Home Depot U.S.A., Inc., 629 F.3d 665, 669 (7th Cir. 2011) (employer not liable for interference with FMLA leave where employee did not seek treatment prior to her termination); Darst v. Interstate Brands Corp., 512 F.3d 903, 908–12 (7th Cir. 2008) (employee offered no evidence that he was receiving treatment for substance abuse on days on which he claimed he was entitled to FMLA leave); Gilmore v. Univ. of Rochester, 654 F. Supp. 2d 141, 149–50 (W.D.N.Y. 2009) (same); Basso v. Potter, 596 F. Supp. 2d 324, 346 (D. Conn. 2009) (summary judgment denied where evidence was not clear about whether employee was absent for substance abuse treatment or because of substance abuse).

because an employee's abuse of alcohol or drugs violated the specific terms of the employer's workplace policy, provided that it is a written policy, applies to all employees, and is communicated to them.[39]

Cosmetic Treatments and Routine Dental Surgeries Versus Restorative Surgeries

Acne and conditions for which cosmetic treatments are available (plastic surgery, for example) rarely require inpatient hospital care or cause an employee to be incapable of performing their job duties for more than three days—even if an employee continues to be treated two or more times in thirty days. So even where employees have elective outpatient plastic surgery, they are unlikely to qualify for FMLA leave unless complications develop. Wearing bandages or showing treatment-related bruising does not, in most cases, render an employee incapable of performing their job duties. The same is true of routine dental surgeries. That being said, cosmetic surgeries and restorative dental surgery done in connection with cancer or with the removal of tumors and other growths may well satisfy the definition of a serious health condition because the underlying condition is itself a serious health condition.[40]

Applying the Medical Facts

In general, determining whether an employee or employee's family member has a condition that meets the definition of a serious health condition is straightforward. The standard is an objective, fact-based one and does not depend on the perceptions of either the employee or the employer. Instead, the employer obtains clinical facts about the health condition from a medical certification form completed by the treating provider.[41]

Once an employer receives a medical certification, it applies the definition of *serious health condition* to the facts presented by the provider to determine whether a serious health condition exists. For example, in *Ramji v. Hospital Housekeeping Systems, LLC*, an employee injured her knee at work, went to the emergency room, and was written out of work for four workdays. That was more than three consecutive full days, so her condition met the first part of the continuing-treatment definition. The employee had a follow-up appointment with a doctor the following week, when he gave her a cortisone injection and prescribed physical therapy for four to six weeks. This met the second part of the definition, which requires a

---

39. Note that there is no ADA protection in this circumstance, either. Current substance abuse is not a protected disability. Alcoholism is a protected disability, but violation of a policy prohibiting the use of alcohol is not excused by the employee's alcoholism. *See* WAGE & HOUR DIV., U.S. DEP'T OF LABOR, FIELD OPERATIONS HANDBOOK, ch. 29, § 39d07 (modernization rev. 693, Aug. 10, 2016), https://www.dol.gov/sites/dolgov/files/WHD/legacy/files/FOH_Ch39.pdf.

40. 29 C.F.R. § 825.113(d).

41. A detailed discussion of the medical certification process may be found in Chapter 5.

second visit or a regimen of continuing treatment.[42] Compare this with another knee-injury case, *Wood v. Gilman Building Products Inc.* There, the employee received care from a doctor who ordered him to stay home from work for two days, which he did. But the employee was not incapacitated for more than three full calendar days and therefore did not meet the first part of the continuing-care definition. He did not receive any subsequent treatment for his knee injury and therefore did not meet the second part of the definition.[43] To take an altogether different condition as a further example, in *Victoriana v. Internal Medicine Clinic of Tangipahoa*, an employee's in vitro fertilization was found not to be a serious health condition because it was not inpatient care and did not involve continuing treatment for an incapacity lasting more than three consecutive days.[44]

Caring for a Family Member: Who Counts as a Spouse, Child, or Parent?

FMLA leave may be taken for an employee's own serious health condition, of course, but also for the serious health condition of an employee's spouse, child, or parent. While that statement appears to be straightforward, closer consideration gives rise to several important questions. Does *spouse* only mean a person to whom the employee is legally married? Are common-law spouses included? What about domestic partners who are in every way like a spouse? Does *child* mean only a minor child? What about adult children who need care? And *parent*—does that include in-laws? What about the aunt who raised the employee because the employee's parents were not in the picture?

Spouse

The text of the FMLA defines *spouse* as a husband or wife.[45] The regulations expand on that definition, explaining that *husband or wife* means a person with whom the employee has entered into marriage as defined or recognized under the law of any state. It includes same-sex marriages as well as common-law marriages entered into in states that recognize common-law marriage.[46] North Carolina, however, does not recognize common-law marriages.[47] So FMLA leave is not available to

---

42. Ramji v. Hosp. Housekeeping Sys., LLC, 992 F.3d 1233, 1242 (11th Cir. 2021).

43. Wood v. Gilman Bldg. Prods. Inc., 769 F. App'x 796, 801–02 (11th Cir. 2019). *Cf.* Blake v. City of Montgomery, 492 F. Supp. 3d 1292, 1302–03 (M.D. Ala. 2020), *aff'd*, No. 20-14229, 2021 WL 5177429 (11th Cir. Nov. 8, 2021) (job burnout and job fatigue do not constitute FMLA-qualifying medical conditions when they are unaccompanied by any medical evidence); Guzman v. Brown Cnty., 884 F.3d 633, 638–39 (7th Cir. 2018) (diagnosis of sleep apnea several years before did not make sleep apnea a serious health condition where there was no evidence that employee sought medical care for the condition at time of request for FMLA leave).

44. *See* Victoriana v. Internal Med. Clinic of Tangipahoa, No. 15-2915, 2016 WL 5404653 (E.D. La. Sept. 28, 2016).

45. 29 U.S.C. § 2611(13).

46. 29 C.F.R. § 825.122(b).

47. Common-law marriages are legally recognized in only ten jurisdictions: Alabama, Colorado, Iowa, Kansas, Montana, Rhode Island, South Carolina, Texas, Utah, and the District

North Carolina employees who seek leave to care for a partner to whom they are not legally married. If evidence of the employee's marriage is not already in the employee's personnel record, the employer may ask for documentation of the marriage.[48]

Child

The FMLA provides leave to take care of a "son or daughter" with a serious health condition and defines *son or daughter* as a "biological, adopted, or foster child, a stepchild, a legal ward, or a child of a person standing *in loco parentis*," who is either incapable of self-care because of a mental or physical disability or younger than 18.[49] This definition contains terms that themselves must be defined to fully understand the scope of the FMLA's reach.

Adopted Child

Some people may use the term *adopted* casually to refer to a minor child whom they have taken into their home. But for FMLA purposes, *adoption* means "legally and permanently assuming the responsibility of raising a child as one's own."[50] In other words, there must be a legal proceeding establishing the adoption.

Foster Child

Similarly, some people may use the term *foster care* casually to refer to a minor child for whom they have temporarily taken responsibility. Here, too, the FMLA regulations require state action for the relationship to be recognized. *Foster care* is defined as "24-hour care for children in substitution for, and away from, their parents or guardian." This definition of foster care requires two types of state action to have occurred. First, there must be either a judge's decision that foster care is needed or an agreement between the state and a child's parent or guardian that foster care is needed. Second, there must be an agreement between the state and the foster family. Although foster care may be with the child's relatives, state action is still required for a foster-care situation to qualify for FMLA leave for the serious health condition of an employee's child.[51]

In Loco Parentis

A person who is acting *in loco parentis* may take FMLA leave to care for a child with a serious health condition. The term *in loco parentis* is a legal one, derived

---

of Columbia. *See* Cornell L. Sch., *Marriage Laws*, Legal Information Institute (last visited Mar. 15, 2024), http://topics.law.cornell.edu/wex/table_marriage.

48. *See* 29 C.F.R. § 825.122(k).

49. 29 U.S.C. § 2611(12).

50. 29 C.F.R. § 825.122(f).

51. *Id.* § 825.122(g). *See* Waltrip v. Conway Hum. Dev. Ctr., No. 4:07CV00103 BSM, 2008 WL 4368788, at *7 (E.D. Ark. Sept. 22, 2008) (no foster care relationship where no state action was taken).

from the Latin phrase meaning "in the place of a parent." The FMLA regulation defines the term thus:

> Persons who are "in loco parentis" include those with *day-to-day responsibilities to care for and financially support* a child . . . . A biological or legal relationship is not necessary.[52]

As one court noted about the inclusion of persons *acting as parents* among those eligible for FMLA leave,

> [t]he very reason that Congress in the FMLA defined "parent" and "son or daughter" to include, respectively, *"an individual who stood in loco parentis to an employee* when the employee" was "under 18 years of age," and "a child of a person standing in loco parentis," was to "reflect *the reality* that *many children* in the United States today *do not* live in traditional 'nuclear' families with their biological father and mother," and are increasingly raised by others including "their grandparents."[53]

In determining whether an employee has an *in loco parentis* relationship with a child, an employer, like a court, should look to the *intention* of the employee to assume the status of a parent toward the child. An employee may assume the care and custody of another's child (including of their own grandchild) under circumstances that are consistent with the continued existence of the relationship between the actual parent and the child without any intention to end that relationship. The intent to assume the status of parent can be inferred from the acts of the parties, the age of the child, the degree to which the child is dependent on the employee claiming to be standing *in loco parentis*, the amount of financial support that the employee provides, and the extent to which the employee exercises the duties commonly associated with parenthood.[54]

Documenting an Employee's Relationship with a Child

As is the case with FMLA to care for a spouse, the employer may require the employee to provide documentation of the parent-child relationship when the employee requests FMLA leave to care for the child's health condition. A child's birth certificate or a court document in the case of an adopted child or a child in foster care will suffice. In the case of an employee standing *in loco parentis* to a child, a simple written statement from the employee is sufficient to satisfy the regulations.[55]

---

52. 29 C.F.R. § 825.122(d)(3) (emphasis added).

53. Coutard v. Mun. Credit Union, 848 F.3d 102, 112 (2d Cir. 2017) (citations omitted).

54. Dillon v. Md.-Nat'l Cap. Park & Planning Comm'n, 382 F. Supp. 2d 777, 786–87 (D. Md. 2005), *aff'd*, 258 F. App'x 577 (4th Cir. 2007).

55. *See* 29 C.F.R. § 825.122(k).

Adult Children Incapable of Self-Care

As we have seen, the FMLA permits employees to take job-protected leave to care for a minor child with a serious health condition. Leave for an adult child is different. The FMLA permits employees to take job-protected leave to care for an *adult* child only when that child is incapable of self-care because of a mental or physical disability. It is easy to determine whether a child is younger than 18, but whether an adult child is incapable of self-care because of a mental or physical disability is a more difficult question. For starters, the FMLA regulations say that in this circumstance, the definition of a mental or physical disability is the same as the one found under the ADA—that is, "a physical or mental impairment that substantially limits" a person in the performance of "one or more major life activities."[56] In other words, the standard is *not* whether an employee's adult child has an FMLA serious health condition. Instead, the employee's adult child must have an ADA disability that renders that child incapable of self-care.

The regulations go on to define *incapable of self-care* as meaning that

> the individual requires active assistance or supervision to provide daily self-care in three or more of the activities of daily living (ADLs) or instrumental activities of daily living (IADLs). Activities of daily living include adaptive activities such as caring appropriately for one's grooming and hygiene, bathing, dressing and eating. Instrumental activities of daily living include cooking, cleaning, shopping, taking public transportation, paying bills, maintaining a residence, using telephones and directories, using a post office, etc.[57]

In addition to having a disability, adult children must need active assistance in taking care of themselves or in accessing the kinds of places or services that allow adults to care for them and their affairs for FMLA leave to be available to their parents. Employees may take FMLA leave to care for adult children with disabilities who need assistance in bathing, dressing, or eating because of a disability. Employees may also take FMLA leave for adult children with disabilities who are able to bathe, dress, and eat but who require assistance in shopping and cooking, for example, or in getting from one place to another, or in managing financial affairs.[58] Whether an adult child has a disability and is incapable of self-care is assessed at the time that leave begins.

As with any form of FMLA leave for a serious health condition, the employer is entitled to a medical certification of the adult child's need for assistance. An

---

56. 29 C.F.R. § 825.122(d)(2).

57. 29 C.F.R. § 825.122(d)(1). For the ADA definitions, see 29 C.F.R. § 1630.2(h)–(j).

58. *See, e.g.,* Bryant v. Delbar Prods., Inc., 18 F. Supp. 2d 799, 803–04 (M.D. Tenn. 1998) (employee sought FMLA leave to care for adult child who had advanced kidney failure, had a physical impairment under the ADA, and required assistance with cooking, cleaning, and transportation).

employee's assertion that the child needs to stay in bed, without more, is not sufficient evidence that the child is incapable of self-care.[59]

FMLA Leave Generally Not Available to Help an Adult Daughter After Childbirth

Employees sometimes desire to take time off to help their adult children with a new baby. Employees may take accrued vacation leave to do this, of course, and sick leave if an employer's policy allows for it, but FMLA leave is not generally available to care for new grandchildren. When an employee takes FMLA leave after the birth, adoption, or foster care placement of a child, the purpose of the leave is to give the new parent bonding time with the child. There is no parallel provision for a grandparent to take time to bond with a new grandchild. However, an employee is entitled to take FMLA leave for an adult daughter who suffers complications during pregnancy or after giving birth if the daughter's condition qualifies as a disability under the ADA and the daughter is incapable of caring for herself.

The case *Voyles v. Lane Furniture Industries, Inc.*, provides a good example of these principles at play. Here, the employee's adult daughter gave birth to a healthy child after a pregnancy beset by complications. As the court noted, the complications might have qualified as a serious health condition before the baby was born, but the employee did not request leave prior to the birth of her grandchild. She applied for leave only after her daughter and grandchild were discharged from the hospital. At that point, the employee's daughter could walk, speak, see, hear, perform manual tasks, use the bathroom, and care for her newborn child without difficulty. She was not, however, allowed to drive for two weeks. The court found that the daughter was not incapable of self-care due to a disability and that the employee was not entitled to FMLA leave.[60]

In another case, *Novak v. MetroHealth Medical Center*, an employee's adult daughter suffered from a postpartum depression that left her unable to care for her newborn child. The court found that the employee was not entitled to FMLA leave in this circumstance because the employee's daughter did not have a disability and was capable of self-care. What she was not capable of doing was caring for her new baby—and it was to care for the baby that the employee sought FMLA leave. "The FMLA," the court said flatly, "does not entitle an employee to leave in order to care for a grandchild."[61] Even if the newborn, newly adopted, or placed grandchild suffered from a serious health condition, a grandparent would not be entitled to FMLA leave to help care for the grandchild unless the employee's child was not able to assume day-to-day responsibility and financial support of the grandchild and the employee was acting *in loco parentis* for the grandchild.

---

59. Sakellarion v. Judge & Dolph, Ltd., 893 F. Supp. 800, 807 (N.D. Ill. 1995).

60. Voyles v. Lane Furniture Indus., Inc., No. 95 C 61, 2009 WL 2392142, at *3–4 (N.D. Miss. July 31, 2009).

61. Novak v. MetroHealth Med. Ctr., 503 F.3d 572, 580–81 (6th Cir. 2007). *But cf.* Gienapp v. Harbor Crest, 756 F.3d 527, 531–32 (7th Cir. 2014) (granting summary judgment to employee who cared for both an adult child incapable of self-care and the child's children).

Parent

Just as the term *son or daughter* is not limited to a biological child, so too for FMLA purposes, an employee's "parent" is not limited to a biological parent. The FMLA regulations explain: "Parent means a biological, adoptive, step or foster father or mother, or any other individual who stood in loco parentis to the employee when the employee was a son or daughter . . . . This term does not include parents 'in law.'"[62]

The same definitions of adoption, foster care, and *in loco parentis* described earlier in this chapter apply in determining whether an employee is entitled to FMLA leave to care for a parent with a serious health condition. And just as FMLA leave may be taken to care for a stepchild with a serious health condition, so too it may be taken to care for a stepfather or stepmother with a serious health condition. Again, grandparents are not included among the family relationships for which FMLA leave applies, unless a grandparent stood *in loco parentis* to the employee when the employee was growing up.[63]

As with employees who stand *in loco parentis* to a child, determining whether an older adult stood *in loco parentis* to an employee can be difficult. The regulations require employers to rely on a written statement from the employee affirming an *in loco parentis* relationship, but that presumes that both employer and employee understand that the person standing *in loco parentis* intended to assume the role of parent in place of the employee's biological or legal parent and provided day-to-day care and financial support of the employee when the employee was a minor.[64] The written statement must provide the employer with sufficient facts indicating that such a relationship existed.[65]

Sometimes it is not clear whether a relationship is one of *in loco parentis* for FMLA purposes. Consider the following hypothetical:

> *Brittany, the single mother of a newborn baby, lives with her parents. Brittany is a student and an army reservist. In addition to housing, Brittany receives substantial financial support from her parents, who also pay for food and health insurance. Brittany's father, Martin, plays a significant role in caring*

---

62. 29 C.F.R. § 825.122(c).

63. *See* Dillon v. Md.-Nat'l Cap. Park & Planning Comm'n, 382 F. Supp. 2d 777, 785 (D. Md. 2005), *aff'd*, 258 F. App'x 577 (4th Cir. 2007) (citing Krohn v. Forsting, 11 F. Supp. 2d 1082, 1092 (E.D. Mo. 1998)).

64. *See id.*, 786–87.

65. *See* Sherrod v. Phila. Gas Works, 57 F. App'x 68, 72–73 (3d Cir. 2003); Ruble v. Am. River Transp. Co., 799 F. Supp. 2d 1017, 1023–24 (E.D. Mo. 2011) (denying employer's motion for summary judgment); Abousaidi v. Mattress Discounters Corp., No. 1:05CV1142, 2005 WL 3797366, at *2 (E.D. Va. Dec. 8, 2005); *see also* Fitzgerald v. Shore Mem'l Hosp., 92 F. Supp. 3d 214, 230 (D.N.J. 2015) (summary judgment in favor of employer where employee referred to relative as her adopted mother, her stepmother, and her aunt and failed to provide documentation to show that the relative stood *in loco parentis* to the employee).

> *for the baby when Brittany is home and takes on sole responsibility when*
> *Brittany is at school or participating in Army Reserve activities. Brittany is*
> *called to active duty and is told that she will be deployed overseas. Martin*
> *requests FMLA leave from his employer to care for Brittany's baby, saying*
> *that he stands* in loco parentis *to the child. Must Martin's employer approve*
> *his FMLA leave?*

Martin cannot take FMLA leave to care for the baby just because he is the baby's grandfather. Grandparents are not entitled to take FMLA leave to care for their grandchildren, whether they are newborns or they have a serious health condition. But Martin can take FMLA leave to care for Brittany's baby if he stands *in loco parentis* to the baby. Is this the nature of Martin's relationship with the baby? Or is he trying to describe his family's needs in a way that will get him a leave to which he is not entitled?

On one hand, he is providing substantial financial support for the child and shares the day-to-day parenting duties with his daughter. In his daughter's absence, he will assume all of those duties. He does not mean to supplant his daughter and there is no suggestion that she will not resume her role as the baby's mother when her deployment concludes. On the other hand, what if her deployment lasts for a substantial period of time—one year, three years, even five years? Will Martin not be acting in the place of a parent during that time? One might even argue that he is acting *in loco parentis* while Brittany is home in that he plays the role of the baby's father. There are no easy answers here.

The facts of this hypothetical are drawn from an Eleventh Circuit case in which the court denied a motion for summary judgment because the facts did not support a finding one way or the other whether, as a matter of law, Martin stood *in loco parentis*. There were facts that suggested an *in loco parentis* relationship and facts that did not. The case needed to be decided by a jury.[66]

A 2020 case from Pennsylvania also resulted in a denial of summary judgment because there were material facts in dispute as to whether an employee had an *in loco parentis* relationship with a niece who had mental health and substance abuse issues. In this case, there was evidence to suggest that the niece spent most of her nights at her aunt's (the employee's) house, that the employee included the niece in her family's activities, and that the employee paid for the niece's gym membership, hair appointments, college class, books, clothing, and food. But there was also evidence that the girl's grandparents (the employee's parents) had legal guardianship of her, and that they also provided her with clothing, food, and medical insurance. The niece spent some nights at her grandparents' house and some with the employee. The court found that the truth of the facts presented by both

---

66. Martin v. Brevard Cnty. Pub. Sch., 543 F.3d 1261, 1266 (11th Cir. 2008). Whether the case went to trial and how the jury found is not reported.

the employee and the employer had to be determined by a jury before it could be determined whether the employee stood *in loco parentis* to her niece and was entitled to FMLA leave.[67]

Being "Needed to Care for" a Family Member

When an employee's plans to care for a family member don't involve physically assisting the family member with activities of daily living, disputes sometimes arise about whether the employee is entitled to FMLA leave simply to provide comfort. When assistance to the family member involves traveling, things can get contentious. Both employers and employees need to understand what "care" means under the FMLA.

The FMLA regulations make clear that an employee doesn't have to be doing anything more than providing psychological and emotional support to the family member with the serious health condition to qualify for FMLA leave.

> The medical certification provision that an employee is needed to care for a family member . . . encompasses both physical and psychological care. It includes situations where, for example, because of a serious health condition, the family member is unable to care for his or her own basic medical, hygienic, or nutritional needs or safety, or is unable to transport himself or herself to the doctor. The term also includes providing psychological comfort and reassurance which would be beneficial to a child, spouse or parent with a serious health condition who is receiving inpatient or home care.[68]

When an employee is sitting by a family member's bedside, at home, or in the hospital, and doing no more than providing the comfort of the employee's presence, that qualifies as care for the purposes of FMLA leave. The family member's serious health condition need not be terminal.[69] Helping to make decisions about a family member's medical care also satisfies the psychological-care standard.[70] The term also includes situations where the employee may be needed to fill in for others who

---

67. Megonnell v. Infotech Sols., Inc., No. 1:07–cv–02339, 2009 WL 3857451, at *9–10 (M.D. Pa. Nov. 18, 2009). *Cf.* Brehmer v. Xcel Energy, Inc., No. 06–3294, 2008 WL 3166265, at *7 (D. Minn. Aug. 4, 2008), *aff'd*, 356 F. App'x 890 (8th Cir. 2009) (question of material fact exists about employee's *in loco parentis* status where employee helped child eat, dress, and go to bed; drove child to doctor appointments and to school; went to child's softball games; visited child's school when he had problems there, and contributed more than half of child's financial support for more than a year).

68. 29 C.F.R. § 825.124(a).

69. *See* Fioto v. Manhattan Woods Golf Enters., LLC, 270 F. Supp. 2d 401, 404–05 (S.D.N.Y. 2003), *aff'd sub nom.* Fioto v. Manhattan Woods Enters. LLC, 123 F. App'x 26 (2d Cir. 2005) (no evidence that employee provided any care to his mother); Plumley v. S. Container Inc., No. 00–140–P–C, 2001 WL 1188469 (D. Me. Oct. 9, 2001) (son who spent time with his hospitalized father providing comfort and reassurance met the FMLA standard of psychological care); Brunelle v. Cytec Plastics, Inc., 225 F. Supp. 2d 67 (D. Me. 2002) (same).

70. *See Brunelle*, 225 F. Supp. 2d at 77.

are caring for the family member or to make arrangements for changes in care, such as transfer to a nursing home.[71]

> The regulations also make clear that the employee doesn't have to be a family member's full-time caregiver to qualify for FMLA leave. An employee's intermittent leave or a reduced leave schedule necessary to care for a family member or covered servicemember includes not only a situation where the condition of the family member or covered servicemember itself is intermittent, but also where the employee is only needed intermittently—such as where other care is normally available, or care responsibilities are shared with another member of the family or a third party.[72]

What may be more surprising to employers is that courts consider an employee to be providing psychological and comfort care when the employee accompanies a family member with a serious health condition on a pleasure trip or vacation. In the Seventh Circuit case *Ballard v. Chicago Park District*, the employer denied an employee FMLA leave to accompany her mother, who was in the final stage of a terminal disease, on a Las Vegas trip whose costs were being borne by a nonprofit benefitting terminally ill adults. The employee went on the trip anyway. Both back home and on the Las Vegas trip, the employee acted as her mother's primary caregiver, bathing and dressing her, administering medication, and draining fluids from her heart. While in Las Vegas, the employee also accompanied her mother in the sort of tourist activities typically enjoyed by visitors to Las Vegas.[73]

The Seventh Circuit concluded that the employee was entitled to FMLA leave to accompany her mother on this trip. It noted that the statutory language does not restrict care to a particular place or geographic location. The court reasoned that if the employee had sought leave to care for her mother in Chicago, where they lived, her request would have fallen within the scope of the FMLA. Her request would have also qualified for FMLA leave if the employee's mother had lived in Las Vegas instead of with the employee, and the employee had requested leave to care for her mother there. The court found no reason to treat the trip to Las Vegas any differently.[74]

---

71. *See* 29 C.F.R. § 825.124(b).
72. *Id.* § 825.124(c). On intermittent and reduced schedule leaves, see Appendix B.
73. Ballard v. Chi. Park Dist., 741 F.3d 838 (7th Cir. 2014).
74. *Id.*, 843.

Summary: The Reasons for Which FMLA Leave Must Be Granted

The reasons for which traditional FMLA must be granted are straightforward: the birth, adoption, or foster care placement of a child; an employee's own serious health condition, or an employee's need to care for an immediate family member with a serious health condition.[75] But as with the ADA, the sheer variety of health conditions and ways in which their symptoms manifest themselves in different individuals makes every circumstance unique. When leave is taken for an employee's or family member's serious health condition, no request for FMLA leave should *automatically* be granted or rejected. Nor should an employer automatically assume or reject the existence of a qualifying relationship when leave is requested to care for a family member. Instead, an employer must carefully examine whether the particular facts set forth by the employee satisfy the several definitions of *serious health condition* and the definitions of *spouse, parent,* and *child.* As with so much of employment law, the devil is in the details.

---

75. The other reasons for which FMLA must be granted, related to family members who serve in the military, will be discussed in Chapter 9.

Chapter 3

Measuring FMLA Leave

Twelve Weeks and the FMLA Year

Measuring FMLA leave can be complicated. An employee is entitled to twelve workweeks of unpaid FMLA leave during any twelve-month period.[1] Conceptually, using a calendar year to measure FMLA leave would appear to be the easiest way to track FMLA leave. But using a calendar year—or any fixed year—to measure an employee's FMLA use has a distinct disadvantage to employers. When an employee needing a leave that exceeds twelve weeks begins FMLA leave toward the end of the year, the employee becomes entitled to another allotment of twelve weeks of leave as soon as the current year ends and a new one begins.[2]

Rick works for the Paradise County public works department. He needs surgery on his shoulder. Rick's job involves manual labor, and his surgeon estimates that he will be out of work for a minimum of four months and possibly as long as six. His surgery is scheduled for the beginning of the second week in October. His employer uses the calendar year to measure the amount of FMLA used in a year. This means that Rick's twelve-week entitlement of FMLA leave (Rick has not used any FMLA leave earlier in the year) will end in the week in which December 31 falls. The new FMLA year begins on January 1, and Rick becomes entitled to a new allotment of twelve weeks of FMLA leave on that date. Because of the combination of the timing of his leave and his employer's use of the calendar year to measure FMLA leave, Rick has a total of twenty-four weeks of continuous job-protected FMLA leave if he needs that much to recuperate from his rotator-cuff repair.

---

1. 29 C.F.R. § 825.200(a).
2. *Id.* § 825.200(c).

Twenty-four weeks of job-protected leave is good news indeed for Rick. It is not good news for his employer. If the surgery were in June, and if Rick used his full twelve-week entitlement, he would have no additional FMLA leave available until the following January 1.[3] If Rick is a good employee, Paradise County might choose to grant him an unpaid administrative leave after his FMLA leave ran out for as long as he needed to recuperate. But what if Rick is working in a critical position that has to be filled, or is simply a terrible employee? If Rick's FMLA leave hadn't spanned two calendar FMLA years, the FMLA would not require the county to hold his job for him after twelve weeks. After that, the county could terminate his employment because he was unavailable to work.

The FMLA does not require employers to use a calendar-year method of measuring the amount of FMLA leave taken. It gives employers four choices: the calendar-year method, the fixed-year method, the rolling-forward method, and the rolling-backward method. Although less straightforward, many employers prefer the rolling-forward and rolling-backward methods because they eliminate the possibility of stacking two twelve-week leave entitlements on top of each other.

The Fixed-Year Method

The fixed-year method is like the calendar-year method, only instead of the new FMLA year beginning on January 1, an employer may choose any day of the year for it to begin. Many local government employers use July 1, the start of their fiscal year, as does the State of North Carolina. But any other fixed date is equally acceptable. Employers may also choose to use the anniversary date of an employee's hire as the fixed date upon which the FMLA year turns. In that case, each employee in the organization has their own individual FMLA year.[4] The fixed-year method has the same disadvantage as the calendar-year method: it allows for the possibility of two entitlements to twelve weeks of FMLA leave being used back-to-back to create a continuous FMLA leave of twenty-four weeks.[5]

The Rolling-Forward Method

Under this method, each employee's FMLA year is independent of one another's. Each employee's FMLA year begins on the first day that the employee starts FMLA leave and extends for twelve months from that date.[6] Under the rolling-forward

---

3. The Americans with Disabilities Act would likely require Paradise County to give him additional leave time as a reasonable accommodation, but an additional twelve weeks of leave would not be required.

4. *See* 29 C.F.R. § 825.200(b)(2).

5. *Id.* § 825.200(c).

6. *Id.* § 825.200(b)(3).

method, a new FMLA year does not begin on the anniversary of the date the first instance of FMLA was taken. Instead, a new FMLA year begins the next time that an employee takes FMLA again after the conclusion of the initial FMLA year—even if that date is more than twelve months after the date when the employee first takes FMLA leave.[7] For example, if the first time that Maria ever takes FMLA leave is August 15, 2025, Maria will have twelve weeks of FMLA leave to use between August 15, 2025, and August 14, 2026. She may take twelve weeks of leave continuously or she may take the twelve weeks in several continuous chunks or in part-week or partial-day increments. Maria's next FMLA year will not begin on August 15, 2026, unless by coincidence she needs to take FMLA leave on August 15, 2026. If Maria does not need to take FMLA leave again until December 8, 2026, then her new FMLA year will begin on December 8, 2026, and she will have twelve weeks of FMLA leave available through December 7, 2027.

The Rolling-Backward Method

Using this method to determine the amount of FMLA leave available, an employer measures how much FMLA leave an employee has already used in the twelve months *preceding* the first day of a new instance of leave.[8] For example, if the first time Lawrence *ever* takes FMLA leave is April 21, 2025, he will have a full twelve weeks available because he has not used any FMLA leave in the preceding twelve months. Lawrence uses four weeks of FMLA leave. Then, on January 7, 2026, he begins a new FMLA leave, this time for the birth of his child. Lawrence does not have his full twelve weeks of FMLA leave available. Rolling back from January 7, 2026, we see that Lawrence used four weeks of FMLA leave in the previous twelve months. This means he only has eight weeks of leave available for the birth of his baby.

If Lawrence's leave for the baby's birth begins on March 3, 2026, the story is different. On March 3, his first day of leave, he again will have used four weeks of FMLA leave in the preceding twelve months. At that point he will have only eight weeks of leave to take going forward. But look at what happens on April 21, 2026, a year after he took his very first instance of FMLA leave. Measuring from that day, the look-back method shows that Lawrence has not used a full twelve weeks in the prior year. He has used one day less than a full twelve weeks, 11⅘ weeks, of FMLA leave in the preceding twelve months. He has "earned back" an additional day of FMLA leave. The same thing is true on April 22, 2026. So Lawrence's FMLA entitlement increases one day at a time and he is able to take a full twelve weeks of leave for the birth of his baby. When using the rolling-back method, employers must calculate the availability of FMLA leave for *each day* that leave is requested. In some

---

7. *See id.* § 825.200(c).
8. *Id.* § 825.200(b)(4).

cases, it is possible, depending on the frequency of FMLA leave and the length of time each instance of leave lasts, for an employee to be on job-protected FMLA leave for part of an absence and on unprotected (not FMLA) leave for another part.[9]

Measuring the Amount of FMLA Leave Taken

Employers Must Record Increments No Greater Than One Hour

When an employee's FMLA leave is taken on an intermittent or reduced schedule basis, measuring the amount of leave can be tricky. When is the twelve-week limit reached? The FMLA regulations require an employer to record both intermittent and reduced schedule leave using the shortest period of time that the employer uses to account for other forms of leave, such as sick, vacation, and personal leave. The period used to account for intermittent or reduced schedule leave, however, *cannot be greater than one-hour increments.*[10] An employer also may not require an employee to take more time off than is necessary to accommodate the need for the intermittent or reduced schedule leave. For example, if an employee needs to be away from work for only two hours a day, the employer may not require the employee to take a half day off.[11]

The Workweek as the Basis for Measuring FMLA Leave

Because an employee is entitled to twelve *weeks* of FMLA leave, the basis of FMLA leave entitlement is the workweek.[12] For example, consider an employee on continuous FMLA leave who normally works five days a week. He begins his FMLA leave on a Monday and returns three weeks and three days later on a Thursday. He will have used 3⅗ weeks of FMLA leave.[13]

Reduced Schedule Leave

Most employees take FMLA leave in continuous blocks of time. But not all health conditions require an employee to be absent for weeks at a time. For example, employees recovering from an illness or a surgical procedure may not be able to work a full day upon their initial return to work, but could still work a partial day. Under the FMLA, such employees would be entitled to a reduced leave schedule. The FMLA regulations define reduced schedule leave as leave that "reduces an employee's usual number of working hours per workweek, or hours per workday. A

---

9. *See id.* § 825.200(c).
10. *Id.* § 825.205(a).
11. *See id.* § 825.203.
12. *Id.* § 825.205(b).
13. *See id.* § 825.205(b)(1).

reduced leave schedule is a change in the employee's schedule for a period of time, normally from full-time to part-time."[14] The FMLA requires employers to grant requests for reduced schedule leave when they are medically necessary.[15]

While reduced schedule leave is usually taken when an employee is recovering from a serious health condition and is unable to work full time,[16] employees who need FMLA leave for the birth or adoption of a child may also request to take FMLA leave on a reduced schedule basis (that is, to work part-time for longer than twelve weeks rather than taking full-time FMLA leave and returning to work full time at the end of twelve weeks). Whether to grant reduced schedule leave in the case of the birth or adoption of a child is within the employer's sole discretion. Reduced schedule leave is not a right in that case.[17] But reduced schedule leave is a right when it is medically necessary due to the circumstances of an employee's or family member's serious health condition.

Measuring the Amount of Reduced Schedule Leave Taken

The measurement of reduced schedule leave is usually straightforward:

- If a full-time employee who normally works eight-hour days temporarily works four-hour days under a reduced leave schedule, that employee will use half a week of FMLA leave each week.
- If an employee who normally works thirty hours a week temporarily works only twenty hours a week under a reduced leave schedule, that employee will use one-third of a week of FMLA leave each week.[18]

Intermittent Leave

Some health conditions are episodic in nature. Employees with serious health conditions that manifest episodically and employees undergoing periodic treatments may need FMLA leave occasionally rather than in a single continuous block of time. This is called intermittent FMLA leave, leave taken in separate blocks of time for a single qualifying reason.[19]

An episodic condition is one that occurs or whose symptoms manifest for only brief periods of time. Those brief periods may be unpredictable. Examples of episodic conditions include epilepsy, migraine headaches, multiple sclerosis,

---

14. *Id.* § 825.202(a).
15. *Id.* § 825.202(b).
16. *See id.* § 825.202(b)(1).
17. *See id.* § 825.202(c).
18. *Id.* § 825.205(b)(1).
19. *Id.* § 825.202(a).

and Crohn's disease, but there are many others. Some medical treatments are also episodic, taking place periodically over a period of time. Examples of episodic treatments include chemotherapy and dialysis. As with reduced schedule leave, the FMLA only requires employers to grant requests for intermittent leave when medically necessary.[20]

Converting Hours to Weeks of Leave

Where an employee takes an instance of intermittent leave in increments of a full workday, it is easy to know how much FMLA leave an employee has used. In a 5-day workweek, 1 workday will be ⅕ of a week of FMLA. A half day would be ¹⁄₁₀ of a week. But the nature of the circumstances that require intermittent leave do not always make for such neat calculations. Often, employees on intermittent leave will take 3 hours here, 5 hours there, and on another occasion, a full day followed by a part day. In these situations, it makes more sense to record an employee's FMLA leave in increments of an hour (or less if appropriate).

The regulations emphasize that when an employer records FMLA leave in hours, it must be sure that it (or its timekeeping and payroll software) does so *proportionately.*[21] *Because leave is based on workweeks, employees who regularly work a 40-hour workweek will be entitled to more hours of FMLA leave than those who regularly work a 35-hour workweek.* For example, the employee who works a 40-hour workweek will be entitled to 480 hours of FMLA leave (40 hours × 12 weeks). A counterpart who works a 35-hour workweek will be entitled to only 420 hours of FMLA leave (35 hours × 12 weeks). The conversion to FMLA hours must be based on the number of hours that the employee is regularly scheduled to work.

Fluctuating Workweeks

It can happen that an employee's schedule fluctuates from week to week to such an extent that an employer is unable to determine with any certainty how many hours the employee would have worked if the employee were not on FMLA leave. In that case, the employer should use a weekly average of the hours the employee had been *scheduled to work* over the 12 months prior to the start of the FMLA leave period. The regulations specify that this calculation *must include* any hours for which the employee took leave of any type. In other words, the calculation should treat those hours for which the employee took leave as hours for which the employee was scheduled to work.[22] The calculation of the number of hours of FMLA leave

---

20. *Id.* § 825.202(b).
21. *See id.* § 825.205(b)(1).
22. *Id.* § 825.205(b)(3).

available to the employee would then proceed as outlined above. For example, if an employee's weekly average turned out to be 46 hours per week, then the employee would be entitled to a total of 552 hours of FMLA leave (46 hours × 12 weeks).

Overtime

The regulations permit employers to count overtime hours that an employee would have been required to work as hours of FMLA leave that count against the employee's 12-week entitlement.[23] Here's an example from the U.S. Department of Labor (DOL). A nonexempt employee who would normally be required to work 48 hours each week (that is, 8 hours' overtime) is currently unable to work more than 40 hours because of a serious health condition. That employee would then use eight hours of FMLA leave out of the 48-hour workweek, or ⅙ of a week of FMLA leave. But if overtime is voluntary, the story is different. Voluntary-overtime hours that an employee does not work due to an FMLA-qualifying reason may not be counted against the employee's leave entitlement.[24]

Intermittent or Reduced Schedule Leave That Is Never Exhausted

One of the more difficult aspects of managing an employee's intermittent FMLA leave is that the leave may be taken in such small increments or in a way that results in an employee's twelve weeks of leave never being exhausted. Consider the following example:

> *Roy suffers from Crohn's disease, a digestive-tract disorder that can be disabling when it flares. He has been approved for intermittent FMLA leave. There are long periods when Roy has no limitations on his daily activities, but the episodes and flare-ups he experiences are unpredictable in their intensity and duration. When he has a Crohn's flare-up, Roy typically uses one to two days of FMLA leave. In any given twelve-month period, Roy usually ends up using something short of the equivalent of twelve weeks for his Crohn's episodes. His supervisor is frustrated because Roy's sometimes frequent and always unplanned absences result in hardship on his co-workers, who must pick up the work he cannot timely complete.*

---

23. *Id.* § 825.205(c).

24. *Id. See also* U.S. Dep't of Labor, Wage & Hour Div., Opinion Letter FMLA2023-1-A (Feb. 9, 2023), https://www.dol.gov/sites/dolgov/files/WHD/opinion-letters/FMLA/2023_02_09_01_FMLA.pdf.

Can Roy's employer do anything about this situation? As mentioned in Chapter 1 (and discussed more fully in Chapter 6), the FMLA prohibits the discipline or dismissal of an employee for reasons connected with the taking of FMLA leave. In Wage and Hour Division opinion letters spanning 1994 to 2023, DOL has reiterated that employees who never exhaust their FMLA leave may work a reduced schedule indefinitely or continue taking intermittent leave indefinitely as long as it is medically necessary.[25] As the Wage and Hour Administrator said in a 1994 opinion letter,

> [y]ou suggest that if the employee requests FMLA leave every Monday and Friday afternoon for the dialysis treatments and incurs no other need for FMLA qualifying leave, the employee's right to take job-protected leave under FMLA could last forever because the employee would never use 12 weeks of leave in any 12-month period.
>
> You are correct in your analysis of FMLA's job protections in this case. . . .
>
> . . . If the employee never uses as much as 12 workweeks of FMLA leave in a 12-month period, the employee would never exhaust his or her statutory entitlement to take FMLA leave.[26]

In this particular situation, the employer has only one option. It may transfer the employee temporarily to a position that better suits the FMLA schedule. The employee must receive equal pay and benefits, but the job duties do not have to be equivalent. The transfer cannot be made permanent and may last only as long as the employee remains on a reduced schedule or intermittent leave. As with all leave taken under the FMLA, the employee must be restored to the same or an equivalent job at the conclusion of the intermittent or reduced schedule leave. For more on managing reduced schedule or intermittent leave, see Appendix B.

Treatment of Holidays During Full-Week, Intermittent, and Reduced Schedule Leave

The rules governing the treatment of paid holidays such as the Fourth of July or Thanksgiving during a period of FMLA leave may be found in section 825.200(h) of title 29 of the Code of Federal Regulations. For any week in which an employee takes a *full week* of FMLA leave, holidays are not taken into account. "[T]he fact that a holiday may occur within the week taken as FMLA leave has no effect; the week

---

25. *See, e.g.,* U.S. Dep't of Labor, FMLA2023-1-A, *supra* note 24; U.S. Dep't of Labor, Wage & Hour Div., Opinion Letter FMLA-29 (Feb. 7, 1994), https://www.dol.gov/sites/dolgov/files/WHD/legacy/files/FMLA-29.pdf; U.S. Dep't of Labor, Wage & Hour Div., Opinion Letter FMLA-67 (July 21, 1995), https://www.dol.gov/sites/dolgov/files/WHD/legacy/files/FMLA-67.pdf.

26. U.S. Dep't of Labor, Opinion Letter FMLA-29, *supra* note 25, at 1.

is counted as a week of FMLA leave."[27] When an employee is using *less than* a full week of FMLA leave—whether it is reduced schedule leave, intermittent leave, or the conclusion of FMLA leave midweek—the holiday is treated differently. When a holiday falls during a week when an employee is taking less than a full workweek of FMLA leave, the holiday is not counted as FMLA leave unless the employee was scheduled and expected to work on the holiday and used FMLA leave for that day.[28]

Examples

Full-Day Intermittent Leave During a Week with a Holiday

For example, imagine that the Fourth of July falls on a Friday. If Jill usually works a 5-day workweek and takes a full day of intermittent leave on Tuesday, then she will have used ⅕ of a week of FMLA leave. If Jill takes a full day of intermittent leave on the Monday of Thanksgiving week and her employer gives Thanksgiving Day and the day after as paid holidays, then again she will have used ⅕ of a week of FMLA leave.

Now imagine the same intermittent leave days if taken by Jared, a firefighter who works a 5-day workweek and is scheduled to work both on the Fourth of July and Thanksgiving and the following day (poor Jared!). He takes 1 day of intermittent leave on the Tuesday of Fourth of July week (again, the Fourth falls on Friday). He takes 1 day of intermittent leave on the Monday of Thanksgiving week. Both times, Jared will have used ⅕ of a week of FMLA leave because the holidays are regular workdays for Jared. They are, for FMLA purposes, the same as the paid holidays are for Jill. That is true even if Jared earns some sort of premium pay for working the holiday.

What if Jared is sick on the holidays he is scheduled to work and needs to use intermittent leave? This situation isn't any different from that of a normal, non-holiday workweek. If Jared is scheduled to work on the Fourth of July and uses intermittent FMLA leave on that day (in addition to the full day of intermittent leave he takes on Tuesday), he will have taken ⅖ of a week of FMLA leave. If he is ill due to his FMLA-qualifying condition on both Thanksgiving Day and the day following and uses intermittent leave (in addition to the 1 day of intermittent leave he took on Monday), he will have used ⅗ of a week of FMLA leave.

Employees Scheduled Under Section 207(k) of the Fair Labor Standards Act

The analysis is the same for law enforcement officers and firefighters scheduled under section 207(k) of the Fair Labor Standards Act (FLSA) and for employees

---

27. 29 C.F.R. § 825.200(h).
28. *Id.*

scheduled under the FLSA's fluctuating workweek. Employers must, however, first calculate the average number of hours worked by an employee over the past 12 months to determine how many hours of FMLA leave to which the particular employee is entitled. This is an important step to ensure that the amount of leave that is being recorded is proportionate to the employee's workweek.

Intermittent Leave Taken in Less Than a Full Workday

When an employee uses intermittent leave in amounts less than a full workday, the principles—and the result—are the same. Let's return to the example of Jill. Jill works a 5-day, 40-hour workweek. During the week in which the Fourth of July falls on Friday, she takes 3 hours of intermittent FMLA leave on Tuesday and 2 hours of intermittent FMLA leave on Wednesday. In this case, she has taken a total of 5 hours of FMLA leave that week, or ⅛ of a week of FMLA leave. The Fourth is a paid holiday, so it is treated as if Jill had worked that day. Another way to understand this example is to say that Jill is entitled to 480 hours of FMLA leave (40 hours × 12 weeks), of which she has now used 5 hours. If she had been scheduled to work on the Fourth of July and had taken 2 hours of intermittent leave on that day instead of on Wednesday, she would still have used ⅛ of a week of leave, or 5 hours of her 480-hour allotment.

What if Jared in the earlier example were taking intermittent leave and were scheduled under FLSA section 207(k)? And the number of hours he worked each week fluctuated? The first thing his employer would have to do is calculate the average number of hours he had worked during the preceding 12 months. Let's say Jared worked an average of 46 hours per week during the preceding 12 months. Applying the rule of proportionality, Jared would be entitled to 46 hours per week multiplied by 12 weeks for a total of 522 hours of FMLA leave. If he used 3 hours of intermittent FMLA leave on Tuesday and 2 hours of intermittent FMLA leave on Wednesday, and he had the Fourth off as a paid holiday, he would use 5 hours of his 552 hours of FMLA leave. If he were scheduled to work on the Fourth, he would again only have used 5 hours of his 552 hours of FMLA leave. For workweeks in which a paid holiday occurs, the paid holiday is treated like a regular workday for FMLA purposes.

Reduced Schedule Leave and Holidays

The same principles apply to reduced schedule leave.[29] If an employee who regularly works an 8-hour day works only 5-hour days on a reduced schedule FMLA leave, then this would be an instance of FMLA leave that is less than an entire workweek. During the week of the Fourth of July, the employee would not have been expected to work during the 3 hours that would otherwise count against the

---

29. *See id.*

FMLA entitlement. The rule dictates that on the Fourth, what would otherwise be the 3 hours of reduced schedule would not count as part of the employee's use of FMLA leave.

Full Week Versus Partial Week: Why the Different Treatment?

The reason that holidays are treated differently when an employee is taking a full workweek of FMLA leave and when FMLA leave is for only part of a workweek is explained in an opinion letter from the Wage and Hour Division in 2023.

> [I]t is clear that the actual workweek includes the day of the holiday. Subtracting the holiday from the workweek when calculating the amount of FMLA leave used in a partial week of leave would impermissibly reduce the employee's leave entitlement, because the employee would have to use a larger amount of FMLA leave than needed. For example, for an employee who normally works a 5-day week and takes one day of FMLA leave, excluding the holiday from the week would result in the employee using ¼ of a workweek of FMLA leave in a workweek that includes a holiday instead of ⅕ of a workweek of FMLA leave. Calculating the amount of leave used in this way would be an interference with the employee's FMLA rights.[30]

Treatment of Periods During Which the Workplace Is Closed

In government, the workplace is rarely entirely closed. Public safety, public works, and utilities are usually on the job even during the worst moments of hurricanes and pandemics. But a city's or county's administrative offices may close and employees in other departments may be told to stay home. Public secondary and postsecondary educational institutions may close down completely during an emergency. In addition, they sometimes close down for a week or more during breaks between semesters or during the winter holidays. In difficult financial times, employers may furlough employees for full or partial weeks. Whenever a workplace or the department or unit to which an employee reports ceases operations, the time during which the employer shuts down does not count against the employee's FMLA entitlement *even when the closing occurs in the middle of an employee's continuous FMLA leave.* This is true whether the employer pays the employees during the shutdown, the employees apply accrued paid leave, or the shutdown is unpaid.[31]

---

30. U.S. Dep't of Labor, Wage & Hour Div., Opinion Letter FMLA2023-2-A, at 3–4 (May 30, 2023), https://www.dol.gov/sites/dolgov/files/WHD/opinion-letters/FMLA/2023_05_30_02_FMLA.pdf.

31. *See* 29 C.F.R. § 825.200(h).

Chapter 4

Compensation and Benefits During FMLA Leave

Salary and Wages

Whether leave taken under the FMLA is paid or unpaid is an issue that confuses employers and employees alike. The FMLA says that leave is unpaid, although employers are required to maintain their contributions to an employee's health insurance premiums during the leave. But it is not as simple as that. To allow employers to limit absences, on one hand, and allow employees to receive some income during a prolonged absence, on the other, the FMLA permits employers to require the use of accumulated paid leave while an employee is on FMLA leave. At the same time, it allows employees, with certain restrictions, to choose to substitute accrued paid leave for unpaid FMLA leave when employers do not require it.[1] These practices turn what would otherwise be unpaid FMLA leave into paid FMLA leave.

Use of Accrued Paid Leave at the Same Time as Unpaid FMLA Leave

Overview

An employer's right to require employees to use all forms of accrued paid leave while on FMLA leave is absolute. An employee has the right to use accrued sick, vacation, or personal leave at the same time as FMLA leave to the extent that the employee's use of accrued paid leave in this instance is consistent with the employer's personnel policies.[2] The FMLA regulation on substitution of paid leave

---

1. 29 CFR § 825.207(a).
2. *Id.* § 825.207(a).

expressly prohibits employers from adopting policies that keep employees from using accrued paid sick, vacation, or personal leave to convert unpaid FMLA leave to paid leave. Note that while employers may require employees to use accrued "comp time" (compensatory time off under the Fair Labor Standards Act (FLSA)) during FMLA leave, employees may use accrued comp time during unpaid FMLA leave only with their employer's permission, although it is unlikely that an employer could meet the FLSA standard for denying the use of comp time in this situation, as discussed below.[3]

Use of Accrued Sick and Vacation Leave at the Same Time as FMLA Leave

Most FMLA-qualifying serious health conditions will also qualify for use of paid sick leave under an employer's local sick-leave policy. Paid vacation leave and personal leave rarely have substantive restrictions on the reasons for which they may be used. Consider the following example:

> *John injured his back while playing softball and requires surgery. His physician says that John will be out of work for 8 weeks, so John requests FMLA leave. John's employer requires employees to use sick and vacation leave when they are on FMLA leave. John has 20 days (4 weeks) of accrued paid sick leave and 15 days (3 weeks) of accrued paid vacation leave. Under his employer's policy, he will have to use all 4 workweeks of his accrued sick leave and all 3 workweeks of his accrued vacation leave during his 8 weeks of FMLA leave. As a result, all but 1 week of his FMLA leave will be paid leave.*

Restrictions on the Use of Sick Leave

The regulation on the substitution of paid leave prohibits employers from restricting an employee's concurrent use of sick leave to turn unpaid FMLA leave into paid FMLA leave. *But employers may restrict an employee's right to use paid sick leave during FMLA leave to those purposes for which sick leave is granted under its policy.*[4] For example, if an employer's sick-leave policy did not allow its use for anything other than the employee's own medical condition, accrued sick leave could not be used during FMLA leave taken to care for a sick spouse or child. In the North Carolina case *Daye v. Potter*, the employer's leave policy included not only personal sick leave, but a specified number of days of paid leave that could be used to care for dependents who were sick. After an employee on FMLA leave to care for his wife used up his accrued dependent-care sick leave, he asked the employer to allow him to use his accrued personal sick leave concurrently with the remainder of this FMLA leave. When his employer denied the request, the employee sued, alleging

---

3. *See id.* § 825.207(f).
4. *Id.* § 825.207(a).

interference with his FMLA rights. The court ruled in favor of the employer, noting that there was no interference since the employee was allowed to take his statutory allotment of FMLA leave. The employee was not, the court said, entitled to convert FMLA leave to paid leave where the employer did not allow the use of personal sick leave for situations other than the employee's own illness.[5]

In addition to limiting the reasons for which sick leave may be used, an employer's sick-leave policies sometimes have other requirements that must also be observed if paid sick leave is being used at the same time as FMLA leave. In *Pellegrino v. Communications Workers of America*, for example, the employer required employees to remain "in the immediate vicinity" of their home while using paid sick leave. To travel outside the area, employees had to request permission in writing.[6] An employee using FMLA leave and sick leave at the same time traveled to Cancun, Mexico, during her recuperation from surgery without asking her employer for permission. The employer fired her for violating its sick-leave policy upon her return. The federal Third Circuit Court of Appeals held that the FMLA did not protect her, because the sick-leave provision in question and the FMLA were not inconsistent with one another.[7] She was not dismissed for taking FMLA leave or even for traveling while on FMLA leave. Instead, she was dismissed for traveling without permission while using paid sick leave. The fact that it would not be lawful to prohibit an employee on *unpaid* FMLA leave from traveling did not change the outcome.

Use of FLSA Comp Time at the Same Time as Unpaid FMLA Leave

Imagine that in the previous example, John is a nonexempt employee under the FLSA. He has forty hours of accrued comp time (pursuant to his employer's policy of giving one-and-one-half hours of paid time off instead of cash for overtime hours worked). He is approved for eight weeks of FMLA leave to recuperate from surgery. He has seven weeks of accrued paid sick leave and vacation leave that he will use to turn the first seven weeks of unpaid FMLA leave into paid FMLA leave. He asks to use his forty hours of comp time to turn his eighth and last week of FMLA leave, which would otherwise be unpaid, into paid leave. Under the FMLA, his employer does not have to grant this request.[8] But under the FLSA, the employer *must* do so. The FLSA regulations at 29 CFR § 553.25 say that an employer must allow an employee to use accrued comp time within a reasonable period of the employee's

---

5. *See* Daye v. Potter, 380 F. Supp. 2d 718, 722 (M.D.N.C. 2005).

6. *See* Pellegrino v. Commc'ns Workers of Am., 478 F. App'x 742, 744 (3d Cir. 2012).

7. See *Pellegrino*, 478 F. App'x at 745–46. *Cf.* Callison v. City of Philadelphia, 430 F.3d 117, 120 (3d Cir. 2005) (finding that sick-leave policy requiring call to hotline when leaving the house is not inconsistent with the FMLA); Allen v. Butler Cnty. Comm'rs, 331 F. App'x 389, 395–96 (6th Cir. 2009) (citing *Callison* and holding that alternate requirements of doctor's note or daily health updates while using sick leave and FMLA at the same time do not violate the FMLA).

8. *See* 29 C.F.R. § 825.207(f).

request unless the use of comp time in that instance would unduly disrupt the employer's operations.[9] Given that John will not be working and will be on FMLA leave anyhow, it would be impossible for his employer to argue that John's use of comp time during this leave would interrupt operations. His employer must grant his request to use comp time to turn the eighth week of his unpaid FMLA leave into paid FMLA leave.

If, for some reason, John does not want to use his accrued comp time during his FMLA leave (perhaps he wishes to save it to use in some other circumstance), his employer may *require* him to use any accrued comp time that he has at the same time as any unpaid FMLA leave.[10]

Workers' Compensation and Payments from Short- and Long-Term-Disability Plans

Workers' compensation leave and short- or long-term-disability leave are considered *paid leave* under the FMLA. As a result, accrued paid leave and accrued comp time may not be used in conjunction with either workers' compensation or disability income benefits during an FMLA leave. Workers' compensation and disability-payment plans, however, usually pay only two-thirds of an employee's regular weekly wage. The FMLA therefore allows employees to use accrued paid leave and accrued comp time to supplement the workers' compensation or disability payments and make the employee whole. The FMLA regulation on the substitution of paid leave says that neither the employer nor the employee may unilaterally insist on the use of accrued paid leave to *supplement* the workers' compensation or disability benefits when leave runs concurrently with FMLA leave. They may, however, *mutually agree* to use paid accrued leave to supplement these benefits.[11]

Light-Duty Workers' Compensation Assignment and FMLA Leave

Sometimes the health care provider treating an employee for a workers' compensation injury will determine that although an employee cannot return to the original job, the employee can do a light-duty assignment. Suppose an employee on FMLA leave declines the employer's offer of a light-duty job. In North Carolina, this usually means that the employee will lose the workers' compensation payments.[12] The employee, however, is still entitled to remain on unpaid FMLA leave. On the date that workers' compensation benefits cease, the employer may require or the employee may choose to use accrued paid leave going forward for the remainder of the FMLA leave. An employee may not accept a light-duty assignment *and* remain on full FMLA leave.[13] The employee could, however, accept a reduced schedule

---

9. *Id.* § 553.25.
10. *See id.* § 825.207(f).
11. *See id.* § 825.207(d)–(e).
12. *See* N.C. Gen. Stat. 97 §§ 32, 2(22).
13. 29 C.F.R. § 825.207(e).

light-duty assignment and remain on a reduced schedule FMLA leave for the other hours in the workweek.

Concurrent Use of Paid Time Off with FMLA Leave: A Summary

Three basic rules govern turning unpaid FMLA leave into paid leave:

- An employer may require an employee on FMLA leave to use accrued vacation and sick leave at the same time as FMLA leave.
- Even if the employer does not require it, an employee has the right to use accrued paid leave at the same time as FMLA leave. However, if the employee wants to use sick leave, then the reason behind the FMLA leave must be a reason for which an employee can take sick leave under the employer's policy.
- An employer may require a nonexempt employee with accrued compensatory time off under the Fair Labor Standards Act to use it concurrently with FMLA leave. Even if the employer does not require it, an employee generally has the right to use FLSA comp time at the same time as FMLA leave.[14]

Holiday Pay and FMLA Leave

The FMLA is silent about whether employers who provide employees with paid holidays must pay employees who are on unpaid FMLA leave on the day a paid holiday occurs. Holiday pay is one of any number of benefits that are not mandated by state or federal law but instead are granted at the discretion of the individual employer. While the FMLA does not address holiday pay, it does require employers to provide employees on FMLA leave the same benefits and opportunities that it offers to employees who are on other forms of leave of absence: "An employee's entitlement to benefits other than group health benefits during a period of FMLA leave (e.g., holiday pay) is to be determined by the employer's established policy for providing such benefits when the employee is on other forms of leave (paid or unpaid, as appropriate)."[15] If an employer pays employees who are on leave other than FMLA leave for holidays, it must pay those who are on FMLA leave. If an employer has a practice, not a written policy, it should treat employees on FMLA leave in accordance with its practice but should also consider putting into writing its policies for benefits granted to employees on leave so they are clear to all.

---

14. *Id.* § 825.207(a).
15. *Id.* § 825.209(h).

Employee Benefits

An employer must continue to cover an employee on FMLA leave under its group health insurance during FMLA leave,[16] but as explained above, the employer is not required to maintain any other benefits, except to the extent that it maintains a benefit when employees are on another form of leave (sick leave or vacation leave, for example) that is comparable to FMLA leave. Employers may choose to maintain any benefit that the law does not require them to maintain.[17]

Health Insurance

An employer must cover an employee on FMLA leave under its group health insurance policy on the same terms as if the employee were working. If an employer pays an employee's entire premium or a share of the premium, it must continue to do so. Similarly, if an employer pays any portion of family coverage, it must continue to do so.[18] The employer share of a key employee's premiums must also continue to be paid since a key employee must be allowed to take FMLA leave and separation only happens when the key employee is denied restoration at the end of leave.[19] Even if all or part of FMLA leave is unpaid, employees are responsible for making any contributions toward payment of the premium that they would normally be required to make. Any employee who fails to make contributions on time may be dropped from coverage.[20]

An employee does not have to continue coverage under employer-sponsored health insurance while on FMLA leave, although that employee will be entitled to immediate reinstatement under the plan as soon as the FMLA leave ends.[21]

Health Insurance Premium Payment Arrangements

Paid FMLA Leave

When an employee uses accrued paid leave to turn unpaid FMLA leave into paid FMLA leave, any required employee contributions to the cost of health insurance premiums will normally continue to be made through payroll deduction. This requires no additional work on the part of the employer or the employee.[22]

---

16. *Id.* § 825.209(a)–(b).
17. *See id.* § 825.209(h).
18. *Id.* §§ 825.209(a), .209(b), .212(a), .212(c).
19. *Id.* § 825.219(c). On key employees, see Chapter 8, pages 113–14.
20. *Id.* §§ 825.210, .212.
21. *Id.* § 825.209(e).
22. *See id.* § 825.210(b).

Unpaid FMLA Leave

When FMLA leave is unpaid, employers must actively seek payment from employees for their share of the cost of health insurance premiums. The FMLA regulations authorize an employer to collect the employee share in any of the following ways:

1. by cash or check at the same time as payment would be made by a payroll deduction;
2. by cash or check at the same time as payment would be made if the employee were covered by continuation coverage under the Consolidated Omnibus Reconciliation Act (COBRA);
3. through prepayment under a section 125 cafeteria plan or through payroll deductions (if the leave is foreseeable and the employee agrees);
4. by using a "catch-up" method where the employer and the employee agree in advance that group coverage will continue during the period of unpaid FMLA leave but that the employee will not pay premiums until the FMLA leave is over (in other words, the employer will advance payment of the premiums on behalf of the employee and the employee will repay the advances upon return from FMLA leave); or
5. by any other means voluntarily agreed to by the employer and the employee.[23]

Employers may not *require* employees to use the pre-payment option. Employers may, on the other hand, require employees to use the catch-up method if that is also required of employees on non-FMLA unpaid leaves of absence.[24]

If an employee misses a premium payment, the employer may but is not required to make up the employee's contribution in order to maintain coverage. If it does so, the employer may recover the amount it advanced.[25] This may be considered akin to an advance on salary or an advance of vacation or sick leave for FLSA purposes and may be deducted from the employee's wages when the employee returns from FMLA leave.[26] This situation is similar to the catch-up method outlined in the fourth option, above.

Steps Required to End an Employee's Health Insurance Coverage for Nonpayment of Premium Contributions

When an employee fails to make a premium payment while on unpaid FMLA leave and the employer chooses not to cover the missing contribution, it may terminate

---

23. *Id.* § 825.210(c); 26 C.F.R. § 1.125-3(A-3) (IRS regulation on FMLA's effect on cafeteria plans).

24. 29 C.F.R. § 825.210(c); 26 C.F.R. § 1.125-3(A-3)(b)(1)–(2).

25. 29 C.F.R. § 825.212(b).

26. For more on repayment of advances and loans, see Diane M. Juffras, A Comprehensive Guide to the Fair Labor Standards Act for Public Employers 44–53 (UNC School of Government, 2020).

the employee's health insurance coverage. There are several requirements an employer must meet, however, before terminating coverage.

First, the employer must provide written notice to the employee that the premium payment was not received. The written notice must be mailed at least fifteen days before coverage will end. It must warn the employee that if payment is not received before then, coverage will be dropped on a specific date that is at least fifteen days after the date of the notice.[27]

If an employer's policies covering insurance payments during other forms of unpaid leave allow the employer to cease coverage retroactively to the date the unpaid premium payment was due, and if the employer has given the fifteen-day notice, the employer may drop the employee from coverage retroactively. If the employer does not have retroactive-drop policies but has given the fifteen-day notice, the employee's coverage may be terminated at the end of the effective thirty-day grace period.[28]

When an Employer's Obligation to Pay for Health Insurance Ends

An employer's obligation to maintain an employee's enrollment in its group health plan is not absolute. It ends in the following circumstances:

- during FMLA leave or at its conclusion, if the employment relationship would have ended because of a reduction-in-force, performance issues, or misconduct that occurred before the employee began FMLA leave;
- when the employee tells the employer that they do not intend to return to work after the leave ends;
- when the employee fails to return from the leave;
- when the employee fails to work for at least thirty calendar days after the leave ends; or
- when the employee remains on a leave of absence after exhausting the FMLA leave entitlement for the twelve-month FMLA year.[29]

Health Insurance and the Conclusion of FMLA Leave

Failure to Pay Health Insurance Contributions

It may come as a shock to some, but employees who fail to pay their share of health insurance premiums while on unpaid FMLA leave do not lose either their right to continue FMLA leave or to be reinstated to the same or an equivalent position when they return to work.[30] They must also be reinstated to all benefits upon their return to work, including health insurance. Even if an employee's participation in an employer's group health insurance plan has been suspended because

---

27. 29 C.F.R. § 825.212(a)(1).

28. *Id.*

29. *See id.* § 825.209(f).

30. 29 C.F.R. § 825.212(a)(3). On reinstatement to the same or an equivalent position, see Chapter 6, *The Return to Work After FMLA Leave.*

the employee failed to pay their share of the premium while on FMLA leave, the employee cannot be subject to any new preexisting-condition waiting periods or be made to wait for open enrollment. The employee cannot be required to submit to a medical examination to have coverage reinstated. An employer who has terminated an employee's health benefits and does not restore them at the conclusion of FMLA leave, either unintentionally or deliberately, may be liable for either the actual replacement cost of the lost health insurance or for the medical expenses incurred by the employee that would have been covered by the insurance plan.[31] This could include the costs of hospitalization, surgery, and other treatments. It is crucial that the employer ensure that all employees returning to work from FMLA leave have maintained their enrollment in the health insurance plan or are immediately reinstated upon their return.

Repayment of Employer's Health Insurance Contributions After a Failure to Return to Work

When an employee fails to return to work after FMLA leave, the employer may recover its share of the cost of health insurance premiums that it paid during a period of *unpaid* FMLA leave.[32] *Return to work* has a technical definition in the FMLA context: for an employee to have "returned to work" means that they have resumed performing their job duties for a minimum of thirty calendar days. An employee who retires during the first thirty calendar days after returning to work is still considered to have "returned to work," meaning that the cost of the employer's share of health insurance premiums paid during the unpaid leave may not be recovered.[33]

An employee who does not return to work owes a legal debt to the employer for the cost of the employer's share of the employee's health insurance during unpaid FMLA leave.[34] An employer in this situation has two options. First, it may recover costs through deductions from any final payments it owes to the employee, such as payouts of accrued vacation or sick leave or accrued comp time. The second option is to initiate a lawsuit to recover the employer's share.[35] Note that employers who

---

31. 29 C.F.R. § 825.212(c). *See* Lubke v. City of Arlington, 455 F.3d 489, 499 (5th Cir. 2006) (remanding to district court for redetermination of damages because jury awarded an undifferentiated sum for benefits); Dollar v. Smithway Motor Xpress, Inc., 787 F. Supp. 2d 896, 917 (N.D. Iowa 2011), *aff'd in part, vacated in part,* 710 F.3d 798 (8th Cir. 2013) (awarding prevailing employee in an FMLA interference suit the amount of lost health insurance contributions); Sherman v. AI/FOCS, Inc., 113 F. Supp. 2d 65, 76 (D. Mass. 2000) (plaintiff in FMLA case entitled to restoration of benefits, including damages sustained because of the termination of her health insurance benefits).

32. 29 C.F.R. § 825.213(a).

33. *Id.* § 825.213(c).

34. Employees using accrued paid leave at the same time as FMLA leave cannot be required to repay the employer share. After all, an employee who quits immediately after using sick or vacation leave cannot be made to reimburse the employer for use of that paid leave.

35. 29 C.F.R. § 825.213(f).

are self-insured may recover only the costs of the *employer's* share of the premium, as would be calculated under COBRA.[36] Self-insured employers may not recover costs paid by the self-insured plan for treatment of the employee's serious health condition or any other health condition.

If an employee fails to return to work after FMLA leave, the employer must still offer COBRA continuation coverage just as it would to any employee who quit or was fired. This is easy to overlook, but failure to do so could result in the employer's being liable for the costs of medical treatment obtained without insurance coverage.

Exceptions to the Repayment Rule

There are three important exceptions to the rule that employees must reimburse the employer's share of health insurance premiums if they fail to return to work. The first is when an employee is receiving workers' compensation benefits while on FMLA leave. Because workers' compensation is a form of paid leave (even though the payments are coming from the insurer or the insurance pool), when an employee fails to return to work at the conclusion of FMLA leave, the employer may not recover the cost of the premiums it paid during the leave.[37]

The second exception is when an employee does not return to work because the employee's serious health condition or that of a family member continues beyond the time when FMLA leave ends.[38] Because the employee still needs treatment or rest, or still needs to care for an immediate family member, the FMLA regulations excuse the employee from having to pay the employer back for the employer's share of the premium. In this situation, the employer may require an additional medical certification at the employee's own cost. The new certification must be returned within thirty days of the day that the employer requests it for the employee to be relieved of the repayment obligation.[39]

The third exception is quite expansive: an employee is not required to reimburse an employer for health premiums if circumstances beyond the employee's control prevent the employee from returning to work. If an employee took FMLA leave because the employee is having a baby, for example, and the baby then had a serious health condition that continued beyond the end of the leave, that would be a circumstance beyond the employee's control. Some other examples include a spouse's being unexpectedly transferred to a work location more than seventy-five miles away; another family member's developing a serious health condition and needing the employee's care; being laid off during FMLA leave; or a key employee deciding not to return to work upon notification of the employer's intention to deny restoration.[40]

---

36. *Id.* § 825.213(e).
37. *Id.* § 825.213(d).
38. *Id.* § 825.213(a).
39. *Id.* § 825.213(a)(3).
40. *Id.* § 825.213(a)(2). See Chapter 8, pages 116–19, for key employees.

Other Benefits

Flexible Spending Plans

Flexible spending accounts (FSAs) are IRS-qualified accounts that allow employees to pay for certain medical costs on a pre-tax basis. There are two types of FSAs: one for medical costs not covered by insurance and one for dependent-care costs. (A health care FSA is distinct from a premium conversion plan, which allows employees to pay their share of health insurance premiums with pre-tax dollars; the rules governing premium conversion plans during FMLA leave are the same as the rules for health insurance generally). With FSAs, participating employees determine, on an annual basis, how much money they wish to deposit in one or both accounts, subject only to an annual limit on each type of account set by the IRS.[41] Employees on FMLA leave must be given the option of either continuing to contribute to their health care FSA during FMLA leave or ceasing contributions. For employees choosing to continue their participation in a health care FSA, deductions will continue to be made from their paychecks if they are on paid FMLA leave. If the FMLA leave is unpaid, then employees' contributions may be made either by pre-paying, paying by check during the course of FMLA leave, or by using the "catch-up" method and contributing the missing amounts upon their return from leave.[42] Employees must continue participation in a health care FSA during their leave if they plan on using funds in the FSA to reimburse themselves for medical expenses incurred during FMLA leave.[43]

There is no requirement that an employer allow an employee on FMLA leave to continue to contribute to a dependent care FSA, however. If the employer allows continued participation, contributions may be made as they would be for health care FSA continuance: by pre-payment, check during leave, or catching up when the employee returns.[44] Because the purpose of allowing dependent care to be paid for using pre-tax dollars is to enable the employee to work, contributions to a dependent care FSA may only be used to pay for child care provided while the employee is actually working and may not be used during a leave of absence longer than two weeks.[45]

TSERS and LGERS

When an employee is on paid FMLA leave, both the employer's and the employee's shares of contributions to the retirement system are made, just as they are when the employee is using accrued paid leave or comp time for ordinary sick or vacation purposes. When FMLA leave is unpaid, no contributions are made.

---

41. FSAs for health care expenses are authorized by 26 U.S.C. § 125, and dependent care FSAs are authorized by 26 U.S.C. § 129.

42. 26 C.F.R. § 1.125-3(A-3), (A-6).

43. *Id.* § 1.125-3(A-6)(b)(1)–(2).

44. *Id.* § 1.125-3(A-3)(b).

45. *Id.* § 1-21-1(c)(2)(ii).

A leave of absence may, however, affect other retirement system issues. Retirement plans do not get specific mention either in the text of the FMLA or in the FMLA regulations. In general, with respect to benefits other than health insurance coverage, employers must treat employees on FMLA leave as they would treat employees on non-FMLA leave, and that general rule would seem to apply to the treatment of FMLA leave for TSERS (Teachers' and State Employees' Retirement System) and LGERS (Local Government Employees' Retirement System) eligibility, vesting, and creditable service purposes.[46] Nevertheless, the U.S. DOL has included the following guidance in its online compliance tool, *elaws Advisor*:

> Any period of unpaid FMLA leave cannot be treated as a break in service for purposes of vesting and eligibility to participate in pension and other retirement plans. If the plan requires an employee to be employed on a specific date in order to be credited with a year of service for vesting, contributions or participation purposes, an employee on unpaid FMLA leave on that date will be deemed to have been employed on that date. Unpaid FMLA leave periods, however, need not be treated as credited service for purposes of benefit accrual, vesting and eligibility to participate.[47]

In other words, unpaid FMLA leave cannot function as a break in service that erases all the employee's previous credits toward eligibility, vesting, or the like. Employers do not, however, have to treat unpaid FMLA leave as time worked for the purposes of creditable service.

Accrual of Sick Leave, Vacation Leave, and Other Paid Time Off

In a perfect world, every government employer would decide whether sick, vacation, or personal leave continues to accrue while an employee is on a leave of absence at the time it adopted its policies for accrued paid time off. Some allow accrual to continue during a leave; some do not. Some employers have practices of allowing or disallowing accrual during leaves of absence but do not have written policies. The FMLA does not require employers to continue crediting employees on FMLA leave with time toward the accrual of paid time off. But if an employer allows employees to accrue paid time off during other forms of paid or unpaid leave, it must also do so for employees on FMLA leave.[48] In comparing how their leave of absence policies apply to different types of leave, employers should remember that for FMLA purposes, workers' compensation leave and short-term disability leave count as forms of paid leave.[49]

---

46. *See* 29 C.F.R. § 825.209(h).

47. *Family and Medical Leave Act Advisor*, U.S. DEP'T OF LABOR (last visited Mar. 24, 2024), https://webapps.dol.gov/elaws/whd/fmla/8e2.aspx.

48. *See* 29 C.F.R. § 825.209(h).

49. *Id.* § 825.207(d)–(e).

Chapter 5

How FMLA Leave Gets Started and How It Is Administered

Notice Requirements and Certifications

The purpose of the Family and Medical Leave Act as set forth in the statute is "to balance the demands of the workplace with the needs of families" and "to entitle employees to take reasonable leave for medical reasons, for the birth or adoption of a child, and for the care of a child, spouse, or parent who has a serious health condition . . . in a manner that accommodates the legitimate interests of employers."[1] The FMLA is a balancing act, a series of negotiated compromises between the interests of employees, on one hand, and employers, on the other. Nowhere is this framework as clear as it is in the carefully delineated series of steps that employees and employers must take in initiating an instance of FMLA leave. To call these steps "Notice Requirements" and "Designation" as the regulations do, or "FMLA paperwork," as employers and employees sometimes do, disguises the importance of this part of the taking of FMLA leave.

Employer General Notice Posting Requirements

Recall that all government employers are covered by the FMLA, although a government employee must work at a worksite that has at least fifty employees within a seventy-five mile radius to be eligible to take FMLA leave.[2] This sometimes leads to the strange situation in which a local government is covered by the FMLA but has no eligible employees. Nevertheless, all government employers, whether they have eligible employees or not, are subject to an FMLA-notice posting requirement.[3] The FMLA requires all public employers to post a notice explaining the FMLA

---

1. 29 U.S.C. § 2601(b)(1)–(3).
2. 29 C.F.R. § 825.104(a).
3. *Id.* § 825.300(a)(1)–(2).

and providing information about filing complaints of violations of the FMLA with the United States Department of Labor (DOL) in conspicuous places inside work areas. The notice must be posted in a prominent position where it will be easily seen by employees. The poster and the text must be large enough to be easy to read.[4] DOL's Wage and Hour Division has a model general notice that employers may download for posting.[5] In 2024, the civil money penalty for violation of the posting requirement is up to $211 for each separate offense.[6]

Employers who do have eligible employees (that is, employers with fifty or more employees over the last twelve months[7]) are subject to one additional general notice requirement. The information provided in DOL's model general notice must also be included *in its entirety* in any employee handbook, personnel manual, or other material provided to employees about employee benefits and leave. If the employer does not have an employee handbook or personnel manual or does not provide any written materials about benefits and the taking of leave, then the employer must give all employees a copy of the general notice when they begin employment. The written material, whether part of a handbook or manual or distributed individually at the time of hire, may be in electronic form.[8]

Employee Notice of Planned or "Foreseeable" Need for Leave

When employees know that they will need FMLA leave (because they are expecting a baby, for example, or because they are having elective surgery), FMLA regulations require employees to give their employer thirty days' advance notice.[9] If the need for leave only becomes apparent fewer than thirty days in advance, then the employee must inform the employer "as soon as is practicable." The regulations define "as soon as is practicable" to mean "as soon as is both possible and practical," which the regulations say should usually be *the same day that the employee realizes the need for leave or the next business day*.[10] An employer may require an employee who fails to provide timely notice of the need for FMLA leave to explain why, and the employer may delay the start of leave if the employee does not provide a reasonable excuse.[11] If the need for leave was apparent thirty days before the date for

---

4. *Id.* § 825.300(a)(1).

5. As of this writing, a PDF of this notice is at https://www.dol.gov/sites/dolgov/files/WHD/legacy/files/fmlaen.pdf.

6. *See* 29 CFR § 825.300(a)(1) (2023). The amount of the penalties US DOL may assess for violations of the FMLA increases annually.

7. See Chapter 2, pages 9–10.

8. 29 C.F.R. § 825.300(a)(3)–(4).

9. *Id.* § 825.302(a). Failure to comply with notice requirements is excused only in unusual circumstances. For example, an employer's policy may require employees to call a specific number to make leave requests. If an employee called that number thirty days in advance to request the leave, no one answered the phone, and the voicemail box were full, then failure to comply with the notice requirement would be excusable.

10. *Id.* § 825.302(a)–(b).

11. *Id.* §§ 825.302(a), .302(d), .304.

which it is requested, the employer may delay the start of FMLA leave until thirty days after it actually received notice.[12] If the need for leave arose fewer than thirty days in advance, then leave may be delayed by the amount of time the employee delayed notifying the employer after it became possible to do so. The regulations give the following example:

> [I]f an employee reasonably should have given the employer two weeks notice but instead only provided one week notice, then the employer may delay FMLA-protected leave for one week (thus, if the employer elects to delay FMLA coverage and the employee nonetheless takes leave one week after providing the notice (*i.e.*, a week before the two week notice period has been met) the leave will not be FMLA-protected).[13]

When employees request leave for planned medical treatment, the regulations require them to consult with their employers before scheduling the treatment to work out a schedule that meets the needs of both employee and employer, subject to the approval of the health care provider. This means that the employee *cannot* simply tell the employer, "I am having surgery on June 1 and am taking FMLA leave." Consider how this very situation played out in a recent case from Ohio. There, a bus driver for a school system had been plagued by a foot injury for many years. Two days before a scheduled foot surgery, the driver informed the system that he needed leave for surgery. The school system terminated the driver after he returned from his surgery. In granting the school system's motion for summary judgment on the bus driver's FMLA retaliation claim, the court found that the driver had not been on FMLA leave at all because he had not given the school system thirty days' advance notice of his surgery. His job, therefore, was not protected and he was not entitled to return to it.[14]

Planned medical treatments are meant to be a cooperative effort between employee, employer, and health care provider. If an employee does not consult with an employer before scheduling the treatment, the employer may require the employee to try to reschedule the treatment to better accommodate the needs of the workplace. Any such rescheduling is, however, "subject to the approval of the health care provider."[15]

"Unforeseeable" Need for FMLA Leave

Not every condition that meets the definition of a serious health condition is predictable or, to use the term preferred by the regulations, "foreseeable." An employee (or an employee's immediate family member) may become ill suddenly or be injured in an accident. A requirement of thirty days' advance notice is unreasonable in

---

12. *See id.* § 825.304(b).

13. *Id.* § 825.304(c).

14. Schwendeman v. Marietta City Schs., 436 F. Supp. 3d 1045, 1066 (S.D. Ohio 2020), *aff'd*, No. 20-3251, 2020 WL 7711327 (6th Cir. Dec. 14, 2020).

15. 29 C.F.R. § 825.302(e).

these situations. That is why the FMLA requires employees to give notice of the need for FMLA "as soon as practicable" when the need for leave is not foreseeable. As with need that is foreseeable but arises with fewer than thirty days' advance notice, the regulations say that "as soon as practicable" will usually be *on the same day or on the next business day*.[16]

Employers may require employees requesting FMLA leave that is unforeseeable to use their "usual and customary notice and procedural requirements" for requesting leave.[17] That may include contacting a specific individual, calling a specific number, or contacting a third-party FMLA administrator.[18] But employers should note that the federal Fourth Circuit Court of Appeals (which has jurisdiction over North Carolina) has held that "'usual and customary procedures' include *any method* that an employer has, by informal practice or course of dealing with the employee, regularly accepted, along with those in the employer's written attendance policy."[19] In that Fourth Circuit case, an employer argued unsuccessfully that an employee had failed to give notice of his need for FMLA leave because he contacted his supervisor by Facebook Messenger rather than by calling the number in the personnel policy. There was ample evidence, however, that the employer had previously allowed the same employee to communicate his absences and his need for FMLA leave to the same supervisor using Messenger. Thus, although not mentioned in the company's employee handbook, Facebook Messenger was a regularly accepted way of communicating absences and the need for leave.[20]

If an employee fails to follow the employer's general leave procedures without a reasonable justification, the employer may delay or deny FMLA leave.[21] This is true for foreseeable leave, unforeseeable leave, and intermittent leave. Sometimes, however, an employer's policies for giving notice of the need for leave are more stringent than the FMLA's requirements. In such a case, an employer cannot deny FMLA leave if the employee has satisfied the FMLA's notice requirements—even if the employee has not satisfied the notice requirements of the employer's policies.[22] Consider the following hypothetical:

> *Paradise City requires every employee requesting FMLA leave to give notice*
> *of an unforeseeable need for FMLA leave to three people: the employee's*

---

16. Waiting eight days to give notice of a family member's need for treatment of a back injury is not "'as soon as practicable' under the facts and circumstances." Torres v. Inspire Dev. Ctr., No. 13–CV–3062–TOR., 2014 WL 3697816, at *9 (E.D. Wash. 2014) (upholding termination on this and other FMLA-related grounds).

17. 29 C.F.R. § 825.303(c).

18. *Id.* § 825.303(a).

19. Roberts v. Gestamp W. Va., LLC, 45 F.4th 726, 734 (4th Cir. 2022) (emphasis added).

20. *Id.* at 734.

21. 29 C.F.R. § 825.302(d).

22. *See* Moore v. GPS Hosp. Partners IV, LLC, 383 F. Supp. 3d 1293, 1303–04 (S.D. Ala. 2019); Hayduk v. City of Johnstown, 580 F. Supp. 2d 429, 455 (W.D. Pa. 2008).

> *immediate supervisor, the department head, and the human resources direc-*
> *tor. When Larissa receives notice that her mother has suffered a traumatic*
> *brain injury, she calls both her supervisor, with whom she speaks in person,*
> *and her department head, for whom she leaves a message. Larissa neglects to*
> *contact the human resources director. Upon her return to work the following*
> *week, Paradise City fires Larissa for absenteeism, telling her that her absences*
> *were not protected by the FMLA because she did not follow the city's reporting*
> *policy for requesting FMLA leave.*

Can Paradise City deny Larissa FMLA leave simply because she forgot to tell one of the three management employees that she needed unforeseeable FMLA leave? The answer to that question is no. Larissa satisfied the FMLA by informing her employer that she would need FMLA leave and explaining why. Although the FMLA requires employees to follow their employer's individual reporting policy, it does not allow employers to add additional requirements. Here, the city required more than a single notice directed to a person designated by the employer. It required the employee to give three separate notices, which is more than the FMLA requires.

Information That Must Be Included in the Notice of the Need for Leave

Whether FMLA leave is foreseeable or unforeseeable, employees must provide their employers with one of the following reasons for the need for leave:

- a health condition makes the employee unable to perform the functions of the job;
- the employee is pregnant;
- the employee has been hospitalized overnight; or
- a family member is under the continuing care of a health care provider.

In the case of a family member, the employee must tell the employer whether the medical condition renders the family member unable to perform daily activities. In any case, if the employee knows the timing (if the need for leave is foreseeable) and the anticipated duration of their absence, the employer must be provided that information, as well.[23]

Neither Mention of the FMLA nor "Magic Words" Are Required

Whether the need for leave is foreseeable or unforeseeable, an employee doesn't need to use any "magic words" or to ask specifically for "family and medical leave" or "FMLA leave" to be entitled to the benefits of the FMLA.[24] An employee's

---

23. 29 C.F.R. §§ 825.302(c) (foreseeable leave), .303(b) (unforeseeable leave).

24. *See* Hannah P. v. Coats, 916 F.3d 327, 345 (4th Cir. 2019) (denying employer's motion to dismiss on plaintiff's FMLA interference claim); Dotson v. Pfizer, Inc., 558 F.3d 284, 295 (4th Cir. 2009).

knowledge of the existence of FMLA leave and the reasons for which it may be taken may be nonexistent or sketchy. But if an employee has been on FMLA leave for the same qualifying reason previously, the employee must specifically mention either the qualifying reason or the need for FMLA leave.[25]

Once an employer knows *or has reason to think* that an employee may qualify for FMLA leave, it is the employer's responsibility to bring the availability of FMLA leave to the employee's attention.[26] But what does it mean to say that an employer knows or has reason to think that an employee may qualify for FMLA leave? As the federal Sixth Circuit Court of Appeals articulates the standard,

> [t]he critical test for substantively-sufficient notice is whether the information that the employee conveyed to the employer was reasonably adequate to apprise the employer of the employee's request to take leave for a serious health condition that rendered him unable to perform his job.[27]

An employee does not need to have been absent for more than three consecutive workdays for an employer to have reason to believe FMLA leave may be appropriate. In the 2019 Fourth Circuit case *Hannah P. v. Coats*, the court held that a reasonable jury could well find that an employee's disclosure to her supervisors that she was suffering from depression (a diagnosis she had told them about several years earlier) and that her psychiatrist was now recommending a four-week leave of absence was sufficient notice to her employer that she was asking for an FMLA leave.[28] Earlier, in *Dotson v. Pfizer, Inc.*, the Fourth Circuit held that a reasonable jury could find that an employee who told his employer that he was adopting a child and asked about whether he could take leave during the adoption process gave his employer enough information that the employer's FMLA obligations were triggered.[29] Once an employee has provided some notice—oral or written—of a potentially qualifying condition or situation, it is the employer's duty to inquire further to determine whether FMLA leave is being sought or whether FMLA is available.[30]

Whether an employee has provided sufficient notice of a qualifying event does not always turn on how much medical information the employee has shared. Consider the case *Coutard v. Municipal Credit Union*. When Frantz Coutard told his employer he needed to take time off to care for his seriously ill grandfather, he did not mention that his grandfather had stood *in loco parentis* to him since he was four years old. The federal Second Circuit Court of Appeals, however, found that

---

25. 29 C.F.R. § 825.303(b).

26. *Hannah P.*, 916 F.3d at 345; *Dotson*, 558 F.3d at 295.

27. Hrdlicka v. Gen. Motors, LLC, 59 F.4th 791, 808 (6th Cir. 2023) (quoting Koch v. Thames Healthcare Grp., LLC, 855 F. App'x 254, 256 (6th Cir. 2021)).

28. *Hannah P.*, 916 F.3d at 346.

29. *Dotson*, 558 F.3d at 291, 295.

30. 29 C.F.R. §§ 825.302(c) (foreseeable leave), .303(b) (unforeseeable leave). *See also* Brushwood v. Wacovia Bank, N.A., 520 F. App'x 154, 157 (4th Cir. 2013).

the mention of caring for his grandfather was enough to put Coutard's employer on notice that he might be eligible for FMLA leave because many people are raised by people who are not their biological parents, and by grandparents in particular, and that this was the reason why Congress included persons standing *in loco parentis* in the FMLA's definition of *parent*.[31] An employer is expected to make additional inquiries to clarify the nature of the employee's condition or situation, and the employee is expected to respond to the employer's questions.

Merely calling in sick, however, is not sufficient to put an employer on notice that the employee may need FMLA leave. In a case from the federal Sixth Circuit Court of Appeals, the court found that an employee's explanation for her recent string of absences, namely, that her head hurt, that she felt sick or that she had a fever, amounted to no more than generalized ailments not rising to the level of a serious health condition. The parties disputed whether the employee had mentioned suffering from depression in a meeting held just before she was terminated for excessive absenteeism, but given that the employee had previously taken FMLA for a different reason and that a warning letter addressing her absenteeism had noted the availability of FMLA leave, the court found that even if the employee had mentioned her depression, this did not make for sufficient notice of the need for FMLA leave without more information.[32]

Consider two other examples of explanations for absences that are not specific enough to give employers notice of the need for FMLA leave. In the first, *Peeples v. Coastal Office Products, Inc.*, an employee on vacation abroad called his employer on his last day of vacation and said that he might have malaria, and that he was waiting to see a doctor and would not be able to return to the United States until he recovered. The court found that he did not provide sufficient notice to his employer that FMLA might apply where the employer was unable to reach the employee to obtain further information.[33] In the second case, the only information an employee provided to his employer at the start of a long absence was an emergency room slip stating that he was under no restrictions. The employee called his supervisor several times to say that he was not ready to return to work. The employee not only failed to give his employer any description of his symptoms or his condition (he was suffering from depression and anxiety), but also misled the supervisor by saying he was seeing a thyroid specialist. The Fourth Circuit found that this did not constitute sufficient notice that the employee had an FMLA-qualifying condition.[34]

---

31. Coutard v. Mun. Credit Union, 848 F.3d 102, 112–13 (2d Cir. 2017). *Cf.* Fitzgerald v. Shore Mem'l Hosp., 92 F. Supp. 3d 214, 230 (D.N.J. 2015) (granting summary judgment to employer where employee's statements about aunt for whom she requested FMLA leave to care for were contradictory and did not indicate their exact relationship, employee did not respond to employer's request for additional information, and employer denied leave).

32. *Hrdlicka*, 59 F.4th at 808–09. *Cf.* Walton v. Ford Motor Co., 424 F.3d 481, 486–87 (6th Cir. 2005) (employee informing supervisor he had "twisted his knee" was not sufficient notice of need for FMLA leave).

33. Peeples v. Coastal Off. Prod., Inc., 64 F. App'x 860, 863 (4th Cir. 2003).

34. Sherif v. Univ. of Md. Med. Ctr., 127 F. Supp. 3d 470, 478 (D. Md. 2015).

In contrast, a Florida employee's email telling her supervisors that she was flying to Pennsylvania, where her dad was in the hospital intensive-care unit, and that she would not be available for calls or video edits, was found sufficient to trigger her employer's FMLA responsibilities.[35]

Employer Responsibilities After Receiving Notice of the Need for FMLA Leave

Once an employer receives a leave request with an FMLA-qualifying reason or learns that an employee is absent for a qualifying reason, it must notify the employee that the employee is eligible for FMLA leave *within five business days*.[36] The five-business-day deadline applies whether the need for leave is foreseeable or arises suddenly. The notice of eligibility may be oral or in writing.[37] The better practice is to put the notice in writing (preferably using the U.S. DOL's combined Notice of Eligibility and Rights and Responsibilities, Form WH-381[38]) in order to have documentary evidence that notice was given in the event of an FMLA interference lawsuit. When employees take a second instance of FMLA leave in the same twelve-month period or FMLA year and there is no change to their eligibility,

> Savvy employees may go straight to human resources when they want FMLA leave or when they are absent, but there is a good chance that some employees will go to a supervisor or department head instead. Suppose an employee (let's call him Stan) says to his supervisor, "Hey, Mr. Jones. I'm going to be having a procedure done on my big toe next month and I'll be out of work for two weeks." What should that supervisor do? The supervisor should, first, refer Stan to human resources and, second, immediately contact human resources himself to let them know that Stan has said he may need FMLA leave. The supervisor should do this *even if FMLA leave was never mentioned.*
>
> Department heads and supervisors should also notify human resources if they learn that an employee will be absent due to a serious accident or hospitalization. In the end, the employee may not be out of work for the three days necessary to meet the definition of a serious health condition, but the probability that their condition will qualify is greater in situations involving accidents and hospital admissions. Alerting the human resources department will give it a head start, as the employer's obligation to respond to a request for FMLA leave (or situation calling for FMLA leave) is still five days even when the need for leave has not been foreseeable.

---

35. Graves v. Brandstar, Inc., 67 F.4th 1117, 1122 (11th Cir. 2023).
36. 29 C.F.R. § 825.300(b)(1).
37. *See id.* § 825.300(b)(2).
38. A PDF of Form WH-381 may be found at https://www.dol.gov/sites/dolgov/files/WHD/legacy/files/WH-381.pdf. A copy of the form may be found in Appendix A.

employers are not required to provide additional notice of eligibility.[39] As described in the previous section, an employer's duty to respond is not triggered unless the employer should reasonably understand, at the time of the request, that the expressed need for leave was covered by the FMLA *or could be* covered by FMLA.[40]

Note that when an employee brings a lawsuit alleging FMLA interference based on an employer's failure to inform them of their right to FMLA leave, the employee must still show that the employer's failure to inform the employee harmed the employee in some way: "If an employer's failure to timely designate leave in accordance with § 825.300 causes the employee to suffer harm, it may constitute an interference with, restraint of, or denial of the exercise of an employee's FMLA rights."[41] In the *Hannah P.* case, the court found that a reasonable jury could have found that her employer's failure to offer and explain FMLA leave had prejudiced Hannah P. because she had used all her sick leave and vacation leave to cover her four-week absence. Had she known of the availability of FMLA leave, Hannah P. claimed, she would have used her sick leave but would have taken unpaid leave instead of using her vacation leave (vacation leave was paid out at separation from her employer, but sick leave was lost).[42] In other words, she would have acted differently had she known she could take unpaid job-protected leave.

The Notice of Eligibility and of Rights and Responsibilities

When an employer notifies an employee that they are eligible for FMLA leave, it must also give the employee a notice that details the specific rights, expectations, and obligations of an employee on FMLA leave. Employers should use Form WH-381, a combined Notice of Eligibility and Rights and Responsibilities (ERR notice), for this purpose. It contains much information that is useful to both employers and employees, and it satisfies the FMLA regulations' employer notification requirement. Section II of the form requires the employer to provide the following information:

- whether the employee must provide a medical certification of the serious health condition (either the employee's or a family member's);
- whether any other information is required, such as documentation of a family or *in loco parentis* relationship (see below, on medical certifications);
- whether the leave will count against the employee's twelve-week FMLA entitlement;

---

39. 29 C.F.R. § 825.300(b)(2).

40. *Id.* §§ 825.300(b), (d)(1), (2), 825.303(b). *See also* Coutard v. Mun. Credit Union, 848 F.3d 102 (2d Cir. 2017).

41. 29 C.F.R. § 825.301(e). *See also* Munoz v. Selig Enters., Inc., 981 F.3d 1265, 1274–75 (11th Cir. 2020) (although her employer never told her of her right to FMLA leave, plaintiff could not show harm as she was not denied time off).

42. Hannah P. v. Coats, 916 F.3d 327, 346–47 (4th Cir. 2019).

- whether the employer requires the use of accrued paid leave in lieu of unpaid leave (see Chapter 4);
- the fact that the employee may elect to use accrued paid leave in place of unpaid leave;
- any conditions related to the substitution of paid leave for unpaid leave (for example, that the employer's policy allows sick leave to be used only for an employee's own illness) (see Chapter 4);
- whether the employee needs to make contributions toward health insurance premium payments and, if so,
  - the arrangements that the employee needs to make,
  - the consequences of a failure to make contribution payments, and
  - the fact that if the employee fails to return to work when FMLA leave is over, the employee is liable for reimbursing the employer's health insurance contributions (see Chapter 4); and
- the employee's right to return to the same or an equivalent job (see Chapter 6).[43]

The notice may but does not have to include other information, such as

- whether the employee must provide periodic updates on their condition during the leave and
- whether the employee must provide a fitness-for-duty certification before returning to work.[44]

If, for some reason, an employer chooses to use its own notice form, it too must contain the information listed above.

If an employee has requested FMLA leave and is ineligible, the ERR notice must give at least one reason why the employee is not eligible—perhaps because the employee has not worked the minimum of twelve months for this employer or the minimum of 1,250 hours in the immediately preceding twelve months.[45]

Section III of Form WH-381 sets forth the employee and the employer's respective rights and responsibilities. It lets the employee know how the employer determines the twelve months within which an employee's twelve-week FMLA entitlement must fall. As described in more detail in Chapter 3, there are four different permissible methods that employers may use for calculating the "FMLA year." Section III is also the place where an employer indicates whether the FMLA leave will be unpaid, whether the employee has requested to use accrued paid leave at the same time as FMLA leave—turning it into paid leave—and whether the employer is requiring the employee to use any accrued paid leave at the same time (see Chapter 4).

---

43. 29 C.F.R. § 825.300(c)(1).
44. *Id.* § 825.300(c)(2). See Chapter 6, pages 86–90.
45. 29 C.F.R. § 825.300(b)(2).

If an employer does not have to provide notice of eligibility because the employee has already taken FMLA leave earlier in the FMLA year, no notice of rights and responsibilities is required. Once a new FMLA calendar year has begun, both a notice of eligibility and a notice of rights and responsibilities are again required.[46]

Certifications and the ERR Notice

The ERR notice must indicate whether the employer is requiring a medical certification of the need for FMLA leave from a health care provider (the content of which is discussed in greater detail later in this chapter).[47] The medical certification form must be given to the employee at the same time as the ERR notice.[48] If the employer wishes to have the health care provider consider the employee's specific job duties in making the assessment that the employee cannot work, it must attach a list of job duties to the medical certification.[49]

If the employer requires a medical certification, the employee has fifteen calendar days from receiving the ERR notice to return it.[50] If the employee does not return the medical certification, the employer may deny FMLA leave, leaving the employee's absence unprotected. Should the certification that is returned be incomplete or insufficient, or should the employer need clarification on one of the answers, the employee has seven days to provide whatever is needed.[51]

The employer may also indicate on the ERR notice whether it plans to require a fitness-for-duty certification before the employee returns to work.

Employee Request Not to Use FMLA Leave for a Qualifying Absence

An employee may wish to "save" FMLA leave. Perhaps they know that they will need FMLA leave in a few months and wish to save it for the birth of a child or for a planned medical procedure. The employee may ask not to have the leave designated as FMLA leave or may refuse to return a required medical certification.

But too bad for the employee! In a 2019 opinion letter, the U.S. DOL made clear that absences that qualify for FMLA leave must be designated as FMLA leave and counted against an employee's annual twelve-week entitlement:

> [A]n employer is prohibited from delaying the designation of FMLA-qualifying leave as FMLA leave. Once an eligible employee communicates a need to take leave for an FMLA-qualifying reason,

---

46. *Id.* § 825.300(b)(2).
47. *Id.* § 825.300(c)(1)(ii).
48. *Id.* 825.300(c)(3).
49. See Form WH-380-E in Appendix A.
50. 29 C.F.R. § 305(b).
51. *Id.* § 825.305(c).

neither the employee nor the employer may decline FMLA protection for that leave. Accordingly, when an employer determines that leave is for an FMLA-qualifying reason, the qualifying leave is FMLA-protected and counts toward the employee's FMLA leave entitlement . . . . [T]he employer may not delay designating leave as FMLA-qualifying, even if the employee would prefer that the employer delay the designation.[52]

If leave qualifies for FMLA protection, it must be counted as FMLA leave. That is true even if the employee fails to return a certification, provided that the employer knows enough about the employee's situation to know that the absence qualifies as a serious health condition. If the employee does not return a certification and the employer remains uncertain whether the circumstances qualify for FMLA leave, then any leave the employee does take will not be protected; the employee may be disciplined or discharged either for failing to follow employer policies or for insubordination by failing to follow a reasonable directive from a supervisor.

Requiring Medical Certification for FMLA Leave

The chief way an employer can get the information it needs to determine whether an employee really qualifies for FMLA leave is to ask for a medical certification from the health care provider involved (or from the health care provider of the employee's family member, where leave is requested to care for a family member with a serious health condition). The FMLA does not *require* employers to obtain a medical certification. It instead *allows* an employer to request certain information from the health care provider to verify that an employee or family member has a serious health condition.[53] An employer may not ask for certification for leave related to the care of a newborn or newly adopted child.[54]

Through the medical certification, the employer may ask for information sufficient to establish the employee's need for leave, including information that answers the following questions:

- Which part of the FMLA's definition of a serious health condition applies to the health condition?
- On what date did the condition begin?
- How long is the condition likely to last, and for how long will either the employee be unable to work or the family member be unable to attend school or tend to daily activities?

---

52. U.S. Dep't of Labor, Wage & Hour Div., Opinion Letter 2019-1-A (Mar. 14, 2019) at https://www.dol.gov/sites/dolgov/files/WHD/legacy/files/2019_03_14_1A_FMLA.pdf (citations omitted).

53. *See* 29 C.F.R. § 825.305(a).

54. *See id.*; U.S. Dep't of Labor, Wage & Hour Div., Opinion Letter FMLA-53 (Dec. 29, 1994), 1, https://www.dol.gov/sites/dolgov/files/WHD/legacy/files/FMLA-53.pdf.

- Will the employee need to take occasional leave, take intermittent leave, or work on a reduced schedule?
- If there is treatment underway, will additional treatments be needed, and if so, how many of these treatments are likely?
- Will the employee be unable to perform work of any kind, be unable to perform any one or more of the essential functions of the employee's position, or be absent from work for treatment?

In sum, employers are entitled to relevant medical facts that support the employee's request for leave, which *may* include symptoms, diagnosis, and treatment plans.[55]

Medical certifications are an excellent tool for ensuring that employees receive their statutory right to FMLA leave when—and only when—they are entitled to it. Adopting a policy requiring all employees who request FMLA leave for their own or a family member's serious health condition to provide medical certifications can also help employers ensure that they are treating all employees equally. The U.S. DOL has developed medical certification forms for use by employers.[56] Employers may develop their own forms, but in almost all cases, they should simply use the DOL forms. The DOL forms ask everything that an employer is entitled to ask but no more. That keeps an employer from inadvertently making prohibited inquiries. The DOL form for certification of the employee's health condition is Form WH-380-E. The form for certification of a family member's health condition is Form WH-380-F. Both forms may be found in Appendix A and on DOL's website.

Written Notice of Need for Medical Certification Required

An employer requiring a medical certification must give an employee requesting FMLA leave written notice of the need for a medical certification within five days of the request for FMLA leave (if the need for leave is foreseeable) or within five days after the leave has begun (if the need was not foreseeable). As discussed earlier in this chapter, employers must also provide employees with a written ERR notice within five days of a request for leave or after leave has begun. If an employer will require a medical certification, it must say so on the ERR notice.[57] In practice, most employers attach the medical certification form to the ERR notice. When employees give advance notice of their need for leave, obtaining medical certification before the leave begins is generally not a problem. Whether the need for leave is foreseeable or unforeseeable, if an employee cannot give the requisite advance notice, the employer must give the employee fifteen calendar days to obtain the certification.[58]

---

55. *See* 29 C.F.R. § 825.306(a).
56. *Id.* § 825.306(b).
57. *Id.* § 825.300(c)(1)(ii).
58. *Id.* § 825.305(b).

Consequences of a Failure to Return a Medical Certification

At the time the employer requests certification, it must also warn the employee of the anticipated consequences of a failure to provide adequate certification. There is no requirement that this warning be in writing, but as with the notice of eligibility, it is better to have contemporaneous documentation of the employer's warning for litigation purposes. If the employer does not advise the employee of these consequences of failing to return a medical certification, it cannot require certification as a condition of granting FMLA leave.[59]

If the employee does not return the certification within the fifteen-day window provided by the regulations, the employer may deny FMLA leave, although the regulations require an employer to make an exception when it has not been "practicable" for the employee to obtain the certification despite "diligent, good faith efforts" to do so.[60] An employee who has not returned a required medical certification is not on FMLA leave.[61] An employee who is not on FMLA leave does not have job protection while out sick. The employee loses the right to return to the same or a substantially equivalent job.[62] Several cases have affirmed the principle that it is *not* a violation of the FMLA to fire an employee who has not returned a medical certification after fifteen days.[63]

As discussed earlier, employees who do not want a leave to count against their twelve weeks of FMLA might intentionally refuse to return a medical certification. If an employer has enough information to designate leave as FMLA leave without the certification, it may count the leave against the employee's FMLA entitlement anyhow. In that case, the FMLA's job-protection provisions apply to the leave.

---

59. *Id.* § 825.305(d).

60. *Id.* §§ 825.305(b); 825.313(b).

61. *See id.* §§ 825.305(d); 825.313(b).

62. *See* 29 C.F.R. § 825.313.

63. *See* Howard v. Inova Health Care Servs., 302 F. App'x 166, 174–75 (4th Cir. 2008) (employer did not violate FMLA by disciplining employee with back injury for unexcused absences where employee failed to update two-year-old certification); Milton v. Texas Dep't of Crim. Just., 707 F.3d 570 (5th Cir. 2013) (employer could administratively terminate employee on FMLA leave after not receiving her monthly medical certification of her continued illness, a condition of her leave, for the third month of that leave); Lockridge v. City of Winston-Salem, 388 F. Supp. 2d 618 (M.D.N.C. 2005) (employer was entitled to deny the request for FMLA leave because the request-for-leave form and medical certification were not received within fifteen days); Frazier v. Honda of Am. Mfg., Inc., 431 F.3d 563 (6th Cir. 2005) (employer did not violate the FMLA by terminating employee who returned medical certification form one day late); Brumbalough v. Camelot Care Ctrs., Inc., 427 F.3d 996, 1002 (6th Cir. 2005) (employee who failed to comply with employer's request for recertification when employee claimed to be unable to return to work after two months of FMLA leave was no longer covered by the FMLA and could be terminated); *cf.* Cooper v. Fulton County, 458 F.3d 1282 (11th Cir. 2006) (upholding trial court's award of damages to employee terminated for failure to return medical certification where county did not give employee fifteen days to return it).

When to Request a Medical Certification

If an employer does not ask for medical certification in the ERR notice, the window for requesting it closes. However, the regulations permit the employer to request certification at some later date if the employer later has reason to question the appropriateness of the leave or its duration.[64]

Employer Entitled to Complete and Sufficient Certification

An employer is entitled to a complete and sufficient medical certification. For a certification to be complete, all the applicable entries on the form must be filled out. *A complete certification may still be insufficient if the information provided is vague, ambiguous, or non-responsive.* If an employer receives an incomplete or insufficient certification, it must tell the employee *in writing* what additional information must be provided. The employee then has seven calendar days to provide that information. FMLA leave may be denied to any employee who fails to return a complete and sufficient certification after being given seven days to resubmit it. In that case, the job-protection provisions of the FMLA do not apply.[65]

Sufficient Certification

A sufficient certification is one that tells the employer the date on which the serious health condition began, how long the condition is likely to last, and appropriate medical facts about the condition.[66] If the need for leave arises from the employee's own health condition, a sufficient certification also contains a statement that the employee is unable to perform the functions of the employee's position.[67] If the certification is for leave to care for a spouse, son, daughter, or parent with a serious health condition, it must include a statement that the employee is needed to care for the family member and an estimate of the amount of time that the employee is needed to care for the family member.[68]

When an employee is requesting intermittent leave or a reduced schedule leave for planned medical treatment (chemotherapy or dialysis, for example), the certification also must provide the dates on which the treatment is scheduled and how long it will last. The certification is not sufficient without that information.[69] Employers do not have to provide intermittent or reduced schedule leave unless it is medically necessary.[70] If intermittent or reduced schedule leave is being requested, a sufficient certification must include a statement of the *medical necessity* for

---

64. 29 C.F.R. § 825.305.

65. *See id.* § 825.305(c).

66. *Id.* § 825.306(a)(2)–(3).

67. *Id.* 825.306(a)(4).

68. *Id.* § 825.306(a)(5).

69. *Id.* § 825.306(a)(6).

70. *Id.* § 825.202(b). A full discussion of intermittent and reduced schedule leave may be found in Appendix B.

intermittent or reduced schedule leave, as well as the expected duration and a schedule of the leave.[71]

Clarification and Authentication

Sometimes the problem with a certification is not whether it is complete and sufficient, but whether the health care provider's answers (or handwriting) are clear. The provider may have used medical jargon or described a condition or a treatment in such abbreviated terms that an employer cannot understand the information. In cases like these, the FMLA allows employers to contact the employee's health care provider for clarification of the medical certification (original or recertification). This may be (and is usually) done by phone. Employers may not ask health care providers for additional information beyond what is required by the certification form. The request for clarification should not be made until the employee has had a chance to fix anything that has made the certification less than complete and sufficient. *Neither the employee's direct supervisor nor anyone in the employee's chain of command should contact the health care provider.* Instead, the employer must use another provider, a human resources professional, a leave administrator, or some other person in management to contact the employee's provider. This is also true when the leave is to care for an employee's family member. Only a human resources professional, a leave administrator, or someone in management who is not in the employee's chain of command may contact the family member's provider.[72]

The Health Insurance Portability and Accountability Act (HIPAA) prohibits health care providers from disclosing a patient's protected health information without specific authorization. An employer seeking clarification of a response on an FMLA certification will therefore need to ask the employee to give the health care provider permission to speak with an employer representative. The employee may have to sign an authorization for the provider to share certain protected information with the employer if the provider requires such authorization. Just as it is the responsibility of an employee to return a complete and sufficient certification, so it is the responsibility of the employee to facilitate contact between the provider and the employer if clarification is needed. An employer may deny FMLA leave if an employee refuses to cooperate.[73] If leave is being taken to care for a family member, an employer will likewise need to ask an employee to obtain the family member's permission to speak with the provider.

There are also times when employers suspect that the provider whose name is on the medical certification did not actually sign the form—or that no such provider exists. In this situation, an employer may seek to *authenticate* the certification. *Authentication* means giving the health care provider a copy of the certification and requesting verification that the information contained on the

---

71. 29 U.S.C. § 2613.
72. 29 C.F.R. § 825.307(a).
73. *Id.*

certification form was completed or authorized by the health care provider who signed it. The employer may not ask for any additional medical information as part of this process.[74] Authentication does not typically require the employee to authorize the disclosure of protected information, since no additional medical information is being requested.

Eligible Health Care Providers for FMLA Certification Purposes

The FMLA regulations specify the types of health care providers eligible to certify an employee's or a family member's need for FMLA leave.[75] The list is exclusive—if a type of provider is not on the list, then the employer need not accept certification from that type of provider—but it is also broad. The following health care professionals may certify the need for FMLA leave *when the qualifying condition is within their area of specialization*:

- licensed doctors of medicine or osteopathy (MDs and DOs),
- nurse practitioners,
- dentists,
- clinical psychologists,
- clinical social workers,
- nurse-midwives,
- physicians' assistants,
- optometrists,
- podiatrists,
- chiropractors (subject to some limitations),
- official Christian Science practitioners (those listed with the First Church of Christ, Scientist, in Boston, Massachusetts),
- health care providers from whom the employer or the benefits manager for the employer's group health plan will accept a medical certification to substantiate a claim for benefits.[76]

If an employer is unsure whether a provider is of a type set forth on this list, it should consult with legal counsel before rejecting the certification.

Second Opinions

If the employer doubts the validity of the information provided on a medical certification, it may require the employee to undergo an examination for a second opinion with a health care provider of the employer's choice at the employer's cost.[77] The employer may not use a health care provider on its own payroll (the

---

74. *Id.*

75. *Id.* § 825.102 (s.v. "health care provider").

76. *Id.* A chiropractor may certify the need for FMLA leave only for treatment consisting of manual manipulation of the spine to correct a subluxation indicated on an X-ray. *Id.*

77. *Id.* § 825.307(b). It is well established that an employer's decision not to seek a second opinion at the time FMLA leave is designated does not prevent it from later questioning the

medical provider for a county health clinic, for example) or with whom it regularly contracts, unless the employer is located in an area where access to health care is extremely limited (like a rural area with only one or two doctors practicing in the relevant specialty).[78] An employer may not seek a second opinion until it has first advised the employee that the medical certification was insufficient or unclear and given the employee seven calendar days to correct the deficiency.[79]

If the employee's provider disagrees with the second opinion, the employee must obtain a certification from a third provider (jointly agreed upon by the employer's provider and the employee's provider), again at the employer's cost. The decision of the third provider is binding.[80] The employer is required to provide the employee with a copy of the second and third medical opinions (if applicable) at the employee's request. There are consequences for both an employer and an employee who fail to act in good faith and to cooperate in obtaining a third opinion. An employer who does not cooperate in selecting a third opinion (by rejecting out of hand all of the providers suggested by the employee or by the employee's provider, for example) will be bound by the first opinion, which was favorable to the employee. An employee who refuses to submit to a third examination or to release the necessary medical information to a third provider will be bound by the second opinion, which disagreed with that of the employee's provider.[81]

If the employer requires the employee to obtain either a second or third opinion, the employer must reimburse the employee or family member for any reasonable out-of-pocket travel expenses involved. The employer generally may not require the employee or family member to travel outside normal commuting distance to obtain either a second or third medical opinion.[82]

If an employer needs a second or third opinion, it must provisionally approve FMLA leave for the employee while the assessment of the employee's condition is taking place. If the employee is ultimately found to have a serious health condition, the designation of the leave as FMLA may be made official as of the date the provisional leave began. If the employee ultimately is not found to have a serious health condition, then the provisional designation of FMLA should be removed and the

---

validity of the original certification if circumstances give rise to questions. *See, e.g.,* Rhoads v. Fed. Deposit Ins. Corp., 257 F.3d 373, 385–86 (4th Cir. 2001) (denying employee's motion for judgment as a matter of law or for a new trial based on the fact that her employer did not pursue second and third opinions and upholding jury's determination that employee did not suffer from an FMLA-qualifying condition); Pollard v. N.Y. Methodist Hosp., 861 F.3d 374, 381–82 (2d Cir. 2017) (upholding hospital's right to contest employee's right to FMLA leave despite not having sought a second opinion).

78. 29 C.F.R. § 825.307(b)(2).

79. *Id.* § 825.307(b).

80. *Id.* § 825.307(c).

81. *See id.*

82. *Id.* § 825.307(e).

employee's absences reclassified as another type of leave available to the employee, including sick leave, vacation leave, or an unpaid leave of absence.[83]

Recertifications

In general, an employer may not ask for recertification of an employee's own serious health condition any more frequently than every thirty days.[84] Recertification every thirty days may be required only when an employee is taking leave for their own serious health condition. Recertification may not be required if the leave is to care for a family member.[85] If the initial certification is for more than thirty days, the employer must wait until the initial leave period provided in the certification is over before asking for recertification. However, in all cases, recertification may be required every six months when an employee is on intermittent or reduced schedule leave for either an employee's own serious health condition and for a family member's serious health condition. For intermittent and reduced schedule FMLA leave, recertification at six months is allowed even if the health care provider's original certification was for more than six months.[86]

The same information that is required for an initial certification may be required for a recertification.[87] As with requiring a second or third opinion on an original medical certification, the cost of a health care provider's visit for recertification is the employee's responsibility.[88] The same fifteen-business-day deadline that applies to returning a first certification form applies to a recertification.[89] The employer may not require a second or third opinion on recertification.[90]

Employers often seek recertifications of the need for intermittent or reduced schedule leave when an employee uses FMLA leave more frequently or in greater blocks of time than the original certification form said were needed. Any change in the frequency of intermittent FMLA leave is suggestive of a change in the employee's condition, in which case a recertification is reasonable—even if requested before the thirty-day mark or before the end of the initial period of certification.[91] Other instances that can make recertification reasonable early are when an

---

83. *See id.* § 825.307(b)(1).

84. *Id.* § 825.308(a).

85. *See id.* § 825.308(b).

86. *Id.*

87. *Id.* § 825.308(e).

88. *Id.* § 825.308(f).

89. *Id.* § 825.308(d).

90. *Id.* 825.308(f).

91. *See id.* § 825.308(c)(2). *See also* Whittington v. Tyson Foods, Inc., 21 F.4th 997, 1001–02 (8th Cir. 2021) (where medical certification for intermittent leave projected that employee would take leave in four-to-five-day increments, a leave of sixteen days made it reasonable to seek recertification); Hansen v. Fincantieri Marine Grp., LLC, 763 F.3d 832, 843 (7th Cir. 2014)); Graham v. BlueCross BlueShield of Tenn., Inc., 521 F. App'x 419, 424 (6th Cir. 2013) (employer's request to submit recertification was reasonable where employee's period of twenty-eight consecutively missed days was twice as long as her previous longest period of absenteeism, constituting significantly changed circumstances). Estimates in the certification

employee exhibits a pattern of using intermittent FMLA leave only on Mondays and Fridays or when an employee is observed engaging in activities that the certification says that the employee cannot perform (an employee with a serious back injury is seen playing in a softball game, for example).[92]

Confidentiality

Employers must keep any medical certification forms and any other FMLA-related medical information in a separate file.[93] Wherever it is located, the medical information is considered confidential under North Carolina's personnel records acts and the Americans with Disabilities Act,[94] but the requirement that FMLA-related information be kept separate makes it easier to ensure that confidential medical information is not seen by anyone who may be reviewing an employee's personnel file for other legitimate reasons. The FMLA allows supervisors, department heads, and managers to have only limited access to information related to an employee's FMLA leave, namely, information about any necessary restrictions on the work or duties of an employee and necessary accommodations. Government officials (most likely investigators from DOL) investigating the employer's compliance with the FMLA, the Americans with Disabilities Act, or the Genetic Information Nondiscrimination Act may be provided with information upon their request.[95]

The Designation Notice

Sooner or later, an employer receives enough information to make the determination about whether an employee's absence qualifies for FMLA leave or not. The notice that FMLA leave has been granted or denied is called the *Designation Notice.* If an employer has sufficient information from the employee, it may provide the employee with the Designation Notice immediately after receiving notice of the need for leave.[96] In most instances, however, the determination will not be made until after the employee returns a medical certification form, in which case a written Designation Notice must be given to the employee *within five business days* once the employer receives the certification.[97] If the employer determines that the leave will not be designated FMLA qualifying (for example, the leave is not for a reason covered by the FMLA or the employee's FMLA leave entitlement has

---

do not act as limitations on the frequency and duration of episodes for which an employee may be entitled to intermittent leave; where the frequency and duration of intermittent leave significantly exceed the certification estimate, recertification must be sought before leave is denied. *Hansen,* 763 F.3d at 843.

92. *See* 29 C.F.R. § 825.308(c)(3). See also Chapter 7.

93. 29 C.F.R. § 825.500(g).

94. *See, e.g.,* N.C. Gen. Stat. §§ 160A-168(b), 153A-98(b), 126-22 to -24.

95. 29 C.F.R. § 825.500(g)(1)–(3).

96. *Id.* § 825.300(d)(2).

97. *Id.* § 825.300(d)(1).

been exhausted), the employer must also notify the employee of that determination. DOL has developed a standard Designation Notice, Form WH-382, to use for this purpose.[98]

Regardless of whether the same information was included in the ERR notice, an employer must include the following information in the Designation Notice:

- whether accrued paid leave will be substituted for unpaid leave;
- whether the employee must provide a fitness-for-duty certification before returning to work;
- a list of the employee's essential job functions, if the fitness-for-duty certification must address the employee's ability to perform essential job functions; and
- notice of the amount of leave that will be counted against the employee's FMLA entitlement.[99]

If an employer fails to indicate on the Designation Notice that a fitness-for-duty certification must be received before the employee will be allowed to return to work, it cannot later ask an employee to provide one. The Designation Notice is an employer's one and only chance to require fitness-for-duty certification and to require that it address an employee's individual essential job functions.

Failure to designate qualifying leave as FMLA leave is a violation of the FMLA and an instance of interference with an employee's right to FMLA leave. But as with a failure to inform an employee of the availability of FMLA, failure to designate cannot be the basis of a lawsuit unless the employee can show that they have been harmed.[100] An employer's failure to designate FMLA leave has harmed an employee when the employee loses compensation or benefits, or has otherwise lost money, as a direct result of the failure to designate, or the employee has suffered a loss in employment status.[101]

What follows is a concrete example of the type of harm an employee could suffer if an employer failed to designate leave as FMLA leave as required by the FMLA regulations. Bhajan Badwal was a faculty member at the University of the District of Columbia in Washington, D.C. He qualified for FMLA leave and received provisional approval for it. He was told, in writing, that he would receive written notification of the final approval and designation of the leave as FMLA leave. But he never received any further communication about his leave, so he assumed he was not on an FMLA leave, with its twelve-week limit, but on an open-ended leave of absence. When Badwal did not return to work after twelve weeks, the university

---

98. A PDF of Form WH-382 may be downloaded from DOL's website at https://www.dol.gov/sites/dolgov/files/WHD/legacy/files/WH-382.pdf. It may also be found in Appendix A.

99. 29 C.F.R. § 825.300(d).

100. *See* Ragsdale v. Wolverine World Wide, Inc., 535 U.S. 81, 88–90, 96 (2002); Badwal v. Bd. of Trs., 139 F. Supp. 3d 295, 317–18 (D.D.C. 2015).

101. *Badwal*, 139 F. Supp. 3d at 317 (quoting Roseboro v. Billington, 606 F. Supp. 2d 104, 108 (D.D.C. 2009).

fired him. Badwal would have returned to work at the conclusion of twelve weeks had he known he was on time-limited FMLA leave, in which case he would not have been fired. Loss of his job was the harm he suffered when the university did not give him a designation notice. The court found that Badwal had adequately pled an FMLA interference claim and denied the employer's motion to dismiss.[102]

A different outcome occurred in a Massachusetts case. There, like Bhajan Badwal, Scott Bellone qualified for FMLA leave. Bellone began his leave, but the school district sent his formal designation notice to him two months late. Bellone completed his twelve-week FMLA leave on June 4; the school year did not end until June 21. Bellone was not medically able to return to the classroom before the end of the school year and remained on a leave of absence. He continued his recovery into the summer months. The school district then terminated him in the fall. Bellone brought suit for wrongful termination under both the Americans with Disabilities Act and the FMLA. His count of FMLA interference—based on the school district's failure timely to designate his leave as FMLA leave—failed because he could show no harm arising from the late delivery of the designation notice. He had his FMLA leave and, at the time it ended in June, he was not medically able to return to teaching.[103]

Employers should do their utmost to observe the deadlines imposed by the FMLA for giving notice of eligibility and for the Designation Notice. But as long as an employee is receiving the job-protected leave to which they are entitled, the employer may take comfort in the fact that it may retroactively designate leave, effectively backdating the start of FMLA-protected leave to the day on which the employee actually began taking leave, and that it will not be liable to an employee for damages for FMLA interference.[104] That should not be read as an invitation to ignore the timelines or to dispense with the Notice of Eligibility and the Designation Notice altogether. The FMLA regulations explicitly require employers to provide notice of a retroactive designation.[105] And as the *Hannah P.* case discussed earlier shows with respect to notice of eligibility, and *Badwal's* case shows with the Designation Notice, employees may sometimes make different decisions based on whether a leave is covered by the FMLA or is simply a leave of absence to which sick or vacation leave may apply.

---

102. *Id.* at 317–18.

103. Bellone v. Southwick-Tolland Reg'l Sch. Dist., 915 F. Supp. 2d 187, 195–96 (D. Mass. 2013).

104. *See* 29 C.F.R. § 825.301(d)

105. *Id.*

Chapter 6

The Return to Work After FMLA Leave

FMLA leave is referred to as "job-protected leave" because employers are required to return employees on FMLA leave to the same position the employee held before the leave began or to an equivalent position, with equivalent benefits, pay, and other terms and conditions of employment. Employers have the right to hire someone else on either a temporary or a permanent basis to take on an employee's duties while the employee is on FMLA leave. They may also restructure employees' duties to ensure that the work gets done during their absence. But in either case, employees must be reinstated to the same or an equivalent position upon their return from FMLA leave.[1] Like so many FMLA rules, the principle that an employee is entitled to reinstatement is easy to state but often difficult to implement without defining key terms and understanding its conditions and exceptions. What is an equivalent position? Are there any prerequisites that an employee must meet before having a right of restoration? Does the reinstatement requirement apply to all employees? Are there circumstances where an employee does not have a right to be restored to the same or equivalent position? Are there circumstances in which an employer may fire an employee upon return from FMLA leave? This chapter discusses those questions.

---

1. 29 C.F.R. § 825.214. *Cf.* Hannah P. v. Coats, 916 F.3d 327, 345, 348 (4th Cir. 2019) (employee could not rebut employer's legitimate, nondiscriminatory reason for failure to reinstate to an equivalent position).

The Same or an Equivalent Position: The Meaning of "Equivalent"

An employee has the right to return to the same *or* an equivalent position upon the conclusion of FMLA leave. "The same position" is just that: the very same position that the employee held at the start of FMLA leave. "An equivalent position," according to the regulations, is one that is "virtually identical" to the employee's original position "in terms of pay, benefits and working conditions, including privileges, perquisites and status."[2] It isn't enough to make the employee whole as far as compensation and benefits go. An equivalent position must also have "the same or substantially similar duties and responsibilities" that call upon the employee to use substantially the same skill, effort, responsibility, and authority.[3] That may make it sound as though an employee cannot actually be moved to a different position from the one held before FMLA leave, but that is not how the courts have interpreted these requirements.

Equivalent Pay

On one hand, equivalent pay means that an employee must be returned to a position that has the same salary or hourly rate that the employee was earning when FMLA leave began. Any across-the-board pay increases, such as cost-of-living increases, that were granted during the period of FMLA leave must also be included in determining that a position offers equivalent pay. If any bonuses or other payments (whether discretionary, such as merit-based pay increases, or nondiscretionary, such as productivity bonuses) have been given to other employees during the period of leave, they must be credited to an employee returning from FMLA leave on the same terms as to employees returning from a comparable form of leave.[4] If a bonus or other payment is based on the achievement of a specified goal and the employee has not met the goal due to FMLA leave, then the payment may be denied, unless it has otherwise been paid to employees on an equivalent non-FMLA leave. For example, if an employee who used paid vacation leave for a non-FMLA purpose would receive a bonus payment despite being absent, then the employee who used paid vacation leave concurrently with FMLA leave must also receive the payment.[5]

For employees who are nonexempt under the Fair Labor Standards Act, the new position must also present the same opportunities for earning overtime pay

---

2. 29 C.F.R. § 825.215(a). *See* Waag v. Sotera Def. Sols., Inc., 857 F.3d 179, 188 (4th Cir. 2017) (employee was returned to equivalent position with salary, benefits, title, worksite, and responsibilities in business development identical to previous position, albeit for a different contract).

3. 29 C.F.R. § 825.215(a).

4. *Id.* § 825.215(c).

5. *Id.* § 825.215(c)(2).

or receiving shift differentials.[6] This means that if an employee's original position regularly required or offered the opportunity to work five to ten hours of overtime each week, for example, then the new position must also afford that opportunity before it can be considered equivalent. If an employee previously worked a less desirable shift, such as a second shift or an overnight shift, or rotated shifts so that the employee regularly (or on rotation) received a higher rate of pay, the employee must have the opportunity to earn a shift differential in the new position before it can be deemed equivalent.

Equivalent Benefits

An employee on FMLA must be returned to a position in which the employee qualifies for the same health insurance plan and continued participation in LGERS (the Local Government Employer Retirement System) or TSERS (the Teachers and State Employees Retirement System).[7] Should the employer change group health insurance plans, the amount of employee premium contributions, or deductibles for all employees, those changes would apply to any employee on FMLA leave when they are made.[8] The employee must continue to receive the same number of days of sick, vacation, and annual leave as before. And any accrued paid leave of any kind that was not used during FMLA leave must remain available upon the employee's return to work.[9] The employee must also be able to continue in any group life insurance plans, disability insurance plans, or tuition benefit plans that the employer may offer.[10]

When employees are on unpaid FMLA leave, any benefits paid for by payroll deduction may lapse if arrangements are not made for the employees to continue paying for them.[11] Even if coverage of health insurance, life insurance, or any other benefit lapses while an employee is on unpaid FMLA leave, the employee must nevertheless be reinstated immediately upon return to work. Employees returning from FMLA leave cannot be required to requalify for any benefit. In other words, there cannot be a waiting period or a preexisting condition exclusion, for example, or a requirement that the employee undergo a medical examination before coverage is reinstated. Indeed, it is the employer's responsibility to make sure that full

---

6. *See* 29 C.F.R. § 825.215(c)(1).

7. In both of these retirement systems, a period of unpaid FMLA leave may not be treated as a break in service. That period does not have to be treated as creditable service, but for the purposes of eligibility and vesting, employees shall be treated as if they had been working during the period of unpaid FMLA leave. 29 C.F.R. § 825.215(d)(4). *See Waag*, 857 F.3d at 188 (health insurance benefits).

8. 29 C.F.R. § 825.215(d)(1).

9. *Id.* § 825.215(d)(2).

10. *Id.* § 825.215(d)(1), (3).

11. On payment of employees' health insurance premiums while on unpaid FMLA leave, see Chapter 4, page 51.

restoration to benefits happens immediately, even if it means that the employer must make payments during the leave to keep certain benefits like life insurance or disability insurance available to the employee upon their return. The FMLA regulations say this explicitly.

> Accordingly, some employers may find it necessary to modify life insurance and other benefits programs in order to restore employees to equivalent benefits upon return from FMLA leave, make arrangements for continued payment of costs to maintain such benefits during unpaid FMLA leave, or pay these costs subject to recovery from the employee on return from leave.[12]

Equivalent Terms and Conditions of Employment

An equivalent position must have substantially similar duties, conditions, responsibilities, privileges, and status as the employee's original position. This means that an employee must be returned to the same worksite[13] or one that is the same distance from the employee's home.[14] An employee must also be assigned to the same work schedule or one that is substantially the same.[15] An equivalent position must also have the same opportunity for both discretionary and nondiscretionary bonuses.[16]

There is one exception to the same-or-equivalent-job rule: it does not cover *de minimis* (very small), intangible, or unmeasurable aspects of a job.[17] What might a court consider *de minimis* differences between two jobs? Consider, as an example, the federal Fourth Circuit Court of Appeals case *Waag v. Sotera Defense Solutions, Inc.* Employee Gary Waag began work at his employer, a defense contractor, as a division director of operations. His job duties included oversight of issues related to recruiting, security, information technology (IT), and facilities as well as developing new business. He was then asked to take on the role of program manager for a new Army program, for which his employer was a prime contractor. In the prime contractor program manager role, most of the initial work involved marketing and business development. Shortly after assuming that role, Waag fell off the roof of his house and severely injured his hand, necessitating FMLA leave. Another employee was assigned to carry out Waag's program manager duties. When Waag returned to work, he was given a different assignment, reporting to a different supervisor. The assignment had the same salary and drew on Waag's experience in modeling and

---

12. 29 C.F.R. § 825.215(d)(1).

13. *See* Waag v. Sotera Def. Sols., Inc., 857 F.3d 179, 188 (4th Cir. 2017) (employee restored to an equivalent position reported to same worksite).

14. 29 C.F.R. § 825.215(e)(1).

15. *Id.* § 825.215(e)(2).

16. *Id.* § 825.215(e)(3). *See Waag*, 857 F.3d at 188 (employee restored to an equivalent position equally eligible for bonuses).

17. 29 C.F.R. § 825.215(f).

simulation in his role as director of operations. Like his program manager position, Waag's new position involved bidding on an important contract.[18]

Unfortunately for Waag, federal budget problems resulted in a significant decrease in work and in revenues for his business unit. The company laid off several senior managers. Waag was chosen for layoff because he was not doing work that was directly billable to the government and his salary was being charged to overhead. In addition, the contract on which he was working was not as important a priority as other projects. The employee who had replaced Waag as program manager when he was on FMLA leave was not let go. So Waag sued, claiming first, that he had not been restored to his original position, and second, that he had not been restored to an equivalent position. His argument was that had he been reinstated to his original program manager position or some other equivalent position, he would not have been laid off. The company, however, claimed that his replacement had been retained not because of his program manager responsibilities but because he had an important role in several other revenue programs.[19]

The Fourth Circuit rejected both of Waag's claims. As to his first claim, that he had a right to be returned to his original position of program manager, the court said,

> Congress provided restoration rights in the disjunctive, meaning that restoration of a covered employee to either position—the employee's original job or a different job that is "equivalent" within the meaning of the statute—will suffice to satisfy [the FMLA]. . . . [T]he restoration provision does not indicate a preference for restoring covered employees to their pre-leave position over "equivalent" positions, and it does not require an employer to hold open an employee's original position while that employee is on leave.[20]

The court found that Waag's position after FMLA leave was substantially equivalent to his position before FMLA leave. His salary and benefits were identical and he was eligible for bonuses in both positions. He reported to the same worksite, held the same title, and reported to a senior vice president in both. His primary focus in both positions was the development of new business. His own testimony supported his employer's claim that in the position to which he was restored, the biggest responsibility was business development. The difference in positions lay in the kinds of contracts on which the pre-FMLA and post-FMLA positions were focused. The court found that "no reasonable factfinder could conclude that Sotera failed to place Waag in 'an equivalent position' or that the differences between the two jobs were more than merely de minimis."[21]

---

18. *Waag*, 857 F.3d at 182–84.
19. *Id.* at 184.
20. *Id.* at 187.
21. *Id.* at 189.

Another Fourth Circuit case addresses job differences that the court found "intangible" and, therefore, not relevant to evaluating the equivalence of the two positions. In *Csicsmann v. Sallada*, the plaintiff's job (server manager in the IT-server group) was eliminated while he was on FMLA leave. On his return he was assigned the responsibility of developing processes for recovering corporate IT infrastructure after a disaster. His salary, title, bonus eligibility, health insurance, and retirement benefits remained the same. He worked the same schedule in the same location. However, his job responsibilities were different, and the plaintiff claimed that his new position was less prestigious and less visible than his original position. The court, however, found that his employer had restored him to an equivalent position, emphasizing that the "concrete and measurable aspects" of the positions were the same. Prestige and visibility, the court said, were "the very intangible aspects of the position appropriately excluded from an equivalency determination."[22]

The Louisiana case *Oby v. Baton Rouge Marriott* presents facts similar to those in the *Waag* case. Here, a court again found in favor of the employer because, as in the *Csicsmann* case above, the jobs in question differed only in "intangible aspects."[23] The plaintiff, who was the executive housekeeper at her hotel employer at the time she began FMLA leave, was restored to the position of food and beverage manager. The plaintiff declined the food and beverage manager position and sued her former employer, alleging that she had not been restored to an equivalent position. The court granted summary judgment to her employer, finding that her salary (third-highest in the hotel), benefits, and terms and conditions of employment were the same in both positions. The court acknowledged that the positions of executive housekeeper and food and beverage manager positions were not identical but found that both positions involved supervisory duties and had "the same goal and responsibility—customer service in and maintenance of the Baton Rouge Marriott in a managerial capacity."[24] The plaintiff did not present evidence that the two positions did not involve the same or substantially the same duties and responsibilities. Instead, she had claimed the positions were not equivalent because she had no expertise in food and beverage management and that she was therefore set up to fail. The court rejected her arguments as being based on either her subjective beliefs about the position or intangible aspects of the job. In its assessment, the positions were equivalent.[25]

---

22. Csicsmann v. Sallada, 211 F. App'x 163, 165–66 (4th Cir. 2006). *Cf.* Corbett v. Richmond Metro. Transp. Auth., 203 F. Supp. 3d 699, 709–10 (E.D. Va. 2016) (fact that employee no longer communicated with governing board or did public relations work in post-FMLA position was *de minimis* where position had same pay, benefits, and working conditions as pre-FMLA position).

23. Oby v. Baton Rouge Marriott, 329 F. Supp. 2d 772, 781–82 (M.D. La. 2004).

24. *Id.* at 781–82.

25. *Id.* at 782.

Finally, in *Montgomery v. Maryland*, another Fourth Circuit case, the court again focused on those aspects of a position that can be measured. Montgomery was an administrative assistant to a state prison warden before she took FMLA leave. Upon her return, she was reassigned to a position as the secretary to a state agency maintenance department. The positions were both in the State of Maryland's classification system as "Administrative Aide Stenographer" and were at the same pay grade and increment level. She received a raise two months after her return into the new position. Montgomery, however, claimed that her duties in her original position were "truly administrative," unlike those of the new position, which were the "most menial of clerical functions." In the new position she shared a work area, while in the original position she had had her own workspace. The court found that the supposed reduction in the difficulty of her work tasks and switch to a shared workspace focused "precisely on the sorts of de minimis, intangible, and unmeasurable aspects of a job that the regulations specifically exclude" and affirmed the dismissal of her claims.[26]

One final note about job restoration: the FMLA allows an employer to restore an employee to a different shift, schedule, or position at the employee's request or to offer a promotion to a better position. An employee does not, however, have to accept an offer of promotion.[27]

Preconditions on an Employee's Return to Work

The FMLA allows employers to impose only two types of preconditions on a return to work: an employee's maintenance of qualifications and the return of a fitness-for-duty certification.

Maintenance of Qualifications

Many jobs in state and local government require employees to maintain certifications or licensures. Think of public safety positions, human services jobs, water and wastewater treatment plant operators, and attorneys, to name just a few. When FMLA leave has prevented an employee from completing the requirements to maintain a required certification or license, the employer must allow the employee to return to work and must grant a reasonable opportunity to meet the recertification or licensure renewal requirements. Employers cannot delay the return to work pending recertification or relicensing.[28]

---

26. *See* Montgomery v. Maryland, 266 F.3d 334, 341–42 (4th Cir. 2001), *cert. granted, judgment vacated on other grounds*, 535 U.S. 1075 (2002).

27. *See* 29 C.F.R. § 825.215(e)(4).

28. *See id.* § 825.215(b).

Fitness-for-Duty Certifications

Whether employees take leave for an entire twelve weeks, for a shorter continuous block of time, or on an intermittent or reduced schedule basis, the FMLA does not require them to provide a certification from a health care provider that they are ready to resume work. All an employee must do is show up for work on the next scheduled workday after the end of the FMLA leave.

If, however, an employer has indicated on the FMLA Designation Notice that an employee must provide a fitness-for-duty certification before returning to work, an employer may delay the return to work until the employee does so.[29] A fitness-for-duty certification is the only way an employer can know whether an employee returning to work from FMLA leave taken for their own serious health condition is sufficiently recovered to perform the job duties safely and well. However, the use of fitness-for-duty certifications following FMLA leave is subject to strict rules. Failure to abide by them leaves an employer open to liability for FMLA interference or for a violation of the Americans with Disabilities Act (ADA).

An employer that wishes to require fitness-for-duty certifications from employees who have taken leave for their own serious health conditions must take affirmative steps to do so with respect to each employee who takes FMLA leave. First, an employer must adopt *a policy requiring fitness-for-duty certifications* upon the conclusion of FMLA leave.[30] But that is not enough by itself. As discussed in Chapter 5, an employer must also indicate on each Designation Notice that a fitness-for-duty certification is required before a return to work.[31] If the employer fails to check the box for a fitness-for-duty certification, it cannot later require that employee to provide one.

Step 1: Adopt a Fitness-for-Duty Certification Policy

Because an employer may require an FMLA fitness-for-duty certification only if it has a uniformly applied policy for *all similarly situated employees,* an employer's first step is to decide the circumstances in which it wants a certification that an employee is physically and mentally able to resume work. Employers may choose to require all employees on FMLA leave for their own serious health condition to return a fitness-for-duty certification (although an employer is prohibited from requiring a fitness-for-duty certification following leave to bond with a newborn child or a child placed for adoption or foster care). Or an employer may designate certain departments or certain positions as ones for which a certification will be required. Employers could also choose to require certifications from all employees who have been out for certain kinds of serious health conditions, such as surgery.[32] The organization's management team and human resources personnel should

---

29. On the required Designation Notice, see pages 76–78.
30. *See* 29 C.F.R. § 825.312(a).
31. *See* 29 C.F.R. § 825.312(b) and (d).
32. *See* 29 C.F.R. § 825.312(a).

consult with department heads and then formulate a policy that meets the needs both of the organization as a whole and of its individual departments.

Step 2: Check the Fitness-for-Duty Certification Box on the Designation Notice and Attach a List of Job Duties

An employer's one and only chance to ask an employee to provide a fitness-for-duty certification when the employee returns from FMLA leave is to check the fitness-for-duty box on the Designation Notice provided when FMLA is approved. On Form WH-382, the standard Designation Notice provided by the U.S. Department of Labor (DOL), there is a box to check that tells an employee that a fitness-for-duty certification is required. It is on the bottom of the second page. Here is what Form WH-382 says in this section:

> **Return-to-work requirements.** To be restored to work after taking FMLA leave, you (☐ will be / ☐ will not be) required to provide a certification from your health care provider (fitness-for-duty certification) that you are able to resume work. This request for a fitness-for-duty certification is *only* with regard to the particular serious health condition that caused your need for FMLA leave. **If such certification is not timely received, your return to work may be delayed until the certification is provided.**
>
> A list of the essential functions of your position (☐ is / ☐ is not) attached. If attached, the fitness-for-duty certification must address your ability to perform the essential job functions.

There is a lot to unpack in those two paragraphs.

First, the fitness-for-duty certification may ask only for information related to the particular health condition for which the employee took FMLA leave.[33] Unless the employer asks the health care provider to address the employee's ability to perform particular job functions (see below), the certification does not have to provide any information beyond the fact that the employee is able to resume work.[34] DOL does not provide a model fitness-for-duty certification, so the burden falls on employers to draft their own forms. The fitness-for-duty certification form should probably reference the reason the employee took FMLA leave in case the employee has the form completed by a health care provider other than the one who completed the original medical certification form before leave began.

As the second paragraph from Form WH-382 quoted above shows, an employer may require that the certification *specifically* address the employee's ability to

---

33. *See* 29 C.F.R. § 825.312(b).

34. *See* Budhun v. Reading Hosp. & Med. Ctr., 765 F.3d 245, 252–53 (3d Cir. 2014); Brumbalough v. Camelot Care Ctrs., Inc., 427 F.3d 996, 1003 (6th Cir. 2005) ("once an employee submits a statement from her health care provider which indicates that she may return to work, the employer's duty to restate has been triggered under the FMLA").

perform the essential functions of the employee's job.[35] To hold the employee to that requirement, the employer must provide the employee with a list of the essential functions along with the Designation Notice and must check the box in the Designation Notice saying that the certification must address the employee's ability to perform those essential functions. If the employer fails to tell the employee that the certification must address the employee's ability to perform those essential job duties, or if the employer does not provide a list of essential job duties, the employee is required only to provide a simple statement of fitness to return to work from the employee's treating physician.[36] Employees are responsible for the cost of the fitness-for-duty certification just as they are responsible for the cost of obtaining the initial medical certification.[37]

Step 3: Follow Up, if Necessary

If the fitness-for-duty certification says that the employee is fit to return to work, the FMLA requires the employer to allow the employee to come back to work.[38] If, however, the certification includes restrictions, then the employer's duty to reinstate the employee is *not* triggered.[39] The employee may be required to remain on FMLA leave if available. If the employee has used all of their twelve-week entitlement, they may be placed on a leave of absence or, after consideration of the employer's responsibilities under the ADA, dismissed.

But what if the certification is unclear, or an employer suspects that the provider who has certified fitness for duty doesn't exist or that the signature has been forged? Employers may always contact the employee's health care provider to clarify and authenticate the fitness-for-duty certification (remember, the regulations define *authentication* as requesting verification from the health care provider that the information contained on the certification form was completed or authorized by the provider who signed the document; *clarification* means contacting the provider to understand the handwriting on the medical certification or to understand the meaning of a response).[40] Clarification and authentication of a fitness-for-duty certification are governed by the same rules as clarifying and authenticating a medical certification.[41] While seeking clarification or authentication, however, the employer *must allow an employee to return to work* while contact with the provider is being made.[42]

---

35. *See* 29 C.F.R. § 825.312(b).

36. *Id. See* Howard v. Inova Health Care Servs., 302 F. App'x 166, 175–77 (4th Cir. 2008) (affirming district court's denial of summary judgment); *Budhun*, 765 F.3d 245, 252–53 (3d Cir. 2014).

37. 29 C.F.R. § 825.312(c).

38. *See Brumbalough*, 427 F.3d at 1004.

39. *See Budhun*, 765 F.3d at 252–53; James v. Hyatt Regency Chi., 707 F.3d 775, 781 (7th Cir. 2013).

40. 29 C.F.R. § 825.307(a).

41. See Chapter 5, pages 72–73.

42. 29 C.F.R. § 825.312(b).

The Intersection of the Family and Medical Leave Act and the Americans with Disabilities Act

The FMLA and the ADA have different purposes and require different things of employers and employees. An employee's FMLA right to a total of twelve workweeks of job-protected, unpaid leave during any twelve-month period reflects the FMLA's purpose: to give employees a reasonable but limited amount of time in which to take care of their own or their family members' health issues without losing their jobs.

The ADA has an entirely different purpose. Like Title VII of the Civil Rights Act of 1964 and the Age Discrimination in Employment Act, the ADA is an antidiscrimination statute. It prohibits employers from discriminating on the basis of disability against a qualified individual in hiring, promotion, and discharge of employees and all other terms and conditions of employment. Under the ADA, an employer's failure reasonably to accommodate an employee's disability so that the employee can continue to work is itself a form of discrimination.

The FMLA's *serious health condition* and the ADA's *disability* are terms of art and do not mean the same thing. This book discusses the meaning of *serious health condition* in Chapter 2. In contrast to the FMLA's focus on medical conditions that make an employee unable to work, the ADA defines disability as a "physical or mental impairment that substantially limits one or more major life activities."[a] Most medical disorders will qualify as impairments under the ADA. While both a serious health condition and a disability have the potential to interfere with an employee's attendance and job performance, they are different concepts, and the existence of each has very different consequences for both employers and employees.

The existence of an ADA disability has no role in determining whether an employee has a serious health condition and is entitled to FMLA leave. Where the ADA and the FMLA tend to intersect is when an employee has taken FMLA leave for their own serious health condition, has now exhausted their twelve weeks of leave, but their condition has not resolved sufficiently for a return to work. At that point, FMLA leave ends and the employee no longer has the FMLA's job protections. But a serious health condition is likely to satisfy the ADA's definition of a disability at this point. The definition of *disability* is broad and is meant to be construed broadly in favor of the employee.

So having exhausted FMLA leave, an employee whose condition satisfies the ADA definition of disability is now entitled to a reasonable accommodation. Most courts have found a leave of absence of an additional four to six weeks following an FMLA leave of twelve weeks to be a reasonable accommodation. An indefinite leave of absence is not considered a reasonable accommodation. Therefore, when an employee cannot return to work at the conclusion of an FMLA leave for their own serious health condition, the employer should consider whether the serious health condition is a disability under the ADA and whether there is an accommodation like an additional leave of absence, a reduced schedule, or a light-duty assignment that can be offered to the employee. For further discussion of the difference between an FMLA serious health condition and a disability under the ADA, see Appendix C.

[a] 42 U.S.C. § 12102(1).

What if an employer just doesn't believe an employee is fit for duty despite what the certification says? In that case, the employer is out of luck. With fitness-for-duty certifications, no second or third opinions may be required, unlike medical certifications.[43]

And what if the employee or the health care provider is uncooperative and does not return certifications in a timely manner? Employees have the same obligation to cooperate in the fitness-for-duty certification process as in the initial certification process. So when an employee ignores or delays responding to an employer's request for a fitness-for-duty certification, the employer may delay the employee's return to work until the employee submits the certification.[44] An employee who does not provide a fitness-for-duty certification (or request additional FMLA leave, if that is what is needed) is no longer entitled to reinstatement under the FMLA.[45]

Fitness-for-Duty Certifications and Intermittent or Reduced Schedule FMLA Leave

Intermittent and reduced schedule FMLA leave present a dilemma when it comes to fitness-for-duty certifications. On one hand, if an employee is taking frequent but short chunks of leave, it would be an unreasonable burden to require a certification after each instance of leave. On the other hand, employers will sometimes need confirmation that an employee is still able to perform their job duties after multiple absences. The FMLA regulations attempt to strike a balance between these competing interests. While an employer is not entitled to a certification of fitness to return to duty for *each* absence taken on an intermittent or reduced leave schedule, it may request a fitness-for-duty certification for intermittent or reduced-leave absences once every thirty days *if* reasonable safety concerns exist regarding the employee's ability to perform the job's duties.[46] Otherwise, employers may only request fitness-for-duty certifications every six months. The FMLA regulations define *reasonable safety concern* as a reasonable belief that there is a significant risk of harm to an individual employee or others (and clarifies that in determining whether such concerns exist, an employer should consider the nature and severity of the potential harm and the likelihood that potential harm will occur).[47]

As with FMLA taken in a continuous block of time, employers must inform employees taking intermittent or reduced schedule leave in the Designation Notice that they will be required to submit a fitness-for-duty certification. In addition to the Designation Notice, employers should give employees written notice that after the first thirty days, the employee will be required to submit a fitness-for-duty

---

43. *Id.*

44. *Id.* § 825.312(a), (e). *See* Howard v. Inova Health Care Servs., 302 F. App'x 166, 175–77 (4th Cir. 2008).

45. *See* Brumbalough v. Camelot Care Ctrs., Inc., 427 F.3d 996, 1004 (6th Cir. 2005); *Howard*, 302 F. App'x at 175–77.

46. 29 C.F.R. § 825.312(f).

47. *Id.*

certification for each subsequent instance of intermittent or reduced schedule leave, unless one has already been submitted within the past thirty days. *An employer may not terminate someone's employment while awaiting that certification for an intermittent or reduced schedule leave absence.*[48]

Fitness-for-Duty Certifications After an Employee Returns to Work

Whether or not an employer has required a fitness-for-duty certification, it sometimes happens that after an employee returns to work, the employer has reason to question whether the same condition for which the employee took FMLA leave is limiting the employee's ability to perform their job functions. Now, the Americans with Disabilities Act applies.[49] The ADA allows an employer to ask an employee to undergo a fitness-for-duty exam if it is related to the employee's ability to perform essential job duties.[50] In this case, an employer may choose to have the exam performed by a medical provider of the employer's choosing at the employer's expense.[51]

---

48. *Id.*

49. *See id.* § 825.312(h).

50. *Id.* 1630.14(c)(1).

51. *See Enforcement Guidance on Disability-Related Inquiries and Medical Examinations of Employees under the ADA*, U.S. EQUAL EMP. OPPORTUNITY COMM'N at Q. 9, 11–12 (last visited Feb. 9, 2024), Available at https://www.eeoc.gov/laws/guidance/enforcement-guidance -disability-related-inquiries-and-medical-examinations-employees#6. Information obtained regarding the medical condition or history of an employee through this exam must be collected and maintained on separate forms in separate medical files and be treated as confidential medical records.

Chapter 7

Limitations on an Employee's Right to Reinstatement: Termination During and at the Conclusion of FMLA Leave

Employees do not have an absolute right to reinstatement to the same position or to an equivalent position. The text of the FMLA and the U.S. Department of Labor's (DOL's) accompanying regulations make that clear. The regulations state it thus:

> An employee has no greater right to reinstatement or to other benefits and conditions of employment than if the employee had been continuously employed during the FMLA leave period. An employer must be able to show that an employee would not otherwise have been employed at the time reinstatement is requested in order to deny restoration to employment.[1]

For example, if an employee would have been laid off had they not been on FMLA, the employer may lay them off during the course of leave or may deny reinstatement at the conclusion of leave. Or if the employee took FMLA leave under false pretenses and lying to the employer would have resulted in termination had the employee been working, the employee may be dismissed during the course of leave or denied reinstatement at the conclusion of leave. FMLA leave is not an absolute shield against termination.

There are seven general situations in which an employer may terminate the employment of an employee on FMLA leave or deny reinstatement at the conclusion of leave. These are examples of situations where an employee "would not otherwise have been employed at the time reinstatement is requested." They are not

---

1. 29 C.F.R. § 825.216(a).

exclusive reasons for which employees may be dismissed or denied reinstatement. The seven general situations are

1. the employee cannot perform one of the essential functions of the job, whether because a serious health condition has still not resolved at the end of FMLA leave or for some other reason;
2. an employee's position is eliminated during FMLA leave and the employee is laid off;
3. the employee would have been terminated for poor performance or misconduct that occurred before the start of FMLA leave;
4. the employee did not comply with the employer's FMLA or leave of absence policies;
5. the employee has engaged in fraud in connection with FMLA leave;
6. the employee has failed to return a required fitness-for-duty certification; and
7. reinstatement of the employee would result in grievous economic harm to the employer organization (this includes denying reinstatement to a key employee).

The following sections will discuss the reasons reinstatement may be denied in more detail. Reason 7 is discussed in Chapter 8, which covers the "key employee" exception to restoration to the same or equivalent position.

Inability to Return to Work

Twelve weeks may be sufficient time for employees or their family members to recover from a serious health condition in most instances. But sometimes, even when a person's health has improved, they are still unable to perform one or more of their essential job duties (in the case of an employee) or return to a daily routine where the assistance of the employee is no longer needed (in the case of a family member). At this point, in the face of an employee's continued unavailability to work, an employer's FMLA obligation to continue their employment ends.[2]

For employees who are unable to return to work because their own serious health condition has not resolved, employers have responsibilities under the Americans with Disabilities Act (ADA) they must consider.[3] Whether granting an additional leave of absence is a reasonable accommodation under the ADA is a determination that may only be made on a case-by-case basis, but when an employer can allow an employee additional time off to recuperate without causing the organization undue hardship, the ADA requires it. If an employer cannot

---

2. *See id.* § 825.216(c).

3. *Id.* §§ 825.216(c), .702. See the sidebar on page 89 and Appendix C on the distinction between an FMLA serious condition and an ADA disability.

reasonably accommodate an employee's need for additional leave, it may terminate the employee once all twelve weeks of FMLA entitlement have been used. If an employee cannot return because they are still needed to care for a family member with a serious health condition, the employer may dismiss the employee. If it chooses, it can put the employee on another form of leave of absence, as allowed by its personnel policy, but under federal and state law, it is not required to do so.

Layoff or Restructuring During FMLA Leave

The FMLA regulations expressly allow employers to include employees on FMLA leave in reductions-in-force and in reorganizations that eliminate their positions, so long as the positions are being eliminated for reasons unrelated to their taking of FMLA leave.[4] The Fourth Circuit case *Yashenko v. Harrah's NC Casino Co.* shows how a reorganization can lawfully result in the termination of an employee on FMLA leave. At the time he took FMLA leave, Yashenko was a casino manager for employee relations. While on leave, casino management informed Yashenko that his position was being eliminated as part of a larger reorganization. Within the human resources department, two eliminated positions were being replaced with a single new position combining the job duties of both. Yashenko was invited to apply for the new position, as well as for other positions within the casino. All other employees whose positions were eliminated as part of the reorganization found other jobs within the casino. Yashenko, however, did not apply for any other position. So, when he returned from FMLA leave, the casino fired him.[5]

Yashenko sued the casino, claiming that it had interfered with his FMLA leave and that it terminated him in retaliation for taking leave. In an FMLA interference case, the employer must show it had a legitimate reason unrelated to the FMLA leave for terminating the employee. In a retaliation case, the employee must show that the FMLA leave was the cause of the termination.[6] Both of Edward Yashenko's

---

4. *See* 29 C.F.R. § 825.216(a)(1).

5. Yashenko v. Harrah's NC Casino Co., 446 F.3d 541 (4th Cir. 2006). *Cf.* White v. Dalton, 225 F.3d 656 (4th Cir. 2000) (unpublished opinion) (reduction-in-force necessitated by declining profits is a legitimate, nondiscriminatory reason for termination in Title VII and ADEA case).

6. An FMLA interference case is brought under 29 U.S.C. § 2615(a)(1), which says that "[i]t shall be unlawful for any employer to interfere with, restrain, or deny the exercise of or the attempt to exercise, any right provided under [the FMLA]." An FMLA retaliation case is brought under 29 U.S.C. § 2615(a)(2), which says that "[i]t shall be unlawful for any employer to discharge or in any other manner discriminate against any individual for opposing any practice made unlawful by [the FMLA]." Both interference and retaliation claims may be proven by direct evidence, but employees more frequently try to prove their cases using indirect evidence through the *McDonnell Douglas* burden-shifting framework used in Title VII discrimination cases. This means that once an employee has made a prima facie case of either interference or retaliation, the burden shifts to the employer to provide a legitimate, non-retaliatory reason for the adverse action. Once the employer has done so, the burden shifts

claims failed. The casino put forth evidence that (1) it had begun considering elimination of Yashenko's position several months before he requested FMLA leave, (2) its human resources department was implementing a general reorganization under a new human resources director, and (3) it had eliminated several other positions in the process. Yashenko offered no evidence that the casino's reasons were merely a pretext for unlawful retaliation.[7] Had the casino not been able to show a comprehensive reorganization plan or had Yashenko's position been the only one eliminated, the result might have been different.

An employer's judgment about the organization's needs will always take priority over an employee's opinion, even if that employee is on FMLA leave. Sometimes, choosing to lay off an employee who happens to be on FMLA leave just makes business sense. In *Propst v. HWS Co.*, the employer implemented a reduction-in-force when its sales decreased significantly at the same time that its costs increased significantly. Propst, the plaintiff, worked in the company's five-person maintenance department and was on FMLA leave when the decision was made. The company decided that it needed to lay off two of the five employees in maintenance and six employees in other departments. Propst's supervisor decided that he needed the three employees who had the best skill sets to service the company's day-to-day maintenance needs and its current and future business needs to remain with the company. As a result of its financial troubles, the company was no longer going to spend money on roofing projects, an area in which the plaintiff had specialized skills, and the plaintiff's supervisor considered one of the department's other employees to be a more skilled welder and machinist than the plaintiff. The court found that Propst had not shown that the company's legitimate, nondiscriminatory reason for choosing him for layoff was a pretext, noting that the company's choice to prioritize some types of work and corresponding skill sets was reasonable and not a pretext for laying off Propst because he was on FMLA leave.[8]

---

back to the employee to show that the employer's reason is merely a pretext. *See* Sharif v. United Airlines, Inc., 841 F.3d 199, 203 (4th Cir. 2016) (retaliation); Tillman v. Ohio Bell Tel. Co., 545 F. App'x 340, 351 (6th Cir. 2013) (interference). The circuits are split on who has the ultimate burden of proof in an interference case, however. *See* Anderson v. Nations Lending Corp., 27 F.4th 1300, 1304 (7th Cir. 2022); Caldwell v. KHOU-TV, 850 F.3d 237, 245 (5th Cir. 2017); Demyanovich v. Cadon Plating & Coatings, LLC, 747 F.3d 419, 427 (6th Cir. 2014). Some courts have rejected the *McDonnell Douglas* framework and ruled that the employer bears the ultimate burden of showing that termination was not caused by the taking of FMLA leave. *See* Herren v. La Petite Acad., Inc., 820 F. App'x 900, 906 (11th Cir. 2020); Metzler v. Fed. Home Loan Bank of Topeka, 464 F.3d 1164, 1180 (10th Cir. 2006); Ross v. Gilhuly, 755 F.3d 185, 192 (3d Cir. 2014); Ballato v. Comcast Corp., 676 F.3d 768, 772 (8th Cir. 2012); Bachelder v. Am. W. Airlines, Inc., 259 F.3d 1112, 1126 (9th Cir. 2001). The Fourth Circuit has not decided whether the ultimate burden of proof in an interference case rests with the employee or the employer. *See Yashenko*, 446 F.3d at 549.

7. *Yashenko*, 446 F.3d at 551.

8. Propst v. HWS Co., 148 F. Supp. 3d 506, 513–21, 525–34 (W.D.N.C. 2015). *Cf.* Fields v. Verizon Servs. Corp., 493 F. App'x 371, 376 (4th Cir. 2012) (selecting an employee for reduction-in-force because she did not have sufficient experience in the area most important

Employers may not consider FMLA leave in making employment decisions.[9] In a typical layoff situation, employers will consider several factors in deciding which employees will lose their jobs. It is crucial for management to ensure that use of FMLA leave is not considered by the supervisors who may be preparing evaluations and recommendations about whom to lay off. A case from the federal Sixth Circuit Court of Appeals shows how a supervisor's consideration of FMLA leave might fly underneath the radar of the ultimate decision maker. In *Cutcher v. Kmart Corp.*, the plaintiff's supervisor gave her an outstanding performance evaluation a mere twenty-six days before she began her FMLA leave. In contrast, her reduction-in-force appraisal score, calculated during her leave, placed her among the six lowest-rated employees at the Kmart store at which she worked. The supervisor made the notation "LOA" (leave of absence) in the comments section of the reduction-in-force evaluation. Not surprisingly, when the employee sued for FMLA retaliation, the court found that a reasonable jury could conclude that the plaintiff was chosen for layoff because she took FMLA leave.[10] In North Carolina local government, either the manager, independent department head (such as the sheriff, register of deeds, director of social services, or local health director), or the human resources department should ask to see all of a supervisor's notes when an employee on FMLA leave is recommended for a reduction-in-force.

Reinstatement After an Employee's Duties Have Been Redistributed to Accommodate FMLA Leave

Sometimes, after redistributing the job duties of an employee on FMLA leave, an employer may conclude that the organization doesn't need that employee and may want to eliminate the position entirely. That would not be an unreasonable judgment, but it would be unlawful for the employer to act on it. The FMLA regulations say clearly that an employee "is entitled to . . . reinstatement even if the employee has been replaced or his or her position has been restructured to accommodate the employee's absence."[11] When the Motorola Corporation, for example, restructured an employee's position to accommodate his absence on FMLA leave, it decided things were working well without him, eliminated his position and terminated

---

to the present and future needs of the company was termination for a legitimate, nondiscriminatory reason in ADA case).

9. 29 C.F.R. § 825.220(c).

10. Cutcher v. Kmart Corp., 364 F. App'x 183, 189 (6th Cir. 2010). *Cf.* Gutierrez v. Grant County, No. CV–10–48–LRS, 2011 WL 1654548, at *4 (E.D. Wash. May 2, 2011) (summary judgment denied where there is circumstantial evidence that employee's use of FMLA leave contributed to decision to include her in layoff); Shaffer v. Am. Med. Ass'n, 662 F.3d 439, 445–46 (7th Cir. 2011) (reasonable jury could find that employer changed his mind about which of two employees to lay off as part of a reduction-in-force because plaintiff took FMLA leave).

11. 29 C.F.R. § 825.214.

his employment. When the employee sued, the court held that the employee was still entitled to reinstatement to the same or a substantially equivalent position.[12]

Elimination of a Shift or of Overtime

Sometimes a reorganization results in the elimination of an entire shift or the need for what had been regular overtime work. Where an entire shift is eliminated or where the need for overtime work goes away during an employee's FMLA leave, the employee has no right to return to the original shift or to work overtime.[13] Long-term temporary employees hired to work on a specific project lose their job-restoration rights if the project concludes while they are on leave.[14]

Termination for Poor Performance or Misconduct

The FMLA does not prevent an employer from terminating an employee for poor performance, misconduct, or insubordinate behavior. Both performance and misconduct issues that arose before an FMLA leave and those discovered during the leave may be grounds for terminating employment during leave or for refusing restoration at the conclusion of the FMLA leave.[15] The touchstone here, as with layoffs, is that the employer must be able to show that it would have taken the same action were the employee at work and not on FMLA leave.[16]

Managers and supervisors who are considering terminating or demoting an employee are sometimes surprised to learn that the very same employee has just requested FMLA leave. Everything grinds to a halt: either the manager or supervisor thinks they are prohibited from dismissing anyone on FMLA leave or they think they cannot fire the person because if they do, the employee will argue that it was FMLA interference or retaliation.

The FMLA is not meant to be a shield against discipline or dismissal, however. Consider the Fourth Circuit case *Fry v. Rand Construction Corp.* Arlene Fry was an administrative assistant to her immediate supervisor, who had long been frustrated with Fry's performance. But it wasn't until after she returned from FMLA leave that her supervisor recommended terminating Fry or, at the very least, replacing

---

12. Breneisen v. Motorola, Inc., 512 F.3d 972, 978 (7th Cir. 2008).

13. 29 C.F.R. § 825.216(a)(2).

14. *Id.* § 825.216(a)(3).

15. *See, e.g.,* Vannoy v. Fed. Rsrv. Bank of Richmond, 827 F.3d 296, 304–05 (4th Cir. 2016) (employer's legitimate, nondiscriminatory reasons for terminating employee included his failure to call in when he did not show up during a work trip, to communicate properly about unscheduled absences, and to complete the employee portion of the performance improvement plan).

16. 29 C.F.R. § 825.216(a).

her as the supervisor's assistant and moving her to another position. The company terminated her. Fry sued, arguing that the many documented mistakes that the employer cited as reasons for her termination were a pretext for FMLA retaliation. Fry argued that if the company had really been dissatisfied with her performance, it would have fired her sooner. The Fourth Circuit, however, affirmed summary judgment for the employer, finding that (1) the supervisor had considered firing Fry before she took leave and (2) the fact that the decision was only finalized after the leave was not evidence that FMLA leave was the real reason for Fry's termination.[17]

There are several other Fourth Circuit cases in which employers identified issues with their employees' performance before the employees requested FMLA leave. Because the performance issues in each of these cases were serious and well documented, the court affirmed summary judgment for the employer in each case. Take *Mercer v. Arc of Prince Georges County, Inc.*, for example. The plaintiff, Adesina Mercer, worked as a finance and benefits coordinator for people with developmental disabilities. Her job responsibilities included applying for and processing initial applications, renewals, and appeals for benefits under social security and the food-stamp program. During Mercer's employment, her supervisors and co-workers had several times identified multiple clients for whom she was responsible who were not receiving benefits to which they were entitled.[18]

When Mercer took FMLA leave to recover from a serious car accident, co-workers assumed her job responsibilities. They discovered that over the course of several months before her accident, Mercer had failed to obtain benefits for 99 of 160 eligible clients. Her employer terminated her employment when she returned from FMLA leave.[19] Mercer sued. In support of her claims of FMLA interference and retaliation, she provided evidence that she had received satisfactory performance evaluations prior to her leave. The Fourth Circuit found that under the circumstances, evidence of the employer's prior satisfaction with her performance did not prove that the employer's reasons for terminating her were pretextual. "[T]he fact that Mercer had previously received satisfactory performance reviews does not negate The Arc's ability to terminate her employment upon the discovery of previously unknown poor performance. This is so even if The Arc discovered the basis for terminating Mercer's employment while she was on FMLA leave.[20]

As this case shows, the courts will not force an employer to retain an employee who has taken FMLA leave when the employer would have fired that employee had they not been on FMLA leave. Nevertheless, employers should always keep in mind the possibility that an employee who is dismissed while on FMLA leave will claim interference or retaliation. The cost of defending against such a claim, in both money and time, can be great even when the employer ultimately prevails.

---

17. Fry v. Rand Constr. Corp., 964 F.3d 239, 247–48 (4th Cir. 2020), *cert. denied*, 141 S. Ct. 2595 (2021).

18. Mercer v. Arc of Prince Georges Cnty., Inc., 532 F. App'x 392, 393–95 (4th Cir. 2013).

19. *Id.* at 393–95.

20. *Id.* at 397.

An employer will be in the best position to respond to a retaliation claim if it can show that it previously took similar action against an employee who was not on FMLA leave. In the Fourth Circuit case *Laing v. Federal Express Corp.*, FedEx was able to show that it had fired another employee who was not on FMLA leave, James Lawton, several months earlier for engaging in the same fraudulent behavior as the plaintiff, Kimberly Laing.

> Lawton was found to have falsified his delivery records by claiming to deliver packages to different addresses miles apart at the exact same time and by delivering multiple packages to the same address at different times instead of delivering them all at once. And the record shows that FedEx treated Lawton and Laing virtually identically: FedEx investigated both by reviewing their route reports and MapQuest maps for suspicious activity. Once it became clear that the reports revealed a pattern of falsification, both were placed on investigative suspension with pay and given an opportunity to submit a written statement; and both were afforded the chance to use FedEx's internal appeals process after they were terminated.[21]

The court granted summary judgment to the employer on both Laing's retaliation and interference claims. It found that Laing had violated a clearly communicated company policy forbidding falsification of delivery records—a policy upon which, the court said, FedEx's commercial viability depended. It found that the company genuinely believed in this reason for terminating Laing. And, the court stressed, Laing was not able to produce any evidence that FedEx treated any other employee any differently.[22]

A recent case from the federal Seventh Circuit Court of Appeals provides another example of a situation where an employer was justified in terminating an employee even though she was on FMLA leave. In *Anderson v. Nations Lending Corp.*, plaintiff Tracy Anderson worked as an underwriting auditor for a residential mortgage lender, analyzing loan files for credit, collateral, capacity, and compliance to identify deficiencies. Right from the beginning, Anderson's employer, Nations Lending, found deficiencies in her work, and her supervisor required her to complete further training. Shortly before Anderson requested FMLA leave, her employer again uncovered multiple errors in her review of a loan. Her supervisor again gave her performance counseling. While Anderson was on FMLA leave, still more errors were discovered in multiple loans. At this point, Anderson's supervisor recommended she be terminated because of poor work performance. Her supervisor concluded that the deficiencies in her audits constituted a violation of Nations Lending's standards of employee conduct. Meanwhile, an additional investigation had uncovered additional mistakes. The investigation did not conclude until several

---

21. Laing v. Fed. Express Corp., 703 F.3d 713, 721 (4th Cir. 2013).
22. *Id.* at 721.

days after her return from FMLA leave and the decision to terminate her was not made until it concluded.[23]

Anderson claimed that her termination constituted FMLA interference and retaliation, saying that her mistakes were pretext for firing her for taking FMLA leave. Anderson argued that her supervisor did not counsel her about the mistakes she made on the loan audits discovered while she was on FMLA leave, which was inconsistent with the supervisor's normal practice. The court did not find this purported inconsistency convincing, noting that the employer's standards of conduct stated that "certain offenses are serious enough to *skip corrective action and warrant immediate termination*," and that it reserved the right "to skip or repeat corrective actions." It concluded that the supervisor's conduct was not necessarily a deviation from her prior practice, and was therefore not evidence of pretext.[24]

These cases show that the courts take seriously the right of employers to dismiss employees whose performance would have justified termination had they not taken FMLA leave. Nevertheless, employers should ask themselves whether the fact that an employee is on FMLA leave is tipping the scale whenever they consider disciplining or dismissing the employee. The FMLA regulations clearly state that "employers cannot use the taking of FMLA leave as a negative factor in employment actions, such as hiring, promotion or disciplinary actions."[25] This goes beyond requiring that FMLA leave not be the *motivating* factor in a dismissal. It says that FMLA leave may not factor into a dismissal decision *at all*. Employers must consider the possibility that an employee's use of FMLA leave is influencing the decision to discipline or dismiss, and they should proceed with a discipline or dismissal only when it is sure that it is not.

Failure to Comply with Employer FMLA or Leave of Absence Policies

Working a Second Job During FMLA Leave

Employees on FMLA leave for their own serious health condition sometimes continue working a second job while on leave. This is not necessarily evidence of FMLA fraud. The second job might not involve the same kinds of duties as the first, and might not prevent the employee from performing the second job's duties. Even so, for an employee to work another job while on FMLA leave from the first may not sit well with the primary employer. Employers have a remedy in this situation provided

---

23. Anderson v. Nations Lending Corp., No. 19-cv-5016, 2021 WL 1517880, at *1–2 (N.D. Ill. Apr. 16, 2021) , *aff'd*, 27 F.4th 1300 (7th Cir. 2022).

24. *Id.* at *3 (quoting Nations Lending's Standards of Employee Conduct and Corrective Action, Employee Handbook p. 5) (emphasis added).

25. 29 C.F.R. § 825.220(c).

they abide by one simple rule: they must have a written policy that prohibits it.[26] A policy prohibiting working a second job during FMLA leave must be uniformly applied. It should include a provision stating that violating the policy may result in immediate termination of both the leave of absence (including FMLA leave) and employment. Without such a formal written policy, an employer may not discipline or discharge an employee simply for working a second job (unless the job involves duties that the FMLA medical certification says the employee cannot do, which is discussed below).

May the Policy Prohibit Outside Employment Only During FMLA Leave?

This is an important but unanswered question. The FMLA regulations say only that a policy prohibiting secondary employment must be a "uniformly-applied" one. In its commentary to the regulations, DOL has said,

> [W]hether an employee may engage in outside employment during FMLA leave is dependent upon the employer's established policy regarding outside employment. For example, the employer may require that all outside employment be pre-approved by the employer. If so, employment while on FMLA leave would be subject to this policy.[27]

This language, coupled with the FMLA's overarching philosophy that employees on FMLA leave must be treated in the same way as employees who are not on FMLA leave, strongly implies that a prohibition on outside employment must be applicable to all employees, or at least to all employees on a leave of absence of any kind, not just to employees on FMLA leave.

There are no cases that directly address this issue. A cautious employer will therefore not limit a ban on outside employment only to those employees on FMLA leave.

Failure to Follow Reporting Procedures During Intermittent Leave

Many employers have policies setting forth a time frame within which employees must call in when unable to work. These policies may also specify a particular person within the employer organization or a third-party administrator to whom employees must give notice. When employees on an approved FMLA leave fail to

---

26. 29 C.F.R. § 825.216(e). *See* Pharakhone v. Nissan N. Am., Inc., 324 F.3d 405, 408 (6th Cir. 2003) (employee violated Nissan policy by working at wife's restaurant while on FMLA leave); Worster v. Carlson Wagon Lit Travel, Inc., 353 F.Supp.2d 257, 268 (D. Conn. 2005) (employee's termination for working in restaurant while on FMLA leave from travel-agency job lawful where travel agency had policy prohibiting secondary employment while on FMLA leave), *aff'd sub nom.* Worster v. Carlson Wagonlit Travel, Inc., 169 F. App'x 602 (2d Cir. 2006).

27. Preamble Commentary to Family and Medical Leave Act Final Rule, 60 Fed. Reg. 2180, 2227 (January 6, 1995). The current rule pertaining to outside employment at 29 C.F.R. § 825.216(e) was originally located at 29 C.F.R. § 825.312 and was moved when DOL amended the FMLA regulations in 2008.

follow their employer's policy for reporting absences, they commit misconduct, just as they would if they failed to abide by any other employer policy. Despite being on FMLA leave, an employee who violates an employer's policy is subject to whatever disciplinary measures the employer typically takes when an employee violating the policy is not on FMLA leave. Disciplinary measures may include dismissal. The Boeing Company, for example, had a policy that employees had to report all absences to their managers. Its separate FMLA policy stated that they had to report all FMLA absences to their managers. Boeing's Puget Sound plant also had a policy that all unscheduled absences had to be reported on or the day before the absence occurred. Considering all these policies, it is hard to see how an employee could not know that absences taken on intermittent FMLA leave had to be reported to the employee's manager. But Anthony Shelton brought suit against Boeing anyway when it dismissed him for failing to report absences to his manager on multiple occasions. Some but not all of those absences at issue were taken as FMLA leave. Shelton claimed that his termination was related to his taking FMLA leave. The court, however, found that Shelton could not show that he was unaware of the policy or that there had been any mitigating circumstances and found that dismissing him for failure to report absences as required, even FMLA absences, was not related to his FMLA leave and that his termination did not constitute an FMLA violation.[28]

It isn't unusual for employers to have general policies about reporting absences in addition to specific FMLA policies. Spirit Aerosystems, a defense contractor, had rules not unlike Boeing's. Spirit had a "General Leave of Absence" policy and an "Attendance and Punctuality" policy. The absence policy required employees to report any absence to Spirit's benefits center within three days in order to have FMLA leave approved. The attendance policy required employees to notify their manager within thirty minutes of a shift's start time if an unexpected need for absence arose. The absence policy made clear that "[n]othing in this procedure is intended to relieve an employee's responsibility to notify management or the Absence Reporting Line . . . of unscheduled absences and/or late arrivals" in accordance with the attendance policy.[29] When Michael Carter failed to report five unscheduled absences that were for FMLA-approved reasons, Spirit fired him. The Tenth Circuit affirmed summary judgment for Spirit, finding that Carter was fired because he violated company policy about reporting absences, not because he used intermittent FMLA leave.[30]

Lewis v. Holsum of Fort Wayne, Inc. provides a twist to these fact-patterns. Rebecca Lewis, the plaintiff employee, suffered from asthma. After suffering an asthma attack at work, she was hospitalized for four days and her employer duly counted those absences as FMLA leave. Lewis had earlier scheduled a week's

---

28. Shelton v. Boeing Co., 702 F. App'x 567, 568–69 (9th Cir. 2017).

29. Carter v. Spirit Aerosystems, Inc., 827 F. App'x 864, 866 (10th Cir. 2020) (quoting Spirit's "General Leave of Absence" policy).

30. *Carter*, 827 F. App'x at 869.

vacation for the week immediately after her hospitalization and was scheduled to return to work following the vacation leave. She did not return to work after her vacation leave ended nor did she contact her employer. The employer's policy, and the collective-bargaining agreement under which Lewis worked, required employees who took time off for medical reasons—whether FMLA or regular sick leave—to call in each day they were absent unless a doctor's note or medical certification had included a return-to-work date. After Lewis remained absent for three days following her return-to-work date, her employer terminated her for violating the company's attendance policy. On the third day, Lewis did drop off a note from her doctor saying that she had been unable to work beginning on the day of her hospital admission and continuing through a week from the date she dropped off the note. The decision to terminate her had already been made, however. The employer did not dispute that Lewis was entitled to FMLA leave for the entire period of her absences. The federal Seventh Circuit Court of Appeals found that the employer's policy was its "usual and customary" method for handling unreported absences and, as such, did not violate the FMLA. Lewis's termination for failure to report her absences was not, therefore, related to her FMLA leave and was lawful.[31]

The takeaway from these cases is that employers have an absolute right to require employees on FMLA leave to follow their usual policies regarding illness and leaves of absence. Failure to follow these policies may be grounds for termination notwithstanding the fact that an employee is on FMLA leave. Employers may not consider the use of FMLA leave in making employment decisions, including decisions to discipline or dismiss an employee because of excessive absenteeism. But note that in the cases discussed above, the courts each time made a distinction between dismissal because of an FMLA absence and dismissal for failure to follow employer's policies related to the taking of leave.

Consider the following hypothetical.

Nick works for the City of Paradise Valley police department. He suffers from migraine headaches that can cause searing pain and leave him incapacitated. Accordingly, he is on intermittent FMLA leave. It goes without saying that having shifts fully covered is of considerable importance in a law enforcement agency. The department has therefore adopted a standing standard operating procedure that requires police officers to alert their supervising officer that they will be absent or late at least thirty minutes before the start of a shift. This requirement applies whether the reason for the absence or tardiness is medical in nature or personal. It expressly applies even when an officer is on intermittent FMLA leave. An officer who accumulates eight or more failures to report is subject to dismissal. When Nick was first diagnosed with migraines

---

31. Lewis v. Holsum of Fort Wayne, Inc., 278 F.3d 706, 709–710 (7th Cir. 2002).

and first went on intermittent FMLA leave, he was diligent about calling in timely when he was going to be absent. Lately, though, he has called in after his shift has begun and sometimes not at all.

The city has an absenteeism policy that applies to all employees, including those in the police department: any employee who is absent for more than ten days in a six-month period—not counting approved FMLA leave, other leaves of absence, or approved vacation leave—is subject to dismissal for excessive absenteeism. The absenteeism policy does not conflict with the police department's standard operating procedure; the policy and the standard operating procedure address different issues.

There comes a day when Nick has been absent for twenty days in a six-month period; fifteen of them are for migraines and count as three weeks against his twelve-week FMLA entitlement. He has also failed to call in on time eighteen of those twenty days. Can the police chief fire Nick?

The police chief may not fire Nick for absenteeism under the city's policy, but may fire him for failure to follow the department's standard operating procedure on calling in when sick or tardy. It doesn't matter that the majority of the time Nick failed to call in, he was on an FMLA-approved absence. Nick has repeatedly engaged in misconduct, a violation of his employer's policy, while on leave. FMLA leave does not protect him even though the policy is one that applies to the taking of leave.

FMLA Fraud

Engaging in Activities Inconsistent with the Medical Certification

Just because an employee is on FMLA leave doesn't necessarily render the employee immobile or confined to bed. The fact that an employee is at the mall or is helping in their child's classroom does not mean that they are engaged in FMLA fraud. But imagine that an employee's FMLA certification form indicates that the employee needs complete bed rest for a month, and the employee is seen playing in a softball game. What is an employer to do?

This is the sort of situation in which one employer found itself in a 2021 case from Delaware, *Snyder v. E.I. DuPont de Nemours, Inc.* Peggy Snyder was on leave for foot surgery. Her medical certification said that she was not able to place any weight on her injured foot and could not drive. But another employee reported seeing Snyder at a pool party walking around freely. The manager in this case had other reasons to be suspicious of Snyder, so he hired an investigator to conduct surveillance. The investigator saw Snyder repeatedly climbing in and out of a Hummer SUV, driving, walking down the stairs and around a backyard, and lifting a child off the ground. During the same time as the surveillance Snyder repeatedly complained of pain to her treating physician, pain that she claimed was made worse by standing, climbing stairs and walking![32]

Snyder returned to work on a reduced schedule, but repeatedly reported to the company nurse that her foot was painful. Her manager restarted surveillance, and sure enough, Snyder was seen walking through a store parking lot, without crutches or a boot and no longer limping; mowing her lawn; and getting a pedicure. At that point, the employer fired her. Snyder sued, alleging that the company had fired her in retaliation for having taken FMLA leave. The court, however, found that she was terminated for legitimate, nondiscriminatory reasons, namely, that she had exploited both the FMLA and the company's short-term disability policy, that while on FMLA leave she had not behaved consistently with her treating physician's restrictions, and that she had mispresented the severity of her foot condition.[33]

Other cases also absolve employers who have terminated employees they believe to be abusing FMLA leave. In *Hyldahl v. AT & T*, for example, an employee had taken intermittent FMLA leave for post-traumatic stress disorder for several years. When the employer began to suspect that the employee was abusing FMLA leave, it hired an investigator. The employer's suspicions turned out to be well founded. The investigator reported that on one of the days for which the employee requested leave for her disorder, she went to a dentist appointment, visited a restaurant with a friend, and had her hair done. The court upheld the employee's termination, finding that the employer sincerely believed that the employee was engaged in FMLA fraud.[34]

Similarly, in *Jaszczyszyn v. Advantage Health Physician Network*, the plaintiff was on FMLA leave for severe back pain. The court found in favor of the employer who terminated Jaszczyszyn after she appeared in photos from several festivals.[35] And in *Weimer v. Honda of America Manufacturing, Inc.*, the court found sufficient evidence for a jury to conclude that Honda had terminated an employee for lying after the employee exaggerated his head injury symptoms when describing them to his physician and then used his FMLA leave to add a porch to his home.[36]

---

32. Snyder v. E.I. Dupont de Nemours, Inc., No. 18-1266-CFC, 2021 WL 412242, at *1–2 (D. Del. 2021).

33. *Id.*

34. Hyldahl v. AT & T, No. 07-14948-BC, 2008 WL 5111910 (E.D. Mich. 2008).

35. Jaszczyszyn v. Advantage Health Physician Network, 504 F. App'x 440 (6th Cir. 2012).

36. Weimer v. Honda of Am. Mfg., Inc., 356 F. App'x 812, 819 (6th Cir. 2019). *Cf.* Dalpiaz v. Carbon County, 760 F.3d 1126, 1132–34 (10th Cir. 2014) (upholding termination of county employee with spine injury who was on four-hour-per week reduced-schedule FMLA leave but was observed playing football); Scruggs v. Carrier Corp., 688 F.3d 821, 826 (7th Cir. 2012) (upholding termination because it was based on employer's "honest belief" that employee misused FMLA leave after video surveillance revealed that he did not leave his house, which would have been necessary to fulfill the purpose of the leave, to care for his mother); Vail v. Raybestos Prods. Co., 533 F.3d 904, 909–10 (7th Cir. 2008), (upholding termination of police officer approved for FMLA leave for migraine headaches after she was seen working for her husband's lawn-mowing business the morning after she had taken FMLA leave for

As these and other cases make clear, when an employer discovers that an employee is engaging in an activity that would appear impossible or prohibited if the reason for FMLA leave were true, *the employer may terminate both the FMLA leave and, if it wishes, the employee.* The employer does not have to wait until FMLA leave ends. That is because the regulations say that "[a]n employee who fraudulently obtains FMLA leave from an employer is not protected by FMLA's job restoration."[37] Nevertheless, before taking that step, an employer should interview the employee and conduct some sort of investigation to make sure its reasons for suspecting fraud are reasonable. There is no required method of investigation or standard of proof that an employer must meet before cancelling the FMLA leave or discharging the employee. Nothing requires an employer to do surveillance of the employee, although nothing (other than cost) prohibits it, either. An employer may interview an employee and ask how the employee is able to engage in an observed activity while being unable to perform their job duties. An employee's implausible or inconsistent answer may lead the employer reasonably to conclude that the employee is lying and that the reason for FMLA leave is fraudulent. An employer may also seek a recertification of the need for FMLA leave, calling the certifying health care provider's attention to the employee's activities. Or the employer might seek a second opinion at this time. At the end of the day, an employer's honest belief that the employee has been lying or has obtained FMLA leave fraudulently is usually enough to absolve an employer of liability for interference with the right to FMLA leave or for retaliation.

Patterns of Absence During Intermittent Leave

The Long Weekend

Sometimes employees use intermittent FMLA to extend a paid holiday or make a long weekend longer.[38] Consider the following hypothetical.

Jordan works for Paradise City Emergency Medical Services (EMS). He is among those with the least seniority in the department and is frequently assigned evening, night, and weekend shifts. Jordan has been on intermittent FMLA leave for a chronic back condition for two years. His medical certification and recertifications have said that he will need leave two to three days a month for back pain flare-ups and doctor's appointments.

The deputy director of EMS realizes that Jordan often takes intermittent FMLA leave on Fridays and on weekend days adjacent to already-scheduled

---

her evening shift); Lineberry v. Richards, No. 11–13752, 2013 WL 438689 (E. Mich. 2013) (upholding termination of hospital nurse for dishonesty in answering questions about vacation in Mexico taken during FMLA leave).

37. 29 C.F.R. § 825.216(d).

38. *See, e.g.,* Tillman v. Ohio Bell Tel. Co., 545 F. App'x 340 (6th Cir. 2013).

time off and holidays. Notwithstanding that his doctor has said that Jordan's flare-ups are unpredictable, Jordan has frequently told his supervisor that he would be using FMLA leave for back pain on a specific day in the future. The deputy director is starting to wonder whether Jordan's use of FMLA leave is legitimate.

The EMS director takes the deputy director's suspicions to Human Resources. After consulting with the city manager, HR hires an investigator to conduct surveillance of Jordan on days that he calls to say he is using FMLA leave. On several days, the investigator observes Jordan working in the yard and the garage, repeatedly bending down and lifting pieces of wood and carrying them into the house. On another day, the investigator observes him driving his family around town: stopping for coffee, visiting stores, and finally stopping at the dentist.

Paradise City interviews Jordan, whose answers about his use of FMLA leave are not believable. Jordan tells HR that he had to use FMLA leave on the weekends because it was the only time he could do the back exercises prescribed by the doctor. He doesn't remember working around the house on the days reported by the investigator but says that he may have been taking Cortisone or opioids, both of which would have masked the pain.

If this hypothetical seems exaggerated, know that it is an abbreviated version of the facts in the federal Sixth Circuit Court of Appeals case, *Tillman v. Ohio Bell Telephone Co.*[39] The court here found that the company held an honest belief that the employee had abused his FMLA leave (and the employee did not deny any of the allegations about his use of the leave).[40] It further found that the employee was not entitled to FMLA leave on the dates the investigator observed him engaging in activities inconsistent with his back condition.[41]

So, how should an employer handle an employee on intermittent FMLA leave whose absences coincide with weekends and holidays so frequently that they become suspicious? One possibility is for the employer to ask the health care provider who certified leave whether there is a medical reason for the pattern. This may put the provider on notice that the employee may be exaggerating symptoms to obtain FMLA certification. Employers should also question the employee about the use of leave, as the employer did in *Tillman*. If the employee's answers are implausible or inconsistent, the employer is entitled to disbelieve them. Not all employers can afford to undertake a full-scale investigation, but hiring an investigator to conduct surveillance of the employee on a day on which the claim of intermittent leave is suspicious may be enough to show that the employee is abusing FMLA leave

---

39. 545 F. App'x 340 (6th Cir. 2013).
40. *Id.* at 350–51.
41. *Id.* at 354–55.

(even if only on that one day). An employer could take away FMLA designation for that single day of misuse. Because FMLA job protection would no longer apply to that day's absence, the employer could terminate the employee if it wished.

Vacation Leave

Weekends and holidays are not the only times that employees abuse intermittent FMLA leave. Sometimes employees use FMLA leave to have time off to vacation or to extend a vacation. The Fourth Circuit case *Sharif v. United Airlines, Inc.* is a good example of this type of FMLA abuse. Employee Masoud Sharif worked for United Airlines, where for more than four years, he had been on intermittent FMLA leave for panic attacks. He received approval for twenty days of vacation leave, with a single workday scheduled in the middle of that period. He and his wife nonetheless planned a trip to South Africa for the entire period.[42]

Sharif called in on the day of his single scheduled shift, saying he was unable to work and asking that the day be recorded as a use of intermittent FMLA leave. Unfortunately for Sharif, United's human resources department noticed that he had taken FMLA leave on the one day he was scheduled to work in the middle of two vacation leaves. To make matters worse, when he was asked about it on his return, Sharif told inconsistent stories, including a claim that there was no room on any flight that would have gotten him back in time for his shift. United, of course, could easily check out this claim, which proved to be false. Sharif was fired for dishonesty, a violation of United's personnel policy. The Fourth Circuit upheld his termination.[43]

Another example of FMLA abuse involving vacation time may be found in the federal Seventh Circuit Court of Appeals case *Crouch v. Whirlpool Corp.*[44] Harold Crouch and his fiancée, who both worked for Whirlpool, tried unsuccessfully to coordinate their vacation time. Crouch then requested FMLA leave for days for which he had been denied vacation leave, claiming that he had injured his knee doing yard work. Crouch's supervisor noticed that the dates of his FMLA leave corresponded to the dates for which he had been denied vacation leave. And worse, his supervisor recalled that Crouch had previously asked for vacation leave at the same time of year. The supervisor checked the records and found that Crouch had previously taken FMLA leave for dates for which he was denied vacation leave and had even claimed to have the same medical condition: a knee injured while doing yard work! Crouch was fired for violating company policy about lying. The Seventh Circuit upheld the termination.[45]

---

42. Sharif v. United Airlines, Inc., 841 F.3d 199, 201 (4th Cir. 2016).
43. *Id.* at 204–06.
44. 447 F.3d 984, 984–85 (7th Cir. 2006).
45. *Id.* at 984–85.

Health Insurance and the Termination of an Employee During FMLA Leave

The FMLA regulations make clear that once an employee is terminated, the employer's FMLA obligation to continue providing health insurance ceases. "If an employee is laid off during the course of taking FMLA leave and employment is terminated, the employer's responsibility to continue FMLA leave, maintain group health plan benefits and restore the employee cease at the time the employee is laid off."[46]

Conclusion

The bar that an employer must meet to terminate an employee on FMLA leave or to deny reinstatement at the end of leave is high. But that is in keeping with the law's purpose of allowing employees to take reasonable leave for a health condition or that of a family member "in a manner that accommodates the legitimate interests of employers."[47] It should be difficult to dismiss an employee exercising their rights under the FMLA. But it is not impossible, nor should it be.

An employer may dismiss an employee on FMLA leave

- if the employee is laid off as the result of a reorganization or reduction-in-force that occurs during the leave, so long as the decision to lay off the employee or eliminate their position is in no way influenced by the employee's requesting FMLA leave or in response to changes made to accommodate that leave;
- if the employer began the process of termination before the employee began FMLA leave;
- if problems with the employee's job performance or evidence of misconduct surface during the leave; or
- if the employee takes FMLA leave fraudulently or violates employer policies during the leave.

With respect to termination for dishonesty in connection with the FMLA leave itself, recall that in both *Sharif v. United Airlines, Inc.* and *Crouch v. Whirlpool Corp.*, the vacation leave cases, the plaintiffs were terminated for dishonesty in violation of company policy rather than for FMLA abuse in itself. These two employers' reasons for dismissal were legitimate, nondiscriminatory, and not FMLA-related. Dismissals based on a violation of an employer's policies are much easier to defend in litigation, provided that the employer has consistently enforced the policies against other employees in the past.

---

46. 29 C.F.R. 825.216(a)(1).
47. 29 U.S.C. § 2601(b)(1)–(3).

Employees on intermittent leave who fail to observe an employer's regular call-out procedures may also be disciplined (and possibly terminated, if the practice continues) because they have violated employer policy as well.

Of course, immediate termination is not required, even when there are grounds to do so. Employers may take disciplinary action short of dismissal. They may also delay dismissal until the conclusion of FMLA leave if, for example, the employee is on leave because of a health condition covered by employer health insurance and the employer wishes to allow the employee to finish out a block of continuous coverage before terminating the health insurance.

Chapter 8

Denying Reinstatement to Key Employees

When a high-ranking employee with important management oversight responsibilities goes on FMLA leave, other employees cannot usually just "pick up the slack." An employer may have to appoint an interim executive, manager, or department head. The interim person may set priorities, adopt a budget, or otherwise direct the organization in ways that the employee on leave would disagree with and that would be difficult to undo upon the employee's return. Sometimes the return of the employee seems likely not just to be awkward but also to interfere with and harm the employer's operations. One of the exceptions to the requirement that an employee be restored to the same or an equivalent position after FMLA leave is when allowing a salaried, eligible employee (a "key employee") to return will cause "substantial and grievous economic injury to the operations of the employer."[1] There is an important distinction here: this is not a denial of FMLA leave, but a denial of restoration to work.

What Is a Key Employee?

First, a key employee is one who must be paid on a "salary basis," as that term is used in the U.S. Department of Labor (DOL) regulations governing the Fair Labor Standards Act.[2] In other words, the employee must be paid a predetermined amount each week that is not reduced because of variations in the quality or quantity of the employee's work.[3] Exempt employees are therefore among the class of employees who might qualify as key employees, as are nonexempt employees

---

1. 29 C.F.R. § 825.216(b).
2. *See id.* § 541.602.
3. *Id.* § 541.602(a).

paid on a salary basis. Nonexempt employees paid hourly may not be designated key employees.

But that is only one part of the definition of a key employee. Key employees are *the highest-paid 10 percent of all an employer's employees*—not just the highest-paid 10 percent of salaried employees but the highest-paid 10 percent of all employees—within seventy-five miles of the employee's worksite.[4] The employer, in this instance, is the city, county, school system, community college, individual university, or individual state agency as a whole. It is not the department or county agency for which an employee works.

Which employees are among the highest-paid 10 percent of employees will vary from time to time. Whether an employee is a key employee must therefore be determined at the time the employee requests leave or the employer becomes aware of an FMLA-qualifying condition. To determine whether an employee is among the highest-paid 10 percent, an employer must divide the employee's year-to-date earnings by the number of weeks the employee has worked (including any weeks during which the employee has used accrued paid leave).[5]

What Is "Substantial and Grievous Economic Injury"?

The FMLA regulations allow an employer to deny job restoration to a key employee only when "necessary to prevent substantial and grievous economic injury to the operations of the employer."[6] It is important to understand that the issue is not whether the employee's use of FMLA leave is causing serious economic injury to the employer—in other words, it isn't about whether the employee's absence is causing the harm—instead, the question is whether the requirement that the employer reinstate the employee would cause serious economic harm.[7]

The regulations are not terribly helpful in understanding what might constitute substantial and grievous economic injury to an employer. The standard is, the regulations say, different from and more stringent than the undue hardship test under the ADA.[8] Minor inconveniences don't count. According to the regulations, it would be a substantial and grievous economic injury if returning the employee to their job threatened the economic viability of the organization. That is a high bar for an employer to meet.

Employers sometimes hire replacements for employees on FMLA leave or have other employees take on their responsibilities. The FMLA allows this (the work

---

4. *Id.* § 825.217(a).

5. *Id.* § 825.217(c)(1).

6. *Id.* § 825.216(b).

7. *Id.* § 825.218(a). *See also* Douglas v. Dreamdealers USA, LLC, 416 F. Supp. 3d 1063, 1073 (D. Nev. 2019) (denying employer's motion for summary judgment where employer assessed harm from employee's absence, not from his return).

8. 29 C.F.R. § 825.218(d). *See generally id.* § 1630.2(p) (defining *undue hardship*).

must get done, after all) so long as the employee on FMLA leave is restored to the same or an equivalent position at the conclusion of leave. Replacement arrangements are therefore usually temporary. An employer is more likely to hire or promote someone into a replacement position when the employee on FMLA leave is a key employee, however. To be one of the most highly paid employees in an organization generally means that an employee is important to its day-to-day operations. To get a new person of the same caliber might require that the replacement be offered a permanent position. The regulations recognize that reinstating the employee on FMLA leave and supporting two positions where there had previously only been one could lead to economic harm.

> An employer may take into account its ability to replace on a temporary basis . . . the employee on FMLA leave. If permanent replacement is unavoidable, the cost of then reinstating the employee can be considered in evaluating whether substantial and grievous economic injury will occur from restoration; in other words, the effect on the operations of the company of reinstating the employee in an equivalent position.[9]

This was the situation in the case *Oby v. Baton Rouge Marriott*. The plaintiff was an executive housekeeper and the third highest-paid employee at the employer hotel. The hotel's housekeeping suffered while the plaintiff was on FMLA leave and, when she was unable to give her employer an approximate date for her return, it decided to replace her. When the employee requested reinstatement, the employer refused, explaining that it could not afford to have two executive housekeepers at the same salary (it did, however, offer her a substantially equivalent position, which she declined). In court, the plaintiff did not produce evidence to the contrary, and the court granted summary judgment to the employer hotel.[10]

Employers should not count on prevailing on a defense that it was necessary to hire a permanent replacement, however. In *Johnson v. Resources for Human Development, Inc.*, another employee took over the plaintiff's duties temporarily when she began her FMLA leave, but the organization soon hired a permanent replacement. In denying summary judgment to the employer, the court noted that it was possible that the human resources department was confused about the legal effect of designating the plaintiff a key employee but held that it had not shown that reinstating her and keeping her replacement would cause grievous harm to the employer.[11]

A similar result can be found in *Kephart v. Cherokee County*. When Rex Kephart, Cherokee County's tax assessor, took FMLA leave, the county had concluded that it needed to have an assessor in place and had appointed the tax appraiser as assessor. The county argued that it could not restore Kephart to the tax assessor

---

9. *Id.* § 825.218(b).
10. Oby v. Baton Rouge Marriott, 329 F. Supp. 2d 772, 782–83 (M.D. La. 2004).
11. Johnson v. Res. for Hum. Dev., Inc., 789 F. Supp. 2d 595, 605–06 (E.D. Pa. 2011).

position because that position had already been filled and no equivalent position existed. Because of this, reinstating Kephart to an equivalent position would have resulted in the expenditure of unbudgeted funds, a situation that would cause grievous economic harm to the county. The court denied the county's motion for summary judgment on Kephart's FMLA interference claim, noting that there was evidence from which a jury could conclude that the board of commissioners could have returned the replacement assessor to her position as tax appraiser and reinstated Kephart with no economic injury resulting to the county.[12]

Interestingly, a key employee's disastrously poor performance can be the basis for concluding that reinstatement after FMLA leave would cause grievous economic harm to the organization. In the 2019 case *Douglas v. Dreamdealers USA, LLC*, the court denied summary judgment to the plaintiff key employee, holding that a reasonable jury could find that the employee's failure to pay the company's taxes (thereby incurring tax penalties) and failure to keep orderly records during a time when the company was experiencing a downturn in sales put the company at economic risk.[13]

Proceeding with a Key Employee Designation

If an employer plans to designate someone a key employee in order to deny that employee reinstatement at the end of FMLA leave, it must proceed carefully. Failure to give the employee the required notice at the right time will result in the employer having to allow the employee to return regardless of whether it results in economic injury to the organization.

Step One: Written Notice of the Key Employee Designation

First, the employer must give the employee written notice that they are being designated a key employee when the employee requests FMLA leave (or when leave begins, if the employee has not been able to give prior notice). In the Designation Notice, the employer must explicitly say that it may deny the employee reinstatement if the employer determines that substantial and grievous economic injury will result from the employee's return. The employer must also explain that even if it subsequently decides not to reinstate the employee, the employee is still entitled to take the full complement of FMLA leave and that the employer will continue to pay its share of the employee's health insurance premiums until the leave is over and employment is terminated. Note that this notice does not have to say that the employer categorically will not reinstate the employee, only that it is *possible* that it will not do so. If the employer has already made the determination that it will

---

12. Kephart v. Cherokee County, 229 F.3d 1142 (4th Cir. 2000).
13. Douglas v. Dreamdealers USA, LLC, 416 F. Supp. 3d 1063, 1073 (D. Nev. 2019).

not restore the employee to the same or an equivalent position, it may inform the employee at the same time that it makes the key employee designation.

Step Two: Determination That Reinstatement Will Cause Substantial and Grievous Injury

Once the employer determines that restoration of the employee will result in substantial and grievous injury to its operations, it must give the employee written notice of that fact. This notice may be separate from the notice that the employee is a key employee. Remember, *the injury to operations must be caused by the return of the employee, not by the fact of the employee's absence.* The written notice must include a representation that the employer *is not denying FMLA leave* but plans to deny restoration of the employee to their previous position once FMLA leave is over. *The employer must also explain* how restoration will cause the employer significant and grievous economic harm. Employers should have such an explanation reviewed by legal counsel since it would be an important piece of evidence if the key employee were to challenge the ultimate dismissal. The written notice must be delivered to the employee in person or sent by certified mail.[14] If the employer does not give the employee the required notice at the right time in the right way, it will have to allow the employee to return regardless of whether doing so results in economic injury to the organization.[15]

The regulations say that ordinarily, an employer should be able to determine that it will deny reinstatement *before* the employee begins leave. This is to allow the employee an opportunity to reevaluate their need for FMLA leave and, if possible, continue working rather than be denied restoration to their position after FMLA leave ends. If, for some reason, an employer is not able to make this determination until after the employee begins the leave, the employer must allow the employee a reasonable amount of time to decide whether to return to work so as not to be denied reinstatement.[16]

Step Three: Return to Work or Continuation of FMLA Leave

Having received the determination notice, the key employee will now either return to work in order not to be denied reinstatement or remain on FMLA leave. An employee who remains on FMLA leave is entitled to the same rights and benefits as anyone else on FMLA leave until that employee seeks to return to work and the employer denies restoration. The employer must continue to pay its share of the employee's health insurance premium during this period. It may not seek reimbursement of the premium costs after employment ends.[17]

---

14. 29 C.F.R. § 825.219(b).

15. *Id.* § 825.219(a).

16. *Id.* § 825.219(b).

17. *Id.* § 825.219(c).

Step Four: Updated Assessment of the Harm Caused by the Employee's Return

Despite receiving a key employee designation notice, the employee may still ask to be restored to their original position at the conclusion of their FMLA leave. At this time the employer *must make an updated assessment* of whether the employee's return will cause substantial and grievous economic harm to the employer's operations. (The employee's replacement may not have worked out, for example, and the employer may want to bring the employee back.) If the employer determines that such economic injury will result, it must notify the employee of the denial in writing (delivered by hand or certified mail) one final time.[18]

The importance of following the steps laid out in the FMLA regulations is well illustrated by a Maryland case, *Neel v. Mid-Atlantic of Fairfield, LLC.* The plaintiff in that case, Elizabeth Neel, was a nursing home administrator employed by Mid-Atlantic. When she requested FMLA leave, her employer indicated that she was a key employee by checking the appropriate box on Form WH-381, the U.S. DOL's form to provide notice of rights and responsibilities under the FMLA. The court held that this was sufficient notice that she was a key employee who might be denied reinstatement at the conclusion of her FMLA leave. Neel's employer, however, failed to give her written notice of its determination that her reinstatement would cause substantial and grievous economic harm to the organization and to explain the basis for that determination.[19]

At trial, her employer argued that the notice of rights and responsibilities contained sufficient information to satisfy the requirements of both step one and step two. The court disagreed, pointing out that

> nowhere in the WH-381 notice from Mid-Atlantic to Neel is the required explanation of the basis for Mid-Atlantic's finding that substantial and grievous economic injury will result. Mid-Atlantic's failure to provide Neel with a clear statement of intent to deny restoration deprived Neel of an important right under the FMLA and, *as important, deprived her of an opportunity to weigh whether taking FMLA leave was in her best interest.*[20]

The court concluded that Mid-Atlantic, by failing to give Neel "unambiguous" notice that it would deny restoration, explain to her the basis for its determination, and offer her a reasonable time in which to return to work after being notified, had interfered with Neel's right to FMLA leave. The court also held that Mid-Atlantic was not entitled to claim the key employee exemption because that exemption is

---

18. *Id.* § 825.219(d).

19. Neel v. Mid-Atl. of Fairfield, LLC, 778 F. Supp. 2d 593 (D. Md. 2011) (summary judgment for the plaintiff employee).

20. *Id.* at 603 (emphasis added).

only available when the employer complies with the requirements set out in the FMLA regulations.[21]

A different court came to a similar conclusion in a 2011 case from Pennsylvania. There, the employer correctly concluded that the employee was a key employee and gave her notice of that fact at the start of her leave. But it never gave the employee notice of its unambiguous determination that her return would cause substantial and grievous economic harm, much less an explanation of that conclusion. The court found that the employer was not entitled to claim the key employee exemption.[22]

Employers wishing to avail themselves of the key employee exemption to the FMLA's reinstatement requirement should, therefore, do a rigorous analysis showing that restoration of the employee to their position will have serious economic consequences for its operations. It must then follow the requirements set forth in the FMLA regulations to the letter.

---

21. *Id.* at 604.
22. Johnson v. Res. for Hum. Dev., Inc., 789 F. Supp. 2d 595, 605–06 (E.D. Pa. 2011).

Chapter 9

Military FMLA: Qualifying Exigency Leave and Military Caregiver Leave

In 2008 and again in 2009, Congress added new provisions to the FMLA for the first time since its passage in 1993. These amendments extended FMLA leave to employees who are the family members of those serving in the armed forces and its reserves. These FMLA amendments added two new types of leave: qualifying exigency leave and military caregiver leave. This book refers to both types as *military FMLA leave* to distinguish them from the original forms of FMLA leave. Although the eligibility, structure, and notice requirements of military FMLA leave are based on original FMLA leave, the two types of military FMLA leave differ in some important respects from original FMLA leave and from each other. This chapter and its discussion of military FMLA leave presumes knowledge of the basic rules governing original FMLA leave, which are discussed in previous chapters.

Qualifying Exigency Leave

Military FMLA requires covered employers to grant up to a total of twelve weeks of leave during the FMLA year to eligible employees to deal with specific types of urgent issues that arise when a *spouse, child of any age, or parent* is a military servicemember ordered to *federal* active duty for deployment to a foreign country in support of a contingency operation. This form of military FMLA leave is known as *qualifying exigency leave* (QEL). For QEL purposes, all public employers are covered employers. As with original FMLA leave, to be eligible for QEL, an employee must work for an employer with fifty or more employees within a seventy-five mile radius. An employee must have worked for that employer for a total of twelve months and for 1,250 hours within the last twelve consecutive months.

QEL is designed to give employees time to deal with some of the informational, financial, and child-related issues common to foreign deployments. An employee may take QEL for any of the following reasons related to a servicemember's foreign deployment:

1. to address issues arising out of deployment with *seven or fewer days' notice* of the deployment;[1]
2. to attend military events, family-support programs, family-assistance programs, or informational briefings related to the servicemember's active duty status or call to active duty status;[2]
3. to provide urgent, immediate child care or parental care to the servicemember's children or parents, or to arrange for alternative child care or eldercare;[3]
4. to enroll a servicemember's child in or transfer the child to a new school or day-care facility and to attend any school or facility meetings;[4]
5. to make new arrangements for the care of a parent of the servicemember, including enrollment in or transfer to a new eldercare facility because of the deployment, and to attend eldercare facility meetings having to do with the parent;[5]
6. to make financial or legal arrangements related to the servicemember's active duty status or call to active duty for deployment abroad, including acting as the servicemember's representative before a government agency to obtain, arrange, or appeal military benefits;[6]
7. to attend counseling sessions for the employee, the servicemember, or a child of the servicemember, provided that the counseling is related to a servicemember's active duty status or call to active duty;[7]
8. to participate in postdeployment activities for ninety days after the termination of the servicemember's foreign deployment;
9. to address issues related to the servicemember's death;[8] or
10. to spend up to fifteen calendar days with the servicemember for each rest-and-recuperation leave granted during the deployment.[9]

As is the case with original FMLA leave, QEL may be taken on an intermittent or reduced schedule.

---

1. 29 C.F.R. § 825.126(b)(1). Leave taken for this reason is limited to the seven calendar days following the servicemember's notification of deployment.

2. *Id.* § 825.126(b)(2).

3. *Id.* § 825.126(b)(3)(i), (3)(ii), (8)(i), (8)(ii).

4. *Id.* § 825.126(b)(3)(iii)–(iv).

5. *Id.* § 825.126(b)(8)(iii)–(iv).

6. *Id.* § 825.126(b)(4).

7. *Id.* § 825.126(b)(5).

8. *Id.* § 825.126(b)(7).

9. *Id.* § 825.126(b)(6).

Covered Servicemembers

It is not just any military servicemember for whom an employee may take QEL. QEL is available for a spouse, child, or parent of members of the regular armed forces who are on active duty or under a call for active duty for deployment to a foreign country.[10] It is also available for members of the National Guard and reserves—the Army National Guard, Army Reserve, Navy Reserve, Marine Corps Reserve, Air National Guard, Air Force Reserve, Coast Guard Reserve, and retired members of the regular armed forces or reserves—who are on federal active duty or under a call to federal active duty in support of a contingency operation in a foreign country or a contingency operation that falls under specified sections of Title 10 of the U.S. Code, which deals with military operations.[11]

There are several things worth noting about QEL taken in connection with a member of the National Guard and reserves. First, the active duty in question must be federal active duty.[12] Employees may not take QEL in support of National Guard members who are called to state active duty. Second, QEL in support of a member of the regular armed forces (that is, full-time career members of the armed forces) may only be taken when the servicemember is being deployed to a foreign country. QEL taken for a member of the National Guard and reserves may be taken only in support of a contingency operation, but here the contingency operation is not limited to one in a foreign country.[13] It may be taken in various other circumstances as well, including a call to "Federal service in the case of insurrections and national emergencies . . . or any other provision of law during a war or during a national emergency declared by the President or Congress."[14]

Finally, human resources personnel responsible for administering FMLA leave and employees requesting QEL are often unable to tell whether a given deployment is to a foreign country or in support of a contingency operation. However, the servicemember's orders (a copy of which may be presented in lieu of certification) will specify whether the member is deployed to a foreign country and whether the deployment is in support of a contingency operation. If the family member of an employee is being deployed for reasons other than a contingency operation in a foreign country, the orders will cite the relevant section of Title 10 of the United States Code under which the family member is being called to duty, or they will refer to the specific name of the contingency operation.[15] Going forward, a servicemember (of either the regular armed forces or the reserves) who meets the requirements set forth above will be referred to as a "covered servicemember."

---

10. *See id.* § 825.126(a)(1).
11. *Id.* § 825.126(a)(2).
12. *Id.* § 825.126(a)(4).
13. *Id.* § 825.126(a)(1)–(2).
14. *Id.* § 825.126(a)(2).
15. *Id.* § 825.126(a)(1), (a)(2)(ii).

Spouses, Children, and Parents of Covered Servicemembers

The FMLA's military leave provisions allow an employee who has a spouse, child, or parent who is a covered servicemember to take QEL for any of the reasons above. The definition of *spouse* for the purposes of QEL is the same as it is for original FMLA leave: a husband or wife in a marriage entered into under the law of a state (or if entered into abroad, a marriage that would meet the requirements of at least one state). This includes same-sex spouses. In North Carolina, it excludes common-law marriages, which are not recognized under state law.[16]

The definition of *son or daughter* is also the same as it is for original FMLA: a biological, adopted, or foster child; a stepchild; a legal ward; or a child for whom an employee stood *in loco parentis*. The difference here is that the child who is a covered servicemember may be of any age (obviously, minors cannot be servicemembers) and does not have to be a dependent incapable of self-care.[17]

When employees take QEL for parents who are covered servicemembers, the same definition of *parent* applies as it does with original FMLA: a biological, adoptive, or foster parent; a stepparent; or any other individual who stood *in loco parentis* to the employee. This does not include "parents-in-law."[18]

QEL to Arrange for Care of a Covered Servicemember's Parent

The third, fourth, and fifth reasons for taking QEL listed above include taking care of the needs of the parent of a covered servicemember. This is where the rules governing QEL start to get tricky. While the definition of *parent* is the same as for original FMLA leave, the U.S. Department of Labor's (DOL's) QEL regulation says that the parent must be incapable of self-care. The regulation goes on to repeat, almost verbatim, the definition of *incapable of self-care* that appears in the DOL's original FMLA regulations, where it typically applies to adult children needing care for a serious health condition.[19]

Imagine now that an employee is taking QEL because a stepson is being deployed to a foreign country and the employee must, as a result of the deployment, arrange for the admission of the stepson's other parent to an eldercare facility. Is that covered?

Ruth asks her employer for qualified exigency leave in connection with the deployment of her stepson Jack to Germany. Ruth is married to Jack's father, Joe. One of the things that Ruth needs to handle for Jack during his deployment

---

16. *See id.* § 825.102.

17. *Compare id.* § 825.126(a)(5) (s.vv. "son or daughter," "incapable of self-care") *with id.* § 825.200 (same).

18. *See id.* § 825.102.

19. *See id.* §§ 825.126(b)(8), .102. Under original FMLA, a child over 18 years of age must be incapable of self-care for an employee to use FMLA leave to care for them when they suffer from a serious health condition.

is the admission of Mary, who is Jack's mother and has dementia, to a memory-care facility. Is she entitled to QEL to take care of this?

Yes, she is. Jack meets the definition of *son* and Ruth is entitled to QEL for a son or daughter who is a covered servicemember being deployed to a foreign country. Mary is covered servicemember Jack's mother and she is incapable of self-care (hence, her admission to a memory-care facility).

Notice of the Need to Take QEL

Employees must give notice of the need for QEL "as soon as practicable," whether the need for leave is known earlier or later than thirty days in advance. This is a different standard from that applied to original FMLA leave or military caregiver leave.[20] As with original leave, no magic words and no mention of FMLA or qualified exigency leave must be made for an employee to be considered to have given notice of the need for leave. So long as an employee has indicated that a spouse, child, or parent is a covered servicemember and that the employee needs leave for one of the reasons for which QEL may be taken, notice will be considered given.[21]

Certification for QEL

Employers may require employees requesting QEL to provide

1. a copy of the covered servicemember's active duty orders or other military-issued documentation indicating the covered servicemember is on active duty or called to active duty, the fact that the servicemember will be deployed abroad, and the dates of the deployment *and*
2. a certification from the employee that provides
   a. facts supporting the employee's need for leave in this situation (Does the employee need, for example, to attend military briefings for family members, meet with a school counselor, or meet with a lawyer?),
   b. the approximate starting date on which the qualifying exigency began or will begin,
   c. the QEL's end date, and,
   d. if the employee is meeting with a third party, identifying and contact information for the third party and a description of the meeting's purposes.[22]

---

20. *Id.* § 825.302(a)–(b).
21. *See id.* § 825.302(c).
22. *Id.* § 825.309(a)–(b).

A copy of the servicemember's active-duty orders will indicate a foreign deployment and, in the case of the reserves, whether the call to duty is in support of a contingency operation. If the QEL will be taken on an intermittent or reduced schedule basis, an employer may ask for an estimate of the frequency and duration of the qualifying exigency.[23] If the qualifying exigency involves the servicemember's rest-and-recuperation leave, the employer may require military documentation indicating the dates of the covered servicemember's rest and recuperation (such as the rest-and-recuperation orders).[24]

An employer may *not* request recertification of the covered servicemember's orders. It may, however, request certification of each individual qualifying exigency arising out of the same call to duty.

As with medical certification for original FMLA leave, DOL has developed a form for use in connection with QEL. It is Form WH-384, a copy of which may be found in Appendix A. *Note that certification of the need for QEL is subject to the same time requirements as FMLA leave*:

1. An employer must provide an employee with Form WH-381, the combined Notice of Eligibility and Rights and Responsibilities. The employer must request certification in writing (usually on the form) within five days of the request for or the beginning of leave.[25]
2. The employee has fifteen days to return the completed form.[26]
3. Once the employer has sufficient information to conclude that an employee is entitled to QEL, it must provide the employee with Form WH-382, the Designation Notice, within five days.[27]

Twelve Weeks of QEL and the FMLA Year

The military FMLA amendments structured QEL as simply one more reason for which an employee may take leave during the twelve-week entitlement to FMLA leave. It does not provide employees with an additional twelve weeks of leave in addition to original FMLA leave. QEL is measured in the same FMLA year as original FMLA. This means that an employee who used twelve weeks of QEL within an FMLA year would have no time left in which to take FMLA leave for the birth of a child or a serious health condition during that same FMLA year. In contrast, military caregiver leave, discussed below, departs from the twelve week FMLA standard.

---

23. *Id.* § 825.309(b)(4).
24. *Id.* § 825.309(b)(6).
25. *Id.* § 825.300(b)–(c).
26. *Id.* § 825.309(b).
27. *Id.* § 825.300(d).

Military Caregiver Leave

Military caregiver leave (MCL) allows FMLA-eligible employees to take *up to twenty-six weeks of leave within a twelve-month period* to care for a spouse, child, parent, or next of kin who has been injured or become ill while serving in the armed forces.[28] MCL differs from original FMLA leave to care for a spouse, child, or parent with a serious health condition in that employees may take MCL to care for an adult child, regardless of the child's ability to care for themselves, and for next of kin. MCL also allows more than double the amount of time an employee may take off to care for a military family member who has a serious injury or illness incurred or aggravated by their military service.

Circumstances That Qualify for MCL

MCL may be taken by an employee whose spouse, child, parent, or next of kin is a current member or veteran of the regular Armed Forces or the National Guard and Reserve, or who is on the temporary disability retired list of the regular armed forces or National Guard and Reserve. The servicemember must have incurred a serious injury or illness in the line of duty while on active duty (or had a preexisting condition aggravated during active duty) and been rendered medically unfit to perform the duties of the servicemember's office, grade, or rating. The servicemember must also be undergoing medical treatment, recuperation, or therapy for that injury or illness or otherwise be in outpatient status or on the temporary disability retired list.[29] If MCL is being requested to care for a veteran, the veteran must have been discharged or released within five years of the date on which the medical treatment, recuperation, or therapy for injuries or illness incurred in the line of duty begins. The veteran may not have received a dishonorable discharge or release from service.[30] In the following sections on MCL, servicemembers and veterans who meet these requirements will also be referred to as "covered servicemembers."

An employee is eligible for twenty-six weeks of MCL during a single twelve-month period. There is a limit of one time per covered servicemember per injury. If the covered servicemember needs care for the original injury beyond the initial twenty-six weeks of MCL, the employee may be able to use the twelve-week FMLA entitlement in a subsequent year to care for the covered servicemember as an immediate family member with a serious health condition. An employee would also be eligible to take twenty-six weeks of leave in a subsequent year *to care for a different covered servicemember* or to care for the first servicemember who has suffered *a different injury* after returning to duty.

---

28. Next-of-kin coverage does not apply to QEL nor to original FMLA.
29. 29 C.F.R. § 825.127(b)(1).
30. *Id.* § 825.127(b)(2).

Definition of *Serious Injury or Illness*

The term *serious injury or illness* is defined slightly differently for current service-members and for veterans. For current servicemembers, a serious injury or illness is

- an injury or illness that was incurred in the line of duty or
- a condition existing at the time the servicemember's active duty began that was aggravated by their service in the line of duty and renders the servicemember medically unfit to perform the duties of the member's office, grade, rank, or rating.[31]

For a veteran, a serious injury or illness is

- an injury or illness incurred in the line of duty;
- a condition existing at the time the servicemember's active duty began that was aggravated by their service in the line of duty, continues into the present, and made the servicemember unable to perform the duties of their office, grade, rank, or rating while an active member of the armed forces, National Guard, or reserves; or
- a condition, physical or mental, for which the veteran has received a disability rating of at least 50 percent from the U.S. Department of Veterans Affairs;
- a physical or mental condition that either substantially impairs the veteran's ability to be gainfully employed or would do so if the individual were not being treated; or
- an injury, physical or psychological, that has caused the veteran to be enrolled in the Department of Veteran Affairs Program of Comprehensive Assistance for Family Caregivers.[32]

Spouse, Child, Parent, or Next of Kin

Spouse, son or daughter, and *parent* have the same meanings in the context of MCL as they do for original FMLA leave, only here, *son or daughter* refers to an employee's *adult* child.[33] *Next of kin* means a covered servicemember's (*not an employee's*) nearest blood relative (other than the servicemember's spouse, son, daughter, or parent) in the order of priority set out in 29 CFR 825.127(d)(3). The servicemember, however, may skip over the regulation's priority list and designate another blood relative as the nearest blood relative and next of kin for purposes of MCL. Note that when there is more than one family member with the same level of relationship to the covered servicemember (one brother and two sisters, for example), all the siblings are considered next of kin. (Brothers and sisters are the first order of priority after spouses, children, and parents.)[34]

---

31. *Id.* § 825.127(c)(1).
32. *Id.* § 825.127(c)(2)
33. *See id.* § 825.127(d)(1)–(2).
34. *Id.* § 825.127(d)(3).

Notice of the Need for MCL

An employer may require an employee to give notice of the need for MCL

- thirty days in advance, if the need for MCL is foreseeable, or
- on either the same day or the next business day, if the need for leave was not foreseeable.

This is the same notice requirement as applies to FMLA leave for the serious health condition of an employee or of an employee's immediate family member. Both QEL and MCL are subject to the same regulations with respect to notice and certification as is original FMLA leave.[35] Thus, an employer may require employees requesting MCL to use its usual and customary notice and procedural requirements for requesting leave. If an employee fails to do so without a reasonable justification, the employer may delay or deny leave.[36] But once an employee gives notice of the need for MCL,[37] the employer must respond within five business days by giving the employee a copy of Form WH-381 (the Notice of Eligibility and Rights and Responsibilities) and tell the employee whether it will be requiring a medical certification of the covered servicemember's condition.[38]

Certification

An employer may ask an employee requesting MCL to provide a medical certification of the need for leave from the servicemember's health care provider. For the purposes of MCL, health care providers who may complete the certification include Department of Defense providers, Department of Veterans Affairs providers, private Tricare-authorized providers, and the types of health care providers who may certify original FMLA leave for a serious health condition (see page 73).[39]

Medical certifications for MCL may ask information sufficient to establish the employee's need for leave, including the following:

1. a statement of medical facts regarding the servicemember's health condition—specifically, facts relating to whether the injury or illness renders the servicemember medically unfit to perform the duties of the member's office, grade, rank, or rating and whether the member is receiving medical treatment, recuperation, or therapy;
2. information sufficient to establish that the servicemember is in need of care;
3. a description of the care to be provided;

---

35. *See id.* §§ 825.302–.305. Notice of an employee's need for leave and certification of the need for leave are discussed in Chapter 5.

36. *Id.* § 825.302.

37. As with original FMLA or QEL, no special language is required. If the employee asks for time off to care for a family member made ill or injured in the line of duty, the burden shifts to the employer to inquire into whether the employee is eligible for MCL.

38. *Id.* § 825.300(b)–(c).

39. *Id.* § 825.310(a).

4. an estimate of the leave needed to provide the care; and

5. the employee's relationship to the servicemember.[40]

Certification of the need for MCL is subject to the same time requirements as FMLA leave: the certification must be completed and returned within fifteen days of its receipt by the employee. In contrast to original FMLA leave, second and third opinions are permitted for MCL only if the heath-care provider signing the certification is not a Department of Defense, Department of Veterans Affairs, or Tricare-authorized provider—although an employer may authenticate or get clarification of the certification, just as it may for original FMLA leave.[41] Again, in contrast to original FMLA leave, recertifications are not permitted for MCL.[42] An employer may also ask for documentation (like a birth certificate) or confirmation (such as a written statement) that the servicemember for whom the employee proposes to care is a spouse, child, parent, or next of kin.[43]

Because MCL differs from FMLA leave to care for a family member with a serious health condition, employers should *not* use the same certification form for traditional FMLA leave and MCL. The U.S. DOL has developed forms specifically for use with requests for MCL. They are Forms WH-385 (current servicemember) and WH-385-V (veteran).[44] They may be found in Appendix A.[45] An employer requiring certification for MCL must accept "invitational travel orders" or invitational travel authorizations issued to a family member to join an ill or injured covered servicemember at the servicemember's bedside in lieu of the DOL's certification form or the employer's own certification form.[46]

Calculating the Amount of MCL an Employee May Take

An employee is entitled to a total of twenty-six workweeks of leave for MCL. This works both concurrently with original FMLA leave and in addition to it. An employee may never take more than a combined twelve weeks of leave in an FMLA year for the reasons allowed for original FMLA leave (the birth or placement of a child or to care for the employee's own or an immediate family member's serious health condition) or for QEL. An employee may never take more than twenty-six weeks of MCL in a twelve-month period, nor may an employee ever take more than twenty-six weeks of *combined* MCL, original FMLA leave, and QEL.

Here is what makes managing MCL difficult. For MCL purposes, the twelve-month period for MCL begins the first day the employee takes MCL and ends

---

40. *Id.* § 825.310(b)–(c).

41. *See id.* § 825.310(d), .307.

42. *Id.* § 825.310(d).

43. *Id.* § 825.122(k).

44. *See id.* § 825.310.

45. The forms may also be downloaded by visiting https://www.dol.gov/general/forms (select heading Forms by Number, then scroll down list to find links to PDFs of Forms WH-385 and WH-385-V) (last visited Apr. 4, 2024).

46. 29 C.F.R. § 825.310(e).

twelve months later, *regardless of the method that the employer uses to determine FMLA entitlement for other forms of FMLA leave.* Consider an easy example first.

> *Paradise County uses a calendar year as its FMLA year. Jonny takes three weeks of FMLA leave for his own serious health condition in February. In April, he asks for six weeks of FMLA leave to bond with his newborn baby from April 10 through May 20. When Jonny returns on May 21, he has used nine of the twelve weeks of FMLA to which he is entitled in that FMLA year.*
>
> *On June 1, Jonny begins MCL to take care of his wife, who was injured in the line of duty shortly after returning from her own FMLA leave for the birth of the baby. This means that Jonny's MCL year begins on June 1. As of June 1, Jonny has his full twenty-six-week MCL entitlement available.*
>
> *Jonny needs twenty weeks of MCL. This is not a problem because the other FMLA leave that he took (the three weeks of FMLA for his own serious health condition and the six weeks for the birth of his baby) were before the start of his MCL year on June 1.*

Now let's add some additional facts to this scenario.

> *Jonny returns to work on October 19. In early November, Jonny injures his rotator cuff while raking leaves. His doctor recommends immediate surgery. Jonny worries that he may not have any FMLA eligibility left because he has taken more than twenty-six weeks of original and military FMLA leave combined. Paradise County Human Resources tells Jonny that he has not used more than twenty-six weeks in the MCL year starting June. He still has three weeks of original FMLA leave left in the regular FMLA year, which he uses for the rotator-cuff surgery and the subsequent post-op healing period.*

Could things get more complicated? Yes.

> *Although Jonny's wife returned to light duty after recovering from her injury and Jonny's MCL has ended, things have not been going so well for her as of late. The bones that were broken in the original injury have not healed properly and will have to be rebroken and reset. Jonny needs additional MCL in February, extending through the end of March. This time Jonny is out of luck. His military caregiver FMLA year started on June 1. Since June 1, he has taken twenty weeks of MCL and three weeks of original FMLA leave. Between February and the start of his new military caregiver FMLA year, Jonny has only three weeks left; his three weeks of leave to deal with his rotator-cuff injury*

> *counted against his twenty-six-week cumulative limit, although his twenty weeks of MCL did not count against his twelve weeks of original FMLA leave.*
>
> *Jonny will not be eligible for MCL to care for his wife for this same injury again. MCL is available one time* per injury. *But Jonny can take original FMLA leave to care for his wife because this is a new original FMLA year and Jonny has not used any of his entitlement for this current year.*

But what if . . .

> *Jonny's father, a member of the regular armed forces, develops a severe illness from his exposure to a noxious agent while in the line of duty. Jonny doesn't bother requesting MCL because he figures that he is not eligible again until June 1, when his MCL year starts again. His wife, however, is better informed and insists that he ask for MCL to help care for his father immediately—in this case, beginning on April 15.*

Who is correct? Jonny's wife is correct. This is MCL for *a family member other than his wife*, so Jonny is entitled to a full twenty-six weeks of leave to care for his father beginning on April 15. That becomes the date on which his military FMLA year begins for the separate and independent MCL to care for his father.

Intermittent and Reduced Leave Schedules

MCL may be taken on an intermittent or reduced leave schedule. As with original FMLA leave, the prerequisite for taking MCL on an intermittent or reduced leave schedule is that a treating provider certify that this is medically necessary for the welfare of the covered servicemember for whom the employee is caring.[47] An employer may transfer an employee on intermittent or reduced schedule MCL to an alternative position if that position is better able to accommodate the employee's need for intermittent or reduced schedule leave so long as the employee's salary and benefits remain the same. As with original FMLA leave, the employee must be returned to their original position when MCL ends.[48]

Compensation and Other Benefits

The same rules governing payment of wages, use of accrued paid leave and compensatory time off, and the continuation of benefits that apply to original FMLA apply to military FMLA leave. Both QEL and MCL are unpaid leave, but employers may require employees to have accrued paid sick, vacation, or personal leave run at the same time as FMLA leave, turning unpaid leave into paid leave. Employees

---

47. *Id.* § 825.202(b).
48. *Id.* § 825.204.

may choose to do this, if their employers don't require it. Use of accrued paid leave in any FMLA circumstance is subject to an employer's policy on the reasons for which each type of leave may be used. If, for example, an employer's sick-leave policy does not allow the use of sick leave to care for a family member, sick leave cannot run concurrently with either QEL or MCL.[49] Employees who are nonexempt under the Fair Labor Standards Act may be required and must be allowed to use accrued compensatory time off (comp time) at the same time as QEL and MCL.[50] And finally, during both QEL and MCL, the employer must continue to contribute to an employee's health insurance on the same basis as it does when the employee is actively working. There is no requirement to continue any other benefit that an employer offers except to the extent that a benefit continues to be offered or paid for by the employer during other comparable leaves of absence.[51]

Return to Work

An employee returning to work after taking MCL must be immediately reinstated to the same or substantially equivalent position. Reinstatement may be denied for the same reasons as it may when an employee returns from original FMLA leave, including being designated a key employee and being informed that the employer might not be required to reinstate the employee.[52]

Conclusion

Administering military FMLA leave offers human resources personnel some distinct challenges. But because the eligibility requirements are the same for all forms of FMLA leave (an employer with fifty or more employees at the same worksite, a cumulative twelve months of service, and 1,250 hours of service in the last twelve consecutive months), human resources professionals are likely to meet their first QEL and MCL request with a sound base of original FMLA experience behind them. The key to successfully managing military FMLA leave is to think of QEL and MCL as variations on a theme, keeping in mind places where the military forms of FMLA diverge from original FMLA.

---

49. *See id.* § 825.207(a).
50. *Id.* § 825.207(f).
51. *See id.* § 825.209.
52. *See id.* §§ 825.214–.219.

APPENDIXES

United States Department of Labor Family and Medical Leave Act Forms

Form WH-380-E: Certification of Health Care Provider for Employee's Serious Health Condition

Certification of Health Care Provider for
Employee's Serious Health Condition
under the Family and Medical Leave Act

U.S. Department of Labor
Wage and Hour Division

**DO NOT SEND COMPLETED FORM TO THE DEPARTMENT OF LABOR.
RETURN TO THE PATIENT.**

OMB Control Number: 1235-0003
Expires: 6/30/2026

The Family and Medical Leave Act (FMLA) provides that an employer may require an employee seeking FMLA protections because of a need for leave due to a serious health condition to submit a medical certification issued by the employee's health care provider. 29 U.S.C. §§ 2613, 2614(c)(3); 29 C.F.R. § 825.305. The employer must give the employee at least 15 calendar days to provide the certification. If the employee fails to provide complete and sufficient medical certification, his or her FMLA leave request may be denied. 29 C.F.R. § 825.313. Information about the FMLA may be found on the WHD website at www.dol.gov/agencies/whd/fmla.

SECTION I - EMPLOYER

Either the employee or the employer may complete Section I. While use of this form is optional, this form asks the health care provider for the information necessary for a complete and sufficient medical certification, which is set out at 29 C.F.R. § 825.306. **You may not ask the employee to provide more information than allowed under the FMLA regulations, 29 C.F.R. §§ 825.306-825.308.** Additionally, you **may not** request a certification for FMLA leave to bond with a healthy newborn child or a child placed for adoption or foster care.

Employers must generally maintain records and documents relating to medical information, medical certifications, recertifications, or medical histories of employees created for FMLA purposes as confidential medical records in separate files/records from the usual personnel files and in accordance with 29 C.F.R. § 1630.14(c)(1), if the Americans with Disabilities Act applies, and in accordance with 29 C.F.R. § 1635.9, if the Genetic Information Nondiscrimination Act applies.

(1) Employee name: ____

               First   Middle   Last

(2) Employer name: ________________________________ Date: ____________ (mm/dd/yyyy)

                                 (List date certification requested)

(3) The medical certification must be returned by ________________________________ (mm/dd/yyyy)
    (Must allow at least 15 calendar days from the date requested, unless it is not feasible despite the employee's diligent, good faith efforts.)

(4) Employee's job title: ________________________ Job description ☐ is / ☐ is not attached.

    Employee's regular work schedule: ____

    Statement of the employee's essential job functions:

    (The essential functions of the employee's position are determined with reference to the position the employee held at the time the employee notified the employer of the need for leave or the leave started, whichever is earlier.)

SECTION II - HEALTH CARE PROVIDER

Please provide your contact information, complete all relevant parts of this Section, and sign the form. Your patient has requested leave under the FMLA. The FMLA allows an employer to require that the employee submit a timely, complete, and sufficient medical certification to support a request for FMLA leave due to the serious health condition of the employee. For FMLA purposes, a "serious health condition" means an illness, injury, impairment, or physical or mental condition that involves **inpatient care** or **continuing treatment by a health care provider**. For more information about the definitions of a serious health condition under the FMLA, see the chart on page 4.

You also may, but are **not required** to, provide other appropriate medical facts including symptoms, diagnosis, or any regimen of continuing treatment such as the use of specialized equipment. Please note that some state or local laws may not allow disclosure of private medical information about the patient's serious health condition, such as providing the diagnosis and/or course of treatment.

     Form WH-380-E, Revised June 2020

Employee Name: ____

Health Care Provider's name: (Print) ____

Health Care Provider's business address: ____

Type of practice / Medical specialty: ____

Telephone: _______________ Fax: _______________ E-mail: _____________________

PART A: Medical Information

Limit your response to the medical condition(s) for which the employee is seeking FMLA leave. Your answers should be your **best estimate** based upon your medical knowledge, experience, and examination of the patient. **After completing Part A, complete Part B to provide information about the amount of leave needed.** Note: For FMLA purposes, "incapacity" means the inability to work, attend school, or perform regular daily activities due to the condition, treatment of the condition, or recovery from the condition. Do not provide information about genetic tests, as defined in 29 C.F.R. § 1635.3(f), genetic services, as defined in 29 C.F.R. § 1635.3(e), or the manifestation of disease or disorder in the employee's family members, 29 C.F.R. § 1635.3(b).

(1) State the approximate date the condition started or will start: ____ (mm/dd/yyyy)

(2) Provide your **best estimate** of how long the condition lasted or will last: _____________________________________

(3) Check the box(es) for the questions below, as applicable. For all box(es) checked, the amount of leave needed must be provided in Part B.

☐ **Inpatient Care:** The patient (☐ has been / ☐ is expected to be) admitted for an overnight stay in a hospital, hospice, or residential medical care facility on the following date(s): ______________________________________

☐ **Incapacity plus Treatment:** (e.g. outpatient surgery, strep throat)

Due to the condition, the patient (☐ has been / ☐ is expected to be) incapacitated for **more than** three consecutive, full calendar days from: _______________ (mm/dd/yyyy) to _______________ (mm/dd/yyyy).

The patient (☐ was / ☐ will be) seen on the following date(s): _______________________________________

The condition (☐ has / ☐ has not) also resulted in a course of continuing treatment under the supervision of a health care provider (e.g. prescription medication (other than over-the-counter) or therapy requiring special equipment).

☐ **Pregnancy:** The condition is pregnancy. List the expected delivery date: _______________ (mm/dd/yyyy).

☐ **Chronic Conditions:** (e.g. asthma, migraine headaches) Due to the condition, it is medically necessary for the patient to have treatment visits at least twice per year.

☐ **Permanent or Long Term Conditions:** (e.g. Alzheimer's, terminal stages of cancer) Due to the condition, incapacity is permanent or long term and requires the continuing supervision of a health care provider (even if active treatment is not being provided).

☐ **Conditions requiring Multiple Treatments:** (e.g. chemotherapy treatments, restorative surgery) Due to the condition, it is medically necessary for the patient to receive multiple treatments.

☐ **None of the above:** If none of the above condition(s) were checked, (i.e., inpatient care, pregnancy) no additional information is needed. Go to page 4 to sign and date the form.

                                                              Form WH-380-E, Revised June 2020

Employee Name: ____

(4) If needed, briefly describe other appropriate medical facts related to the condition(s) for which the employee seeks FMLA leave. (e.g., use of nebulizer, dialysis)

____

PART B: Amount of Leave Needed

For the medical condition(s) checked in Part A, complete all that apply. Several questions seek a response as to the frequency or duration of a condition, treatment, etc. Your answer should be your **best estimate** based upon your medical knowledge, experience, and examination of the patient. Be as specific as you can; terms such as "lifetime," "unknown," or "indeterminate" may not be sufficient to determine FMLA coverage.

(5) Due to the condition, the patient (☐ had / ☐ will have) **planned medical treatment(s)** (scheduled medical visits) (e.g.psychotherapy, prenatal appointments) on the following date(s): ____

____

(6) Due to the condition, the patient (☐ was / ☐ will be) **referred to other health care provider(s)** for evaluation or treatment(s).

State the nature of such treatments: (e.g. cardiologist, physical therapy) ____

Provide your **best estimate** of the beginning date _________________ (mm/dd/yyyy) and end date _________________ (mm/dd/yyyy).

for the treatment(s).

Provide your **best estimate** of the duration of the treatment(s), including any period(s) of recovery (e.g. 3 days/week)

____

(7) Due to the condition, it is medically necessary for the employee to work a **reduced schedule**.

Provide your **best estimate** of the reduced schedule the employee is able to work. From _________________ (mm/dd/yyyy)

to _________________ (mm/dd/yyyy) the employee is able to work: (e.g., 5 hours/day, up to 25 hours a week)

____

(8) Due to the condition, the patient (☐ was / ☐ will be) **incapacitated for a continuous period of time**, including any time

for treatment(s) and/or recovery.

Provide your **best estimate** of the beginning date _________________ (mm/dd/yyyy) and end date _________________ (mm/dd/yyyy).

for the period of incapacity.

(9) Due to the condition, it (☐ was / ☐ is / ☐ will be) medically necessary for the employee to be absent from work on an

intermittent basis (periodically), including for any episodes of incapacity i.e., episodic flare-ups. Provide your **best estimate** of how often (frequency) and how long (duration) the episodes of incapacity will likely last.

Over the next 6 months, episodes of incapacity are estimated to occur _________________________________ times per

(☐ day ☐ week ☐ month) and are likely to last approximately _________________________ (☐ hours ☐ days) per episode.

     Form WH-380-E, Revised June 2020

Employee Name: ____

PART C: Essential Job Functions

If provided, the information in Section I question #4 may be used to answer this question. If the employer fails to provide a statement of the employee's essential functions or a job description, answer these questions based upon the employee's own description of the essential job functions. An employee who must be absent from work to receive medical treatment(s), such as scheduled medical visits, for a serious health condition is considered to be **not able** to perform the essential job functions of the position during the absence for treatment(s).

(10) Due to the condition, the employee (☐ was not able / ☐ is not able / ☐ will not be able) to perform **one or more** of the essential job function(s). Identify at least one essential job function the employee is not able to perform:

____

Signature of Health Care Provider ______________________________________ Date: _________________ (mm/dd/yyyy)

Definitions of a Serious Health Condition (See 29 C.F.R. §§ 825.113-.115)
Inpatient Care
• An overnight stay in a hospital, hospice, or residential medical care facility. • Inpatient care includes any period of incapacity or any subsequent treatment in connection with the overnight stay.
Continuing Treatment by a Health Care Provider (any one or more of the following)

Incapacity Plus Treatment: A period of incapacity of more than three consecutive, full calendar days, and any subsequent treatment or period of incapacity relating to the same condition, that also involves either:
   o Two or more in-person visits to a health care provider for treatment within 30 days of the first day of incapacity unless extenuating circumstances exist. The first visit must be within seven days of the first day of incapacity; or,
   o At least one in-person visit to a health care provider for treatment within seven days of the first day of incapacity, which results in a regimen of continuing treatment under the supervision of the health care provider. For example, the health provider might prescribe a course of prescription medication or therapy requiring special equipment.

Pregnancy: Any period of incapacity due to pregnancy or for prenatal care.
Chronic Conditions: Any period of incapacity due to or treatment for a chronic serious health condition, such as diabetes, asthma, migraine headaches. A chronic serious health condition is one which requires visits to a health care provider (or nurse supervised by the provider) at least twice a year and recurs over an extended period of time. A chronic condition may cause episodic rather than a continuing period of incapacity.
Permanent or Long-term Conditions: A period of incapacity which is permanent or long-term due to a condition for which treatment may not be effective, but which requires the continuing supervision of a health care provider, such as Alzheimer's disease or the terminal stages of cancer.
Conditions Requiring Multiple Treatments: Restorative surgery after an accident or other injury; or, a condition that would likely result in a period of incapacity of more than three consecutive, full calendar days if the patient did not receive the treatment.

PAPERWORK REDUCTION ACT NOTICE AND PUBLIC BURDEN STATEMENT

If submitted, it is mandatory for employers to retain a copy of this disclosure in their records for three years. 29 U.S.C. § 2616; 29 C.F.R. § 825.500. Persons are not required to respond to this collection of information unless it displays a currently valid OMB control number. The Department of Labor estimates that it will take an average of 15 minutes for respondents to complete this collection of information, including the time for reviewing instructions, searching existing data sources, gathering and maintaining the data needed, and completing and reviewing the collection of information. If you have any comments regarding this burden estimate or any other aspect of this collection information, including suggestions for reducing this burden, send them to the Administrator, Wage and Hour Division, U.S. Department of Labor, Room S-3502, 200 Constitution Avenue, N.W., Washington, D.C. 20210.

DO NOT SEND COMPLETED FORM TO THE DEPARTMENT OF LABOR. RETURN TO THE PATIENT.

                                        Form WH-380-E, Revised June 2020

Form WH-380-F: Certification of Health Care Provider for Family Member's Serious Health Condition

Certification of Health Care Provider for
Family Member's Serious Health Condition
under the Family and Medical Leave Act

U.S. Department of Labor
Wage and Hour Division

DO NOT SEND COMPLETED FORM TO THE DEPARTMENT OF LABOR.
RETURN TO THE PATIENT.

OMB Control Number: 1235-0003
Expires: 6/30/2026

The Family and Medical Leave Act (FMLA) provides that an employer may require an employee seeking FMLA leave to care for a family member with a serious health condition to submit a medical certification issued by the family member's health care provider. 29 U.S.C. §§ 2613, 2614(c)(3); 29 C.F.R. § 825.305. The employer must give the employee **at least 15 calendar days** to provide the certification. If the employee fails to provide complete and sufficient medical certification, his or her FMLA leave request may be denied. 29 C.F.R. § 825.313. Information about the FMLA may be found on the WHD website at www.dol.gov/agencies/whd/fmla.

SECTION I - EMPLOYER

Either the employee or the employer may complete Section I. While use of this form is optional, this form asks the health care provider for the information necessary for a complete and sufficient medical certification, which is set out at 29 C.F.R. § 825.306. **You may not ask the employee to provide more information than allowed under the FMLA regulations, 29 C.F.R. §§ 825.306-825.308.** Additionally, you **may not** request a certification for FMLA leave to bond with a healthy newborn child or a child placed for adoption or foster care.

Employers must generally maintain records and documents relating to medical information, medical certifications, recertifications, or medical histories of employees or employees' family members created for FMLA purposes as confidential medical records in separate files/records from the usual personnel files and in accordance with 29 C.F.R. § 1630.14(c)(1), if the Americans with Disabilities Act applies, and in accordance with 29 C.F.R. § 1635.9, if the Genetic Information Nondiscrimination Act applies.

(1) Employee name: ____
                          First   Middle   Last

(2) Employer name: ____ Date: __________________ (mm/dd/yyyy)
                                                                  (List date certification requested)

(3) The medical certification must be returned by ____ (mm/dd/yyyy)
      (Must allow at least 15 calendar days from the date requested, unless it is not feasible despite the employee's diligent, good faith efforts.)

SECTION II - EMPLOYEE

Please complete and sign Section II before providing this form to your family member or your family member's health care provider. The FMLA allows an employer to require that you submit a timely, complete, and sufficient medical certification to support a request for FMLA leave due to the serious health condition of your family member. If requested by your employer, your response is required to obtain or retain the benefit of the FMLA protections. 29 U.S.C. §§ 2613, 2614(c)(3). **You are responsible for making sure the medical certification is provided to your employer within the time frame requested, which must be at least 15 calendar days.** 29 C.F.R. §§ 825.305-825.306. Failure to provide a complete and sufficient medical certification may result in a denial of your FMLA leave request. 29 C.F.R. § 825.313.

(1) Name of the family member for whom you will provide care: ____

(2) Select the relationship of the family member to you. The family member is your:

☐ Spouse   ☐ Parent   ☐ Child, under age 18

☐ Child, age 18 or older and incapable of self-care because of a mental or physical disability

Spouse means a husband or wife as defined or recognized in the state where the individual was married, including in a common law marriage or same-sex marriage. The terms "child" and "parent" include in loco parentis relationships in which a person assumes the obligations of a parent to a child. An employee may take FMLA leave to care for an individual who assumed the obligations of a parent to the employee when the employee was a child. An employee may also take FMLA leave to care for a child for whom the employee has assumed the obligations of a parent. No legal or biological relationship is necessary.

Form WH-380-F, Revised June 2020

Employee Name: ____

(3) Briefly describe the care you will provide to your family member: (**Check all that apply**)

    ☐ Assistance with basic medical, hygienic, nutritional, or safety needs   ☐ Transportation

    ☐ Physical Care   ☐ Psychological Comfort   ☐ Other: ____

(4) Give your **best estimate** of the amount of leave needed to provide the care described:

____

(5) If a **reduced work schedule** is necessary to provide the care described, give your **best estimate** of the reduced schedule
you are able to work.   From ______________ (mm/dd/yyyy) to ______________ (mm/dd/yyyy),   I am able to work
____________ (hours per day)   ____________ (days per week)

Employee Signature ____   **Date** ________________ (mm/dd/yyyy)

SECTION III - HEALTH CARE PROVIDER

Please provide your contact information, complete all relevant parts of this Section, and sign the form below. A family member of your patient has requested leave under the FMLA to care for your patient. The FMLA allows an employer to require that the employee submit a timely, complete, and sufficient medical certification to support a request for FMLA leave to care for a family member with a serious health condition. For FMLA purposes, a "serious health condition" means an illness, injury, impairment, or physical or mental condition that involves inpatient care or continuing treatment by a health care provider. For more information about the definitions of a serious health condition under the FMLA, see the chart at the end of the form.

You also may, but are **not required** to, provide other appropriate medical facts including symptoms, diagnosis, or any regimen of continuing treatment such as the use of specialized equipment. Please note that some state or local laws may not allow disclosure of private medical information about the patient's serious health condition, such as providing the diagnosis and/or course of treatment.

Health Care Provider's name: (Print)   ____

Health Care Provider's business address: ____

Type of practice / Medical specialty: ____

Telephone: ______________   Fax: ______________   E-mail: _______________________________

PART A: Medical Information

Limit your response to the medical condition for which the employee is seeking FMLA leave. Your answers should be your **best estimate** based upon your medical knowledge, experience, and examination of the patient. **After completing Part A, complete Part B to provide information about the amount of leave needed.** Note: For FMLA purposes, "incapacity" means the inability to work, attend school, or perform regular daily activities due to the condition, treatment of the condition, or recovery from the condition. Do not provide information about genetic tests, as defined in 29 C.F.R. § 1635.3(f), genetic services, as defined in 29 C.F.R. § 1635.3(e), or the manifestation of disease or disorder in the employee's family members, 29 C.F.R. § 1635.3(b).

(1) Patient's Name: ____

(2) State the approximate date the condition started or will start: ___________________________ (mm/dd/yyyy)

(3) Provide your **best estimate** of how long the condition lasted or will last: _____________________________

(4) For FMLA to apply, care of the patient must be medically necessary. Briefly describe the type of care needed by the patient (e.g., assistance with basic medical, hygienic, nutritional, safety, transportation needs, physical care, or psychological comfort).

____

    Form WH-380-F, Revised June 2020

Employee Name: ____

(5) Check the box(es) for the questions below, as applicable. For all box(es) checked, the amount of leave needed must be provided in Part B.

☐ **Inpatient Care**: The patient (☐ has been / ☐ is expected to be) admitted for an overnight stay in a hospital, hospice, or residential medical care facility on the following date(s): ____

☐ **Incapacity plus Treatment**: (e.g. outpatient surgery, strep throat)

Due to the condition, the patient (☐ has been / ☐ is expected to be) incapacitated for more than three consecutive, full calendar days from: _______________ (mm/dd/yyyy) to _______________ (mm/dd/yyyy).

The patient (☐ was / ☐ will be) seen on the following date(s): ____

The condition (☐ has / ☐ has not) also resulted in a course of continuing treatment under the supervision of a health care provider (e.g. prescription medication (other than over-the-counter) or therapy requiring special equipment)

☐ **Pregnancy**: The condition is pregnancy.   List the expected delivery date: _______________ (mm/dd/yyyy).

☐ **Chronic Conditions**: (e.g. asthma, migraine headaches) Due to the condition, it is medically necessary for the patient to have treatment visits at least twice per year.

☐ **Permanent or Long Term Conditions**: (e.g. Alzheimer's, terminal stages of cancer) Due to the condition, incapacity is permanent or long term and requires the continuing supervision of a health care provider (even if active treatment is not being provided).

☐ **Conditions requiring Multiple Treatments**: (e.g. chemotherapy treatments, restorative surgery) Due to the condition, it is medically necessary for the patient to receive multiple treatments.

☐ **None of the above**: If none of the above condition(s) were checked, (i.e., inpatient care, pregnancy) no additional information is needed. Go to page 4 to sign and date the form.

(6) If needed, briefly describe other appropriate medical facts related to the condition(s) for which the employee seeks FMLA leave. (e.g., use of nebulizer, dialysis)

____

PART B: Amount of Leave Needed

For the medical condition(s) checked in Part A, complete all that apply. Several questions seek a response as to the frequency or duration of a condition, treatment, etc. Your answer should be your **best estimate** based upon your medical knowledge, experience, and examination of the patient. Be as specific as you can; terms such as "lifetime," "unknown," or "indeterminate" may not be sufficient to determine if the benefits and protections of the FMLA apply.

(7) Due to the condition, the patient (☐ had / ☐ will have) **planned medical treatment(s)** (scheduled medical visits) (e.g. psychotherapy, prenatal appointments) on the following date(s): ____

____

(8) Due to the condition, the patient (☐ was / ☐ will be) **referred to other health care provider(s)** for evaluation or treatment(s).

State the nature of such treatments: (e.g. cardiologist, physical therapy) ____

Provide your **best estimate** of the beginning date _______________ (mm/dd/yyyy) and end date _______________ (mm/dd/yyyy). for the treatment(s).

Provide your **best estimate** of the duration of the treatment(s), including any period(s) of recovery (e.g. 3 days/week)

____

Employee Name: ____

(9) Due to the condition, the patient (☐ was / ☐ will be) **incapacitated for a continuous period of time**, including any time for treatment(s) and/or recovery.

Provide your **best estimate** of the beginning date _____________________ (mm/dd/yyyy) and end date _____________________ (mm/dd/yyyy). for the period of incapacity.

(10) Due to the condition, it (☐ was / ☐ is / ☐ will be) medically necessary for the employee to be absent from work to

provide care for the patient on an **intermittent basis** (periodically), including for any episodes of incapacity i.e., episodic flare-ups. Provide your **best estimate** of how often (frequency) and how long (duration) the episodes of incapacity will likely last.

Over the next 6 months, episodes of incapacity are estimated to occur ____ times per

(☐ day ☐ week ☐ month) and are likely to last approximately _____________________ (☐ hours ☐ days) per episode.

Signature of Health Care Provider ____ Date: _____________________ (mm/dd/yyyy)

Definitions of a Serious Health Condition (See 29 C.F.R. §§ 825.113-.115)
Inpatient Care
• An overnight stay in a hospital, hospice, or residential medical care facility. • Inpatient care includes any period of incapacity or any subsequent treatment in connection with the overnight stay.
Continuing Treatment by a Health Care Provider (any one or more of the following)

Incapacity Plus Treatment: A period of incapacity of more than three consecutive, full calendar days, and any subsequent treatment or period of incapacity relating to the same condition, that also involves either:
    o Two or more in-person visits to a health care provider for treatment within 30 days of the first day of incapacity unless extenuating circumstances exist. The first visit must be within seven days of the first day of incapacity; or,
    o At least one in-person visit to a health care provider for treatment within seven days of the first day of incapacity, which results in a regimen of continuing treatment under the supervision of the health care provider. For example, the health provider might prescribe a course of prescription medication or therapy requiring special equipment.

Pregnancy: Any period of incapacity due to pregnancy or for prenatal care.
Chronic Conditions: Any period of incapacity due to or treatment for a chronic serious health condition, such as diabetes, asthma, migraine headaches. A chronic serious health condition is one which requires visits to a health care provider (or nurse supervised by the provider) at least twice a year and recurs over an extended period of time. A chronic condition may cause episodic rather than a continuing period of incapacity.
Permanent or Long-term Conditions: A period of incapacity which is permanent or long-term due to a condition for which treatment may not be effective, but which requires the continuing supervision of a health care provider, such as Alzheimer's disease or the terminal stages of cancer.
Conditions Requiring Multiple Treatments: Restorative surgery after an accident or other injury; or, a condition that would likely result in a period of incapacity of more than three consecutive, full calendar days if the patient did not receive the treatment.

PAPERWORK REDUCTION ACT NOTICE AND PUBLIC BURDEN STATEMENT

If submitted, it is mandatory for employers to retain a copy of this disclosure in their records for three years. 29 U.S.C. § 2616; 29 C.F.R. § 825.500. Persons are not required to respond to this collection of information unless it displays a currently valid OMB control number. The Department of Labor estimates that it will take an average of 15 minutes for respondents to complete this collection of information, including the time for reviewing instructions, searching existing data sources, gathering and maintaining the data needed, and completing and reviewing the collection of information. If you have any comments regarding this burden estimate or any other aspect of this collection information, including suggestions for reducing this burden, send them to the Administrator, Wage and Hour Division, U.S. Department of Labor, Room S-3502, 200 Constitution Avenue, N.W., Washington, D.C. 20210.

DO NOT SEND COMPLETED FORM TO THE DEPARTMENT OF LABOR. RETURN TO THE PATIENT.

Form WH-380-F, Revised June 2020

Form WH-381: Notice of Eligibility & Rights and Responsibilities

**Notice of Eligibility & Rights and Responsibilities
under the Family and Medical Leave Act**

**U.S. Department of Labor
Wage and Hour Division**

**DO NOT SEND TO THE DEPARTMENT OF LABOR.
PROVIDE TO EMPLOYEE.**

OMB Control Number: 1235-0003
Expires: 6/30/2026

In general, to be eligible to take leave under the Family and Medical Leave Act (FMLA), an employee must have worked for an employer for at least 12 months, meet the hours of service requirement in the 12 months preceding the leave, and work at a site with at least 50 employees within 75 miles. While use of this form is optional, a fully completed Form WH-381 provides employees with the information required by 29 C.F.R. §§ 825.300(b), (c) which must be provided within five business days of the employee notifying the employer of the need for FMLA leave. Information about the FMLA may be found on the WHD website at www.dol.gov/agencies/whd/fmla.

Date: _____________________________ *(mm/dd/yyyy)*

From: _____________________________ *(Employer)* To: _____________________________ *(Employee)*

On _______________ *(mm/dd/yyyy)*, we learned that you need leave *(beginning on)* _______________ *(mm/dd/yyyy)* for one of the following reasons: *(Select as appropriate)*

☐ The birth of a child, or placement of a child with you for adoption or foster care, and to bond with the newborn or newly-placed child

☐ Your own serious health condition

☐ You are needed to care for your family member due to a serious health condition. Your family member is your:

    ☐ Spouse   ☐ Parent   ☐ Child under age 18   ☐ Child 18 years or older and incapable of self-care because of a mental or physical disability

☐ A qualifying exigency arising out of the fact that your family member is on covered active duty or has been notified of an impending call or order to covered active duty status. Your family member on covered active duty is your:

    ☐ Spouse   ☐ Parent   ☐ Child of any age

☐ You are needed to care for your family member who is a covered servicemember with a serious injury or illness. You are the servicemember's:

    ☐ Spouse   ☐ Parent   ☐ Child   ☐ Next of kin

Spouse means a husband or wife as defined or recognized in the state where the individual was married, including in a common law marriage or same-sex marriage. The terms "child" and "parent" include *in loco parentis* relationships in which a person assumes the obligations of a parent to a child. An employee may take FMLA leave to care for an individual who assumed the obligations of a parent to the employee when the employee was a child. An employee may also take FMLA leave to care for a child for whom the employee has assumed the obligations of a parent. No legal or biological relationship is necessary.

SECTION I – NOTICE OF ELIGIBILITY

This Notice is to inform you that you are:

☐ **Eligible** for FMLA leave. *(See Section II for any Additional Information Needed and Section III for information on your Rights and Responsibilities.)*

☐ **Not eligible** for FMLA leave because: *(Only one reason need be checked)*

    ☐ You have not met the FMLA's 12-month length of service requirement. As of the first date of requested leave, you will have worked approximately: _____________ towards this requirement.
        (months)

    ☐ You have not met the FMLA's 1,250 hours of service requirement. As of the first date of requested leave, you will have worked approximately: _____________ towards this requirement.
        (hours of service)

    Form WH-381, Revised June 2020

Employee Name: ____

☐ You are an airline flight crew employee and you have not met the special hours of service eligibility requirements for airline flight crew employees as of the first date of requested leave (i.e., worked or been paid for at least 60% of your applicable monthly guarantee, and worked or been paid for at least 504 duty hours.)

☐ You do not work at and/or report to a site with 50 or more employees within 75-miles as of the date of your request.

If you have any questions, please contact: ___________________________________ *(Name of employer representative)*

at ____ *(Contact information).*

SECTION II – ADDITIONAL INFORMATION NEEDED

As explained in Section I, you meet the eligibility requirements for taking FMLA leave. Please review the information below to determine if additional information is needed in order for us to determine whether your absence qualifies as FMLA leave. Once we obtain any additional information specified below we will inform you, **within 5 business days**, whether your leave will be designated as FMLA leave and count towards the FMLA leave you have available. **If complete and sufficient information is not provided in a timely manner, your leave may be denied.**

(Select as appropriate)

☐ No additional information requested. If no additional information requested, go to Section III.

☐ We request that the leave be supported by a certification, as identified below.

    ☐ Health Care Provider for the Employee   ☐ Health Care Provider for the Employee's Family Member
    ☐ Qualifying Exigency   ☐ Serious Illness or Injury *(Military Caregiver Leave)*

    Selected certification form is ☐ attached / ☐ not attached.

    If requested, medical certification must be returned by _______________________ *(mm/dd/yyyy) (Must allow at least 15 calendar days from the date the employer requested the employee to provide certification, unless it is not feasible despite the employee's diligent, good faith efforts.)*

☐ We request that you provide reasonable documentation or a statement to establish the relationship between you and your family member, including *in loco parentis* relationships (as explained on page one). The information requested must be returned to us by _______________________ *(mm/dd/yyyy).* You may choose to provide a simple statement of the relationship or provide documentation such as a child's birth certificate, a court document, or documents regarding foster care or adoption-related activities. Official documents submitted for this purpose will be returned to you after examination.

☐ Other information needed *(e.g. documentation for military family leave)*: ___________________________________.

    The information requested must be returned to us by _______________________ *(mm/dd/yyyy).*

If you have any questions, please contact: ___________________________________ *(Name of employer representative)*

at ____ *(Contact information).*

SECTION III – NOTICE OF RIGHTS AND RESPONSIBILITIES

Part A: FMLA Leave Entitlement

You have a right under the FMLA to take unpaid, job-protected FMLA leave in a 12-month period for certain family and medical reasons, including up to **12 weeks** of unpaid leave in a 12-month period for the birth of a child or placement of a child for adoption or foster care, for leave related to your own or a family member's serious health condition, or for certain qualifying exigencies related to the deployment of a military member to covered active duty. You also have a right

Employee Name: ____

under the FMLA to take up to **26 weeks** of unpaid, job-protected FMLA leave in a single 12-month period to care for a covered servicemember with a serious injury or illness (*Military Caregiver Leave*).

The 12-month period for FMLA leave is calculated as: *(Select as appropriate)*

    ☐   The calendar year (January 1st - December 31st)

    ☐   A fixed leave year based on ____
                                  (e.g., a fiscal year beginning on July 1 and ending on June 30)

    ☐   The 12-month period measured forward from the date of your first FMLA leave usage.

    ☐   A "rolling" 12-month period measured backward from the date of any FMLA leave usage. *(Each time an employee takes FMLA leave, the remaining leave is the balance of the 12 weeks not used during the 12 months immediately before the FMLA leave is to start.)*

If applicable, the single 12-month period for *Military Caregiver Leave* started on ____________________ *(mm/dd/yyyy)*.

You (☐ are / ☐ are not) considered a key employee as defined under the FMLA. Your FMLA leave cannot be denied for this reason; however, we may not restore you to employment following FMLA leave if such restoration will cause substantial and grievous economic injury to us.

We (☐ have / ☐ have not) determined that restoring you to employment at the conclusion of FMLA leave will cause substantial and grievous economic harm to us. Additional information will be provided separately concerning your status as key employee and restoration.

Part B: Substitution of Paid Leave – When Paid Leave is Used at the Same Time as FMLA Leave

You have a right under the FMLA to request that your accrued paid leave be substituted for your FMLA leave. This means that you can request that your accrued paid leave run concurrently with some or all of your unpaid FMLA leave, provided you meet any applicable requirements of our leave policy. Concurrent leave use means the absence will count against both the designated paid leave and unpaid FMLA leave at the same time. If you do not meet the requirements for taking paid leave, you remain entitled to take available unpaid FMLA leave in the applicable 12-month period. Even if you do not request it, the FMLA allows us to require you to use your available sick, vacation, or other paid leave during your FMLA absence.

(Check all that apply)

☐ **Some or all of your FMLA leave will not be paid.** Any unpaid FMLA leave taken will be designated as FMLA leave and counted against the amount of FMLA leave you have available to use in the applicable 12-month period.

☐ **You have requested to use some or all of your available paid leave** *(e.g., sick, vacation, PTO)* during your FMLA leave. Any paid leave taken for this reason will also be designated as FMLA leave and counted against the amount of FMLA leave you have available to use in the applicable 12-month period.

☐ **We are requiring you to use some or all of your available paid leave** *(e.g., sick, vacation, PTO)* during your FMLA leave. Any paid leave taken for this reason will also be designated as FMLA leave and counted against the amount of FMLA leave you have available to use in the applicable 12-month period.

☐ **Other:** *(e.g., short- or long-term disability, workers' compensation, state medical leave law, etc.)*________________
Any time taken for this reason will also be designated as FMLA leave and counted against the amount of FMLA leave you have available to use in the applicable 12-month period.

The applicable conditions for use of paid leave include: ____.

For more information about conditions applicable to sick/vacation/other paid leave usage please refer to ____________

____ available at: ____.

Employee Name: ____

Part C: Maintain Health Benefits

Your health benefits must be maintained during any period of FMLA leave under the same conditions as if you continued to work. During any paid portion of FMLA leave, your share of any premiums will be paid by the method normally used during any paid leave. During any unpaid portion of FMLA leave, you must continue to make any normal contributions to the cost of the health insurance premiums. To make arrangements to continue to make your share of the premium payments on your health insurance while you are on any unpaid FMLA leave, contact _____________________________ at

____.

You have a minimum grace period of (☐ 30-days or ☐ _____________ *indicate longer period, if applicable)* in which to make premium payments. If payment is not made timely, your group health insurance may be cancelled, provided we notify you in writing at least 15 days before the date that your health coverage will lapse, or, at our option, we may pay your share of the premiums during FMLA leave, and recover these payments from you upon your return to work.

You may be required to reimburse us for our share of health insurance premiums paid on your behalf during your FMLA leave if you do not return to work following **unpaid** FMLA leave for a reason other than: the continuation, recurrence, or onset of your or your family member's serious health condition which would entitle you to FMLA leave; or the continuation, recurrence, or onset of a covered servicemember's serious injury or illness which would entitle you to FMLA leave; or other circumstances beyond your control.

Part D: Other Employee Benefits

Upon your return from FMLA leave, your other employee benefits, such as pensions or life insurance, must be resumed in the same manner and at the same levels as provided when your FMLA leave began. To make arrangements to continue your employee benefits while you are on FMLA leave, contact ____ at ____.

Part E: Return-to-Work Requirements

You must be reinstated to the same or an equivalent job with the same pay, benefits, and terms and conditions of employment on your return from FMLA-protected leave. An equivalent position is one that is virtually identical to your former position in terms of pay, benefits, and working conditions. At the end of your FMLA leave, all benefits must also be resumed in the same manner and at the same level provided when the leave began. You do not have return-to-work rights under the FMLA if you need leave beyond the amount of FMLA leave you have available to use.

Part F: Other Requirements While on FMLA Leave

While on leave you (☐ will be / ☐ will not be) required to furnish us with periodic reports of your status and intent to return to work every ____.

(Indicate interval of periodic reports, as appropriate for the FMLA leave situation).

If the circumstances of your leave change and you are able to return to work earlier than expected, you will be required to notify us at least two workdays prior to the date you intend to report for work.

PAPERWORK REDUCTION ACT NOTICE AND PUBLIC BURDEN STATEMENT

DO NOT SEND THE COMPLETED FORM TO THE DEPARTMENT OF LABOR. EMPLOYEE INFORMATION.

Form WH-382: Designation Notice

**Designation Notice
under the Family and Medical Leave Act**

**U.S. Department of Labor
Wage and Hour Division**

**DO NOT SEND TO THE DEPARTMENT OF LABOR.
PROVIDE TO EMPLOYEE.**

OMB Control Number: 1235-0003
Expires: 6/30/2026

Leave covered under the Family and Medical Leave Act (FMLA) must be designated as FMLA-protected and the employer must inform the employee of the amount of leave that will be counted against the employee's FMLA leave entitlement. In order to determine whether leave is covered under the FMLA, the employer may request that the leave be supported by a certification. If the certification is incomplete or insufficient, the employer must state in writing what additional information is necessary to make the certification complete and sufficient. While use of this form is optional, a fully completed Form WH-382 provides employees with the information required by 29 C.F.R. §§ 825.300(d), 825.301, and 825.305(c), which must be provided within five business days of the employer having enough information to determine whether the leave is for an FMLA-qualifying reason. Information about the FMLA may be found on the WHD website at www.dol.gov/agencies/whd/fmla.

SECTION I - EMPLOYER

The employer is responsible in **all** circumstances for designating leave as FMLA-qualifying and giving notice to the employee. Once an eligible employee communicates a need to take leave for an FMLA-qualifying reason, an employer may not delay designating such leave as FMLA leave, and neither the employee nor the employer may decline FMLA protection for that leave.

Date: _________________________ *(mm/dd/yyyy)*

From: _________________________ *(Employer)*   To: _________________________ *(Employee)*

On _________________________ *(mm/dd/yyyy)* we received your most recent information to support your need for leave due to:
(Select as appropriate)

- ☐ The birth of a child, or placement of a child with you for adoption or foster care, and to bond with the newborn or newly-placed child
- ☐ Your own serious health condition
- ☐ The serious health condition of your spouse, child, or parent
- ☐ A qualifying exigency arising out of the fact that your spouse, child, or parent is on covered active duty or has been notified of an impending call or order to covered active duty with the Armed Forces
- ☐ A serious injury or illness of a covered servicemember where you are the servicemember's spouse, child, parent, or next of kin *(Military Caregiver Leave)*

We have reviewed information related to your need for leave under the FMLA along with any supporting documentation provided and decided that your FMLA leave request is: *(Select as appropriate)*

- ☐ **Approved.** All leave taken for this reason will be designated as FMLA leave. Go to Section III for more information.

- ☐ **Not Approved:** *(Select as appropriate)*
  - ☐ The FMLA does not apply to your leave request.
  - ☐ As of the date the leave is to start, you do not have any FMLA leave available to use.
  - ☐ Other _________________________

- ☐ **Additional information** is needed to determine if your leave request qualifies as FMLA leave. *(Go to Section II for the specific information needed. If your FMLA leave request is approved and no additional information is needed, go to Section III.)*

SECTION II – ADDITIONAL INFORMATION NEEDED

We need additional information to determine whether your leave request qualifies under the FMLA. Once we obtain the additional information requested, we will inform you **within 5 business days** if your leave will or will not be designated as FMLA leave and count towards the amount of FMLA leave you have available. **Failure to provide the additional information as requested may result in a denial of your FMLA leave request.**

If you have any questions, please contact: _________________________ at _________________________
      (Name of employer FMLA representative)   *(Contact information)*

Incomplete or Insufficient Certification
The certification you have provided is incomplete and/or insufficient to determine whether the FMLA applies to your leave request. *(Select as applicable)*

- ☐ The certification provided is incomplete and we are unable to determine whether the FMLA applies to your leave request. *"Incomplete" means one or more of the applicable entries on the certification have not been completed.*

Employee Name: ____

☐ The certification provided is insufficient to determine whether the FMLA applies to your leave request. *"Insufficient" means the information provided is vague, unclear, ambiguous or non-responsive.*

Specify the information needed to make the certification complete and/or sufficient: _________________________________

You must provide the requested information no later than *(provide at least 7 calendar days)* _________________ *(mm/dd/yyyy),* unless it is not practicable under the particular circumstances despite your diligent good faith efforts, or your leave may be denied.

Second and Third Opinions

☐ We request that you obtain a (☐ second / ☐ third opinion) medical certification at our expense, and we will provide further details at a later time. *Note: The employee or the employee's family member may be requested to authorize the health care provider to release information pertaining <u>only</u> to the serious health condition at issue.*

SECTION III – FMLA LEAVE APPROVED

As explained in Section I, your FMLA leave request is approved. All leave taken for this reason will be designated as FMLA leave and will count against the amount of FMLA leave you have available to use in the applicable 12-month period. The FMLA requires that you notify us as soon as practicable if the dates of scheduled leave change, are extended, or were initially unknown. Based on the information you have provided to date, we are providing the following information about the amount of time that will be counted against the total **amount of FMLA leave** you have available to use in the applicable 12-month period: *(Select as appropriate)*

☐ Provided there is no change from your **anticipated FMLA leave schedule**, the following number of hours, days, or weeks will be counted against your leave entitlement: ____.

☐ Because the leave you will need will be **unscheduled**, it is not possible to provide the hours, days, or weeks that will be counted against your FMLA entitlement at this time. You have the right to request this information once in a 30-day period (if leave was taken in the 30-day period).

Please be advised: *(check all that apply)*

☐ **Some or all of your FMLA leave will not be paid.** Any unpaid FMLA leave taken will be designated as FMLA leave and counted against the amount of FMLA leave you have available to use in the applicable 12-month period.
☐ **Based on your request, some or all of your available paid leave** *(e.g., sick, vacation, PTO)* **will be used during your FMLA leave.** Any paid leave taken for this reason will also be designated as FMLA leave and counted against the amount of FMLA leave you have available to use in the applicable 12-month period.
☐ **We are requiring you to use some or all of your available paid leave** *(e.g., sick, vacation, PTO)* **during your FMLA leave.** Any paid leave taken for this reason will also be designated as FMLA leave and counted against the amount of FMLA leave you have available to use in the applicable 12-month period.
☐ **Other:** ____
(e.g., Short- or long-term disability, workers' compensation, state medical leave law, etc.) Any time taken for this reason will also be designated as FMLA leave and counted against the amount of FMLA leave you have available to use in the applicable 12-month period.

Return-to-work requirements. To be restored to work after taking FMLA leave, you (☐ will be / ☐ will not be) required to provide a certification from your health care provider (fitness-for-duty certification) that you are able to resume work. This request for a fitness-for-duty certification is *only* with regard to the particular serious health condition that caused your need for FMLA leave. **If such certification is not timely received, your return to work may be delayed until the certification is provided.**

A list of the essential functions of your position (☐ is / ☐ is not) attached. If attached, the fitness-for-duty certification must address your ability to perform the essential job functions.

PAPERWORK REDUCTION ACT NOTICE AND PUBLIC BURDEN STATEMENT
It is mandatory for employers to inform employees in writing whether leave requested under the FMLA has been determined to be covered under the FMLA. 29 U.S.C. § 2617; 29 C.F.R. § 825.300(d), (e). It is mandatory for employers to retain a copy of this disclosure in their records for three years. 29 U.S.C. § 2616; 29 C.F.R. § 825.500. Persons are not required to respond to this collection of information unless it displays a currently valid OMB control number. The Department of Labor estimates that it will take an average of 10 minutes for respondents to complete this collection of information, including the time for reviewing instructions, searching existing data sources, gathering and maintaining the data needed, and completing and reviewing the collection of information. If you have any comments regarding this burden estimate or any other aspect of this collection of information, including suggestions for reducing this burden, send them to the Administrator, Wage and Hour Division, U.S. Department of Labor, Room S-3502, 200 Constitution Avenue, N.W., Washington, D.C. 20210.
DO NOT SEND THE COMPLETED FORM TO THE DEPARTMENT OF LABOR. EMPLOYEE INFORMATION.

   Form WH-382, Revised June 2020

Form WH-384: Certification for Military Family Leave for Qualifying Exigency

Certification for Military Family Leave for Qualifying Exigency under the Family and Medical Leave Act

U.S. Department of Labor Wage and Hour Division

DO NOT SEND FORM TO THE DEPARTMENT OF LABOR. RETURN THE COMPLETED FORM TO THE EMPLOYER.

OMB Control Number: 1235-0003 Expires: 6/30/2026

The Family and Medical Leave Act (FMLA) provides that eligible employees may take FMLA leave for a qualifying exigency while the employee's spouse, child, or parent (the military member) is on covered active duty or has been notified of an impending call or order to covered active duty. The FMLA allows an employer to require an employee seeking FMLA leave due to a qualifying exigency to submit a certification. 29 U.S.C. §§ 2613, 2614(c)(3). The employer must give the employee **at least 15 calendar days** to provide the certification. 29 C.F.R. § 825.305(b). If the employee fails to provide complete and sufficient certification, the employee's FMLA leave request may be denied. 29 C.F.R. § 825.313. Information about the FMLA may be found on the WHD website at http://www.dol.gov/agencies/whd/fmla.

SECTION I - EMPLOYER

Either the employee or the employer may complete Section I. While use of this form is optional, it asks the employee for the information necessary for a complete and sufficient qualifying exigency certification, which is set out at 29 C.F.R. § 825.309. **You may not ask the employee to provide more information than allowed under the FMLA regulations, 29 C.F.R. § 825.309.**

(1)   Employee name: ____
           First   *Middle*   *Last*

(2)   Employer name: _________________________________ Date: _________________ *(mm/dd/yyyy)*
                                                     (List date certification requested)

(3)   This certification must be returned by____ *(mm/dd/yyyy)*.
         (Must allow at least 15 calendar days from the date requested, unless it is not feasible despite the employee's diligent, good faith efforts.)

SECTION II - EMPLOYEE

Please complete all Parts of Section II and sign the form before returning it to your employer. The FMLA allows an employer to require that you submit a timely, complete, and sufficient certification to support a request for FMLA leave due to a qualifying exigency. If requested by your employer, your response is required to obtain the benefits and protections of the FMLA. 29 C.F.R. § 825.309. Failure to provide a complete and sufficient certification may result in a denial of your FMLA leave request. A complete and sufficient certification to support a request for FMLA leave due to a qualifying exigency includes written documentation confirming a military member's covered active duty or call to covered active duty status. **You are responsible for making sure the certification is provided to your employer within the time frame requested, which must be at least 15 calendar days.** 29 C.F.R. § 825.313.

(1)   Provide the name of the military member on covered active duty or call to covered active duty status:

____
          First   *Middle*   *Last*

(2) Select your relationship of the military member. The military member is your:

     ☐ Spouse   ☐ Parent   ☐ Child, of any age

Spouse means a husband or wife as defined or recognized in the state where the individual was married, including a common law marriage or same-sex marriage. The terms "child" and "parent" include *in loco parentis* relationships in which a person assumes the obligations of a parent to a child. An employee may take FMLA leave for a qualifying exigency related a military member who assumed the obligations of a parent to the employee when the employee was a child. An employee may also take FMLA leave for a qualifying exigency related a military member for whom the employee has assumed the obligations of a parent. No legal or biological relationship is necessary.

Employee Name: ____

PART A: COVERED ACTIVE DUTY STATUS

Covered active duty or call to covered active duty in the case of a member of the Regular Armed Forces means duty during the deployment of the member with the Armed Forces to a foreign country. Covered active duty or call to covered active duty in the case of a member of the Reserve components means duty during the deployment of the member with the Armed Forces to a foreign country under a Federal call or order to active duty in support of a contingency operation pursuant to: Section 688 of Title 10 of the United States Code; Section 12301(a) of Title 10 of the United States Code; Section 12302 of Title 10 of the United States Code; Section 12304 of Title 10 of the United States Code; Section 12305 of Title 10 of the United States Code; Section 12406 of Title 10 of the United States Code; chapter 15 of Title 10 of the United States Code; or, any other provision of law during a war or during a national emergency declared by the President or Congress so long as it is in support of a contingency operation. 10 U.S.C. § 101(a)(13)(B).

An employer may require the employee to provide a copy of the military member's active duty orders or other documentation issued by the military which indicates that the military member is on covered active duty or call to covered active duty status, and the dates of the military member's covered active duty service. **This information need only be provided to the employer once, unless additional leave is needed for a different military member or different deployment.**

(3)   Provide the dates of the military member's covered active duty service: _______________________________

(4)   Please check one of the following and attach the indicated written document to support that the military member is on covered active duty or call to covered active duty status:

   ☐   A copy of the military member's covered active duty orders

   ☐   Other documentation from the military indicating that the military member is on covered active duty or has been notified of an impending call to covered active duty, such as official military correspondence from the military member's chain of command

   ☐   I have previously provided my employer with sufficient written documentation confirming the military member's covered active duty or call to covered active duty status

PART B: APPROPRIATE FACTS

Under the FMLA, leave can be taken for a number of qualifying exigencies. 29 C.F.R. § 825.126(b). Complete and sufficient certification to support a request for FMLA leave due to a qualifying exigency includes available written documentation which supports the need for leave such as a copy of a meeting announcement for informational briefings sponsored by the military, a document confirming the military member's Rest and Recuperation leave, or other documentation issued by the military which indicates that the military member has been granted Rest and Recuperation leave, or a document confirming an appointment with a third party (*e.g.*, a counselor or school official, or staff at a care facility, a copy of a bill for services for the handling of legal or financial affairs). Please provide appropriate facts related to the particular qualifying exigency to support the FMLA leave request, including information on the type of qualifying exigency and any available written documentation of the exigency event.

(5)   Select the appropriate **Qualifying Exigency Category** and, if needed, provide additional information related to the event:

   ☐   Short notice deployment (*i.e.*, deployment within seven or fewer days of notice)

   ☐   Military events and related activities *(e.g., official ceremonies or events, or family support and assistance programs):*

   ____

   ☐   Childcare related activities for the child of the military member *(e.g., arranging for alternative childcare):*

   ____

Employee Name: ____

    ☐ Care for the military member's parent *(e.g., admitting or transferring the parent to a new care facility):*
____

    ☐ Financial and legal arrangements related to the deployment *(e.g., obtaining military identification cards)*

    ☐ Counseling related to the deployment *(i.e., counseling provided by someone other than a health care provider)*

    ☐ Military member's short-term, temporary Rest and Recuperation leave (R&R) (leave for this reason is limited to 15 calendar days for each instance of R&R)

    ☐ Post deployment activities *(e.g., arrival ceremonies, or reintegration briefings and events):*_______________
____

    ☐ Any other event that the employee and employer agree is a qualifying exigency: _______________________
____

(6)   **Available written documentation** supporting this request for leave is (☐ attached / ☐ not attached / ☐ not available).

PART C: AMOUNT OF LEAVE NEEDED

Provide information concerning the amount of leave that will be needed. Several questions in this section seek a response as to the frequency or duration of the qualifying exigency leave needed. Be as specific as you can; terms such as *"unknown"* or *"indeterminate"* may not be sufficient to determine FMLA coverage.

(7)   List the approximate date exigency started or will start: ____ *(mm/dd/yyyy)*

(8)   Provide your best estimate of how long the exigency lasted or will last:

    From _______________________________ *(mm/dd/yyyy)* to _______________________________ *(mm/dd/yyyy)*

(9)   Due to a qualifying exigency, I need to work a **reduced schedule**. Provide your **best estimate** of the reduced schedule you are able to work:

    From _______________________________ *(mm/dd/yyyy)* to _______________________________ *(mm/dd/yyyy)*

    I am able to work ____
                               (e.g., 5 hours/day, up to 25 hours a week)

(10)   Due to a qualifying exigency, I will need to be absent from work for a **continuous period of time**. Provide your **best estimate** of the beginning and ending dates for the period of absence:

    From _______________________________ *(mm/dd/yyyy)* to _______________________________ *(mm/dd/yyyy)*

Employee Name: ____

(11) Due to a qualifying exigency, I will need to be absent from work on an **intermittent basis** (periodically).

Provide your **best estimate** of the frequency (how often) and duration (how long) of each appointment, meeting, or leave event, including any travel time.

Over the next 6 months, absences on an **intermittent basis** are estimated to occur: _______________ times per (☐ day / ☐ week / ☐ month) and are likely to last approximately ____________ (☐ hours / ☐ days) per episode.

(12) My leave is due to a qualifying exigency that involves **Rest and Recuperation leave** (R & R) of the military member (leave for this reason is limited to 15 calendar days for each instance of R & R leave).

List the dates of the military member's R &R leave:

From ______________________________________ *(mm/dd/yyyy)* to ______________________________________ *(mm/dd/yyyy)*

PART D: THIRD PARTY INFORMATION

If applicable, please provide information below that may be used by your employer to verify meetings or appointments with a third party related to the qualifying exigency. Examples of meetings with third parties include: arranging for childcare or parental care, to attend non-medical counseling, to attend meetings with school, childcare or parental care providers, to make financial or legal arrangements, to act as the military member's representative before a federal, state, or local agency for purposes of obtaining, arranging or appealing military service benefits, or to attend any event sponsored by the military or military service organizations. This information may be used by your employer to verify that the information contained on this form is accurate.

Individual *(e.g., name and title)* or Entity / Organization: ____

Address: ____

Telephone: (____) _______________ Fax: (____) _______________ E-mail: _________________________________

Describe purpose of meeting: ____

**Employee
Signature** ____ **Date** _______________ *(mm/dd/yyyy)*

PAPERWORK REDUCTION ACT NOTICE AND PUBLIC BURDEN STATEMENT

If submitted, it is mandatory for employers to retain a copy of this disclosure in their records for three years. 29 U.S.C. § 2616; 29 C.F.R. § 825.500. Persons are not required to respond to this collection of information unless it displays a currently valid OMB control number. The Department of Labor estimates that it will take an average of 15 minutes for respondents to complete this collection of information, including the time for reviewing instructions, searching existing data sources, gathering and maintaining the data needed, and completing and reviewing the collection of information. If you have any comments regarding this burden estimate or any other aspect of this collection information, including suggestions for reducing this burden, send them to the Administrator, Wage and Hour Division, U.S. Department of Labor, Room S-3502, 200 Constitution Avenue, N.W., Washington, D.C. 20210.

**DO NOT SEND THE COMPLETED FORM TO THE DEPARTMENT OF DEPARTMENT OF LABOR.
RETURN FORM TO THE EMPLOYER.**

Form WH-385: Certification for Serious Injury or Illness of a Current Servicemember for Military Caregiver Leave

Certification for Serious Injury or Illness of a Current Servicemember for Military Caregiver Leave under the Family and Medical Leave Act

U.S. Department of Labor
Wage Hour Division

DO NOT SEND COMPLETED FORM TO THE DEPARTMENT OF LABOR. RETURN TO THE PATIENT.

OMB Control Number: 1235-0003
Expires: 6/30/2026

The Family and Medical Leave Act (FMLA) provides that eligible employees may take FMLA leave to care for a covered servicemember with a serious illness or injury. The FMLA allows an employer to require an employee seeking FMLA leave for this purpose to submit a medical certification. 29 U.S.C. §§ 2613, 2614(c)(3). The employer must give the employee **at least 15 calendar days** to provide the certification. If the employee fails to provide complete and sufficient certification, his or her FMLA leave request may be denied. 29 C.F.R. § 825.313. Information about the FMLA may be found on the WHD website at www.dol.gov/agencies/whd/fmla.

SECTION I - EMPLOYER

Either the employee or the employer may complete Section I. While use of this form is optional, it asks the health care provider for the information necessary for a complete and sufficient medical certification. **You may not ask the employee to provide more information than allowed under the FMLA regulations, 29 C.F.R. § 825.310. Recertifications are not allowed for FMLA leave to care for a covered servicemember. Where medical certification is requested by an employer, an employee may not be held liable for administrative delays in the issuance of military documents, despite the employee's diligent, good-faith efforts to obtain such documents.** An employer requiring an employee to submit a certification for leave to care for a covered servicemember **must** accept as sufficient certification invitational travel orders (ITOs) or invitational travel authorizations (ITAs) issued to any family member to join an injured or ill servicemember at the servicemember's bedside. An ITO or ITA is sufficient certification for the duration of time specified in the ITO or ITA.

Employers must generally maintain records and documents relating to medical information, medical certifications, recertifications, or medical histories of employees or employees' family members created for FMLA purposes as confidential medical records in separate files/records from the usual personnel files and in accordance with 29 C.F.R. § 1630.14(c)(1), if the Americans with Disabilities Act applies, and in accordance with 29 C.F.R. § 1635.9, if the Genetic Information Nondiscrimination Act applies.

(1) Employee name: ____
       First   Middle   Last

(2) Employer name: ______________________________________ Date: _______________ *(mm/dd/yyyy)*
                                                                      (List date certification requested)

(3) This certification must be returned by: _______________________________________ *(mm/dd/yyyy)*
       (Must allow at least 15 calendar days from the date requested, unless it is not feasible despite the employee's diligent, good faith efforts.)

SECTION II - EMPLOYEE and/or CURRENT SERVICEMEMBER

Please complete all Parts of Section II before having the servicemember's health care provider complete Section III. The FMLA allows an employer to require that an employee submit a timely, complete, and sufficient certification to support a request for FMLA leave due to a serious injury or illness of a covered servicemember. If requested by your employer, your response is required to obtain or retain the benefit of FMLA-protected leave.

PART A: EMPLOYEE INFORMATION

(1) Name of the current servicemember for whom employee is requesting leave:_______________________

Employee Name: ____

(2) Select your relationship to the current servicemember. You are the current servicemember's:

☐ Spouse ☐ Parent ☐ Child ☐ Next of Kin

Spouse means a husband or wife as defined or recognized in the state where the individual was married, including a common law marriage or same-sex marriage. The terms "child" and "parent" include *in loco parentis* relationships in which a person assumes the obligations of a parent to a child. An employee may take FMLA leave to care for a covered servicemember who assumed the obligations of a parent to the employee when the employee was a child. An employee may also take FMLA leave to care for a covered servicemember for whom the employee has assumed the obligations of a parent. No biological or legal relationship is necessary. "Next of kin" is the servicemember's nearest blood relative, other than the spouse, parent, son, or daughter, in the following order of priority: (1) a blood relative as designated in writing by the servicemember for purposes of FMLA leave, (2) blood relatives granted legal custody of the servicemember, (3) brothers and sisters, (4) grandparents, (5) aunts and uncles, and (6) first cousins.

PART B: SERVICEMEMBER INFORMATION AND CARE TO BE PROVIDED TO THE SERVICEMEMBER

(3) The servicemember (☐ is / ☐ is not) a current member of the Regular Armed Forces, the National Guard or Reserves. If yes, provide the servicemember's military branch, rank and unit currently assigned to: ______________

____

(4) The servicemember (☐ is / ☐ is not) assigned to a military medical treatment facility as an outpatient or to a unit established for the purpose of providing command and control of members of the Armed Forces receiving medical care as outpatients, such as a medical hold or warrior transition unit. If yes, provide the name of the medical treatment facility or unit: ____

(5) The servicemember (☐ is / ☐ is not) on the Temporary Disability Retired List (TDRL).

(6) Briefly describe the care you will provide to the servicemember: *(Check all that apply)*
  ☐ Assistance with basic medical, hygienic, nutritional, or safety needs
  ☐ Psychological Comfort   ☐ Physical Care
  ☐ Transportation   ☐ Other: ___________________________________

(7) Give your **best estimate** of the amount of leave needed to provide the care described: ______________________

____

(8) If a reduced work schedule is necessary to provide the care described, give your **best estimate** of the reduced work schedule you are able to work. From _________________ *(mm/dd/yyyy)* to _________________ *(mm/dd/yyyy)*, I am able to work: ___________________________________ *(hours per day)* _________________ *(days per week)*.

SECTION III - HEALTH CARE PROVIDER

Please provide your contact information, complete all Parts of this Section fully and completely, and sign the form below. The employee listed at Section I has requested leave under the FMLA to care for a family member who is a current member of the Regular Armed Forces, the National Guard, or the Reserves who is undergoing medical treatment, recuperation, or therapy, is otherwise in outpatient status, or is otherwise on the temporary disability retired list for a serious injury or illness. Note: For purposes of FMLA leave, a serious injury or illness is one that was incurred in the line of duty on active duty in the Armed Forces or that existed before the beginning of the member's active duty and was aggravated by service in the line of duty on active duty in the Armed Forces that may render the servicemember medically unfit to perform the duties of the servicemember's office, grade, rank, or rating. "Need for care" includes both physical and psychological care. It includes situations where, for example, due to his or her serious injury or illness, the servicemember is not able to care for his or her own basic medical, hygienic, or nutritional needs or safety, or needs transportation to the doctor. It also includes providing psychological comfort and reassurance which would be beneficial to the servicemember who is receiving inpatient or home

                                  Form WH-385, Revised June 2020

Employee Name: ____

care. A complete and sufficient certification to support a request for FMLA leave due to a current servicemember's serious injury or illness includes written documentation confirming that the servicemember's injury or illness was incurred in the line of duty on active duty or if not, that the current servicemember's injury or illness existed before the beginning of the servicemember's active duty and was aggravated by service in the line of duty on active duty in the Armed Forces, and that the current servicemember is undergoing treatment for such injury or illness by a health care provider listed above.

PART A: HEALTH CARE PROVIDER INFORMATION

Health Care Provider's Name: *(Print)* ____

Health Care Provider's business address: ____

Type of practice/Medical specialty: ____

Telephone: (___) _____________ Fax: (___) _____________ E-mail: ____

Please select the type of FMLA health care provider you are:

    ☐ DOD health care provider

    ☐ VA health care provider

    ☐ DOD TRICARE network authorized private health care provider

    ☐ DOD non-network TRICARE authorized private health care provider

    ☐ Health care provider as defined in 29 C.F.R. § 825.125

PART B: MEDICAL INFORMATION

Please provide appropriate medical information of the patient as requested below. Limit your responses to the servicemember's condition for which the employee is seeking leave. If you are unable to make some of the military-related determinations contained below, you are permitted to rely upon determinations from an authorized DOD representative, such as a DOD recovery care coordinator. Do not provide information about genetic tests, as defined in 29 C.F.R. § 1635.3(f), or genetic services, as defined in 29 C.F.R. §1635.3(e).

(1)   Patient's Name: ____

(2)   List the approximate date condition started or will start: _______________________________ *(mm/dd/yyyy)*

(3)   Provide your **best estimate** of how long the condition will last: _______________________________

(4)   The servicemember's injury or illness: *(Select as appropriate)*

        ☐ Was incurred in the line of duty on active duty.
        ☐ Existed before the beginning of the servicemember's active duty and was
            aggravated by service in the line of duty on active duty.
        ☐ None of the above.

(5)   The servicemember (☐ is / ☐ is not) undergoing medical treatment, recuperation, or therapy for this condition.
        If yes, briefly describe the medical treatment, recuperation or therapy: _______________________________

Employee Name: ____

(6)   The current servicemember's medical condition is classified as: *(Select as appropriate)*

  ☐ **(VSI) Very Seriously Ill/Injured** Illness/Injury is of such a severity that life is imminently endangered. Family members are requested at bedside immediately. *Please note this is an internal DOD casualty assistance designation used by DOD healthcare providers.*

  ☐ **(SI) Seriously Ill/Injured** Illness/injury is of such severity that there is cause for immediate concern, but there is no imminent danger to life. Family members are requested at bedside. *Please note this is an internal DOD casualty assistance designation used by DOD healthcare providers.*

  ☐ **OTHER Ill/Injured** A serious injury or illness that may render the servicemember medically unfit to perform the duties of the member's office, grade, rank, or rating.

  ☐ **NONE OF THE ABOVE.** *Note to Employee: If this box is checked, you may still be eligible to take leave to care for a covered family member with a "serious health condition" under 29 C.F.R. § 825.113 of the FMLA. If such leave is requested, you may be required to complete DOL FORM WH-380-F or an employer-provided form seeking the same information.*

PART C: AMOUNT OF LEAVE NEEDED

For the medical condition checked in Part B, complete all that apply. Some questions seek a response as to the frequency or duration of a condition, treatment, etc. Your answer should be your **best estimate** based upon your medical knowledge, experience, and examination of the patient. Be as specific as you can; terms such as "lifetime," "unknown," or "indeterminate" may not be sufficient to determine FMLA coverage.

(7)   Due to the condition, the servicemember will need care for a **continuous period of time**, including any time for treatment and recovery. Provide your **best estimate** of the beginning date ________________ *(mm/dd/yyyy)* and end date ____________ *(mm/dd/yyyy)* for this period of time.

(8)   Due to the condition, it is medically necessary for the servicemember to attend **planned medical treatment** appointments (scheduled medical visits). Provide your **best estimate** of the duration of the treatment(s), including any period(s) of recovery ____ *(e.g. 3 days/week)*

(9)   Due to the condition, it is medically necessary for the servicemember to receive care on an **intermittent basis** (periodically), such as the care needed because of episodic flare-ups of the condition or assisting with the servicemember's recovery. Provide your **best estimate** of how often (frequency) and how long (the duration) the intermittent episodes will likely last.

   Over the next 6 months, intermittent care is estimated to occur ___________________________ times per (☐ day / ☐ week / ☐ month) and are likely to last approximately ____________ (☐ hours / ☐ days) per episode.

Signature of
Health Care Provider ____ **Date** ______________ *(mm/dd/yyyy)*

Form WH-385-V: Certification for Serious Injury or Illness of a Veteran for Military Caregiver Leave

Certification for Serious Injury
or Illness of a Veteran for
Military Caregiver Leave
(Family and Medical Leave Act)

U.S. Department of Labor
Wage and Hour Division

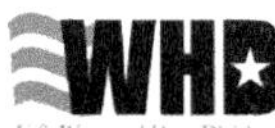

DO NOT SEND COMPLETED FORM TO THE DEPARTMENT OF LABOR; RETURN TO THE EMPLOYEE

OMB Control Number: 1235-0003
Expires: 8/31/2021

Notice to the EMPLOYER

The Family and Medical Leave Act (FMLA) provides that an employer may require an employee seeking military caregiver leave under the FMLA leave due to a serious injury or illness of a covered veteran to submit a certification providing sufficient facts to support the request for leave. Your response is voluntary. While you are not required to use this form, you may not ask the employee to provide more information than allowed under the FMLA regulations, 29 CFR 825.310. Employers must generally maintain records and documents relating to medical certifications, recertifications, or medical histories of employees or employees' family members, created for FMLA purposes as confidential medical records in separate files/records from the usual personnel files and in accordance with 29 CFR 1630.14(c)(1), if the Americans with Disabilities Act applies, and in accordance with 29 CFR 1635.9, if the Genetic Information Nondiscrimination Act applies.

SECTION I: For completion by the EMPLOYEE and/or the VETERAN for whom the employee is requesting leave

INSTRUCTIONS to the EMPLOYEE and/or VETERAN: Please complete Section I before having Section II completed. The FMLA permits an employer to require that an employee submit a timely, complete, and sufficient certification to support a request for military caregiver leave under the FMLA leave due to a serious injury or illness of a covered veteran. If requested by the employer, your response is required to obtain or retain the benefit of FMLA-protected leave. 29 U.S.C. 2613, 2614(c)(3). Failure to do so may result in a denial of an employee's FMLA request. 29 CFR 825.310(f). The employer must give an employee at least 15 calendar days to return this form to the employer.

(This section must be completed before Section II can be completed by a health care provider.)

Part A: EMPLOYEE INFORMATION

Name and address of employer (this is the employer of the employee requesting leave to care for a veteran):

____

Name of employee requesting leave to care for a veteran:

____

| First | Middle | Last |

Name of veteran (for whom employee is requesting leave):

____

| First | Middle | Last |

Relationship of employee to veteran:

Spouse☐   Parent☐   Son☐   Daughter☐   Next of Kin ☐ (please specify relationship):

Part B: VETERAN INFORMATION

(1)   Date of the veteran's discharge:

____

(2)   Was the veteran **dishonorably** discharged or released from the Armed Forces (including the National Guard or Reserves)? Yes☐   No☐

(3)   Please provide the veteran's military branch, rank and unit at the time of discharge:

____

(4)   Is the veteran receiving medical treatment, recuperation, or therapy for an injury or illness?
       Yes☐   No☐

Part C: CARE TO BE PROVIDED TO THE VETERAN

Describe the care to be provided to the veteran and an estimate of the leave needed to provide the care:

____

____

SECTION II: For completion by: (1) a United States Department of Defense ("DOD") health care provider; (2) a United States Department of Veterans Affairs ("VA") health care provider; (3) a DOD TRICARE network authorized private health care provider; (4) a DOD non-network TRICARE authorized private health care provider; or (5) a health care provider as defined in 29 CFR 825.125.

INSTRUCTIONS to the HEALTH CARE PROVIDER: The employee named in Section I has requested leave under the military caregiver leave provision of the FMLA to care for a family member who is a veteran. For purposes of FMLA military caregiver leave, a serious injury or illness means an injury or illness incurred by the servicemember in the line of duty on active duty in the Armed Forces (or that existed before the beginning of the servicemember's active duty and was aggravated by service in the line of duty on active duty in the Armed Forces) and manifested itself before or after the servicemember became a veteran, and is:

> (i) a continuation of a serious injury or illness that was incurred or aggravated when the covered veteran was a member of the Armed Forces and rendered the servicemember unable to perform the duties of the servicemember's office, grade, rank, or rating; or
> (ii) a physical or mental condition for which the covered veteran has received a U.S. Department of Veterans Affairs Service Related Disability Rating (VASRD) of 50 percent or greater, and such VASRD rating is based, in whole or in part, on the condition precipitating the need for military caregiver leave; or
> (iii) a physical or mental condition that substantially impairs the covered veteran's ability to secure or follow a substantially gainful occupation by reason of a disability or disabilities related to military service, or would do so absent treatment; or
> (iv) an injury, including a psychological injury, on the basis of which the covered veteran has been enrolled in the Department of Veterans' Affairs Program of Comprehensive Assistance for Family Caregivers.

A complete and sufficient certification to support a request for FMLA military caregiver leave due to a covered veteran's serious injury or illness includes written documentation confirming that the veteran's injury or illness was incurred in the line of duty on active duty or existed before the beginning of the veteran's active duty and was aggravated by service in the line of duty on active duty, and that the veteran is undergoing treatment, recuperation, or therapy for such injury or illness by a health care provider listed above. Answer fully and completely all applicable parts. Several questions seek a response as to the frequency or duration of a condition, treatment, etc. Your answer should be your best estimate based upon your medical knowledge, experience, and examination of the patient. Be as specific as you can; terms such as "lifetime," "unknown," or "indeterminate" may not be sufficient to determine FMLA military caregiver leave coverage. Limit your responses to the veteran's condition for which the employee is seeking leave. Do not provide information about genetic tests, as defined in 29 CFR 1635.3(f), or genetic services, as defined in 29 CFR 1635.3(e).

(Please ensure that Section I has been completed before completing this section. Please be sure to sign the form on the last page and return this form to the employee requesting leave (See Section I, Part A above). **DO NOT SEND THE COMPLETED FORM TO THE WAGE AND HOUR DIVISION.**)

Part A: HEALTH CARE PROVIDER INFORMATION

Health care provider's name and business address:

____

Telephone: (   ) _________________ Fax: (   ) _________________ Email: ____

Type of Practice/Medical Specialty: ____

Please indicate if you are:
☐ a DOD health care provider

☐ a VA health care provider

☐ a DOD TRICARE network authorized private health care provider

☐ a DOD non-network TRICARE authorized private health care provider

☐ other health care provider

              CONTINUED ON NEXT PAGE   Form WH-385-V Revised May 2015

PART B: MEDICAL STATUS

Note: If you are unable to make certain of the military-related determinations contained in Part B, you are permitted to rely upon determinations from an authorized DOD representative (such as, DOD Recovery Care Coordinator) or an authorized VA representative.

(1)   The Veteran's medical condition is:

☐ A continuation of a serious injury or illness that was incurred or aggravated when the covered veteran was a member of the Armed Forces and rendered the servicemember unable to perform the duties of the servicemember's office, grade, rank, or rating.

☐ A physical or mental condition for which the covered veteran has received a U.S. Department of Veterans Affairs Service Related Disability Rating (VASRD) of 50% or higher, and such VASRD rating is based, in whole or in part, on the condition precipitating the need for military caregiver leave.

☐ A physical or mental condition that substantially impairs the covered veteran's ability to secure or follow a substantially gainful occupation by reason of a disability or disabilities related to military service, or would do so absent treatment.

☐ An injury, including a psychological injury, on the basis of which the covered veteran is enrolled in the Department of Veterans' Affairs Program of Comprehensive Assistance for Family Caregivers.

☐ None of the above.

(2)   Is the veteran being treated for a condition which was incurred or aggravated by service in the line of duty on active duty in the Armed Forces?   Yes☐ No☐

(3)   Approximate date condition commenced: ____

(4)   Probable duration of condition and/or need for care: ____

(5)   Is the veteran undergoing medical treatment, recuperation, or therapy for this condition?   Yes☐   No☐

If yes, please describe medical treatment, recuperation or therapy:

____

PART C: VETERAN'S NEED FOR CARE BY FAMILY MEMBER

"Need for care" encompasses both physical and psychological care. It includes situations where, for example, due to his or her serious injury or illness, the veteran is unable to care for his or her own basic medical, hygienic, or nutritional needs or safety, or is unable to transport him or herself to the doctor. It also includes providing psychological comfort and reassurance which would be beneficial to the veteran who is receiving inpatient or home care.

(1)   Will the veteran need care for a single continuous period of time, including any time for treatment and recovery?
Yes☐   No☐

If yes, estimate the beginning and ending dates for this period of time: _____________________________

(2)   Will the veteran require periodic follow-up treatment appointments? Yes☐   No☐

If yes, estimate the treatment schedule: ____

(3)   Is there a medical necessity for the veteran to have periodic care for these follow-up treatment appointments?
Yes☐   No☐

(4)   Is there a medical necessity for the veteran to have periodic care for other than scheduled follow-up treatment appointments (<u>e.g.</u>, episodic flare-ups of medical condition)?   Yes☐   No☐

If yes, please estimate the frequency and duration of the periodic care:

____

____

Signature of Health Care Provider: _________________________________ **Date:** ___________________

A Comprehensive Discussion of Intermittent and Reduced Schedule FMLA Leave

FMLA leave taken on an intermittent or reduced schedule basis has been discussed throughout this book. Chapter 2 discusses the circumstances under which it must be granted to employees. Chapter 3 explains how to calculate the amount of time an employee has used for intermittent or reduced schedule leave. Chapter 4 discusses how to handle benefits while an employee is on it. Nevertheless, seeing all the material related to intermittent and reduced schedule leave in one place may be helpful to some employers. This appendix, therefore, consolidates the discussions of intermittent and reduced schedule leave that appear throughout the book here in one place so that employers may get a unified discussion of the challenges these types of leave pose.

Intermittent and reduced schedule leave are designed for those serious health conditions (whether of an employee or a family member) that do not require leave in continuous blocks of time. Intermittent and reduced schedule leave are not an accommodation—the FMLA requires employers to grant requests for reduced schedule or intermittent leave when it is medically necessary.[1] Reduced schedule FMLA leave is more straightforward than intermittent leave, so it is discussed first.

Reduced Schedule Leave

The FMLA regulations define "reduced leave schedule" as "a leave schedule that reduces an employee's usual number of working hours per workweek, or hours per workday. A reduced leave schedule is a change in the employee's schedule for

---

1. *See* 29 C.F.R. § 825.202(b).

a period of time, normally from full-time to part-time."[2] In other words, reduced schedule leave is a temporary reduction in the number of hours an employee works during the week. It is usually taken when an employee is recovering from a serious health condition and is unable to work full time.[3] It may also be taken when an employee is caring for a family member with a serious health condition who does not need assistance full time. Employees who need FMLA leave for the birth, adoption, or foster care placement of a child may request to take it on a reduced schedule basis (that is, to work part-time for longer than twelve weeks rather than taking full-time FMLA leave and returning to work full-time at the end of twelve weeks). Whether to grant reduced schedule leave for the birth, adoption, or foster care placement of a child is within the employer's sole discretion. It is not a right.[4] But reduced schedule leave is a right when it is *medically necessary* due to the circumstances of an employee's or a family member's serious health condition.

Intermittent Leave

The FMLA regulations define *intermittent leave* as "FMLA leave taken in separate blocks of time due to a single qualifying reason."[5] Intermittent leave may be needed because the nature of the employee's illness is episodic. Episodic illnesses include but are hardly limited to diabetes, asthma, cardiac arrythmias, migraine headaches, Crohn's disease, and seizures. Intermittent leave may also be needed because the treatment of an employee's serious health condition is episodic, as dialysis is, for example, or because it takes place periodically over a period of time, like chemotherapy.

How to Know if Reduced Schedule
or Intermittent Leave Is Appropriate

Reduced schedule leave and intermittent leave are two distinct variations of FMLA leave. As mentioned above, they share a requirement for their use, namely that such leave best accommodates an employee's or family member's serious health condition.[6] In other words, they must be medically necessary for an employee to be entitled to them. The need for intermittent or reduced schedule leave must be indicated on the FMLA medical certification, either Form WH-380-E (for the employee's health condition) or Form WH-380-F (for the family member's), on page 3, section II, part B (shown in Figure 1).

---

2. *Id.* § 825.202(a).
3. *See id.* § 825.202(b)(1).
4. *See id.* § 825.202(c).
5. *Id.* § 825.202(a).
6. *Id.* § 825.202(b).

Figure 1

PART B: Amount of Leave Needed

For the medical condition(s) checked in Part A, complete all that apply. Several questions seek a response as to the frequency or duration of a condition, treatment, etc. Your answer should be your **best estimate** based upon your medical knowledge, experience, and examination of the patient. Be as specific as you can; terms such as "lifetime," "unknown," or "indeterminate" may not be sufficient to determine FMLA coverage.

(5) Due to the condition, the patient (☐ had / ☐ will have) **planned medical treatment(s)** (scheduled medical visits) (e.g.psychotherapy, prenatal appointments) on the following date(s): _______________________________________

____

(6) Due to the condition, the patient (☐ was / ☐ will be) **referred to other health care provider(s)** for evaluation or treatment(s).

State the nature of such treatments: (e.g. cardiologist, physical therapy) _______________________________________

Provide your **best estimate** of the beginning date _________________ (mm/dd/yyyy) and end date _______________ (mm/dd/yyyy).

for the treatment(s).

Provide your **best estimate** of the duration of the treatment(s), including any period(s) of recovery (e.g. 3 days/week)

(7) Due to the condition, it is medically necessary for the employee to work a **reduced schedule**.

Provide your **best estimate** of the reduced schedule the employee is able to work. From _________________ (mm/dd/yyyy)

to _________________ (mm/dd/yyyy) the employee is able to work: (e.g., 5 hours/day, up to 25 hours a week)

(8) Due to the condition, the patient (☐ was / ☐ will be) **incapacitated for a continuous period of time**, including any time

for treatment(s) and/or recovery.

Provide your **best estimate** of the beginning date _________________ (mm/dd/yyyy) and end date _______________ (mm/dd/yyyy).

for the period of incapacity.

(9) Due to the condition, it (☐ was / ☐ is / ☐ will be) medically necessary for the employee to be absent from work on an

intermittent basis (periodically), including for any episodes of incapacity i.e., episodic flare-ups. Provide your **best estimate** of how often (frequency) and how long (duration) the episodes of incapacity will likely last.

Over the next 6 months, episodes of incapacity are estimated to occur ____________________________________ times per

(☐ day ☐ week ☐ month) and are likely to last approximately ____________________ (☐ hours ☐ days) per episode.

The employer's approval of reduced schedule or intermittent leave must be indicated on the Designation Notice, Form WH-382. When the need for intermittent or reduced schedule leave is foreseeable because of a planned course of medical treatment, the employer and employee must attempt to work out a treatment schedule that does not unduly disrupt the employer's operations, subject to the approval of the medical provider.[7]

Managing Reduced Schedule and Intermittent Leave

It does not diminish the great benefits that the FMLA provides to individual employees to say that FMLA leave is almost always an inconvenience to an employer. The work that an employee on leave was hired to do does not go away, and employers must figure out how to get that work done in the employee's absence. Reduced schedule and intermittent leave complicate matters even more because

---

7. *Id.* § 825.302(f).

the employee is there some of the time, but not enough of the time to get all the work done. In addition, intermittent leave frequently involves leave that is unforeseeable. For example, an employee cannot predict when they will have a seizure or a flare-up of a condition. Consequently, the employer cannot plan for how to cover the employee's work. And for all the employees who use intermittent leave only for its intended purpose, there are always a few who abuse their intermittent leave. There are two primary strategies for dealing with the difficulties posed by reduced schedule and intermittent leave.

Temporary Transfer to an Alternate Position

In its regulations, the U.S. Department of Labor (DOL) expressly allows an employer to transfer an employee on intermittent or reduced schedule leave when the employee's position is one that requires someone to work full time or to be regularly and reliably present. The transfer to an alternate position that better suits the FMLA schedule must be temporary, and the employee must receive equal pay and benefits. The job duties, however, do not have to be equivalent. The employee must be restored to the same or an equivalent job at the conclusion of the leave.[8]

Stringent Call-In Procedures

The regulations make clear that employees on intermittent leave may still be required to comply with the employer's usual notice and procedure requirements for reporting absences, unless unusual circumstances prevent notification.[9] Failure to comply with the employer's call-in or reporting policy may be cause for termination.[10] And while employers may not ask an employee on intermittent leave to return a medical certification or medical fitness-for-duty certification each time the employee takes an instance of intermittent leave, they may ask employees to themselves certify that they were absent due to already-approved FMLA intermittent leave rather than allowing employees simply to call in "sick" without specifying whether the call is for job-protected FMLA leave. Absences for illnesses or other events not covered by intermittent FMLA leave are not job protected and may be the basis of discipline or even discharge. Employers need to know (and track) which absences are which.

---

8. *Id.* § 825.204. *See* Howard v. Inova Health Care Servs., 302 F. App'x 166, 172–74 (4th Cir. 2008) (transfer to alternate position was not FMLA interference); Claffey v. Wegmans Food Mkts., Inc., No. 07–CV–6430, 2010 WL 811306, at *5 (W.D.N.Y. Mar. 2, 2010) (same).

9. 29 C.F.R. § 825.302(d).

10. *See, e.g.,* , Ritenour v. Tenn. Dep't of Hum. Servs., 497 F. App'x 521 at **7 (6th Cir. 2012); Bacon v. Hennepin Cnty. Med. Ctr., 550 F.3d 711, 714–15 (8th Cir. 2008); *see also* Lewis v. Holsum of Fort Wayne, Inc., 278 F.3d 706, 710–11 (7th Cir. 2002) (employee failed to call in after requesting indefinite leave to spend time with newborn child).

Recertification

Employers may require recertification of reduced schedule leave and intermittent leave every six months. They may reasonably expect the absences of employees on intermittent leave to be consistent with their medical certification. Employees whose health care providers certify that they will likely need leave two or three days each month are not entitled to FMLA job-protected leave for eight to ten days per month, or to leave every Friday and Monday. When the number of FMLA-leave absences an employee reports is greater than what the medical certification calls for, the regulations allow an employer to ask for a recertification.[11] It may well be that the severity of an employee's illness has increased or that the employee is suffering complications from the disease or from treatment. Or the employee may be abusing intermittent leave. The employer has a right to know.

Consider the case *Whittington v. Tyson Foods.* There, an employee with anxiety and depression was certified by his psychiatrist for occasional leave in four-to-five-day increments. When the employee took a ten-day leave as FMLA leave and later took sixteen consecutive days of FMLA leave, his employer asked for recertification. The employee did not, however, provide a recertification showing a need for longer increments of leave. His employer fired him. The employee sued, alleging that the employer had interfered with his FMLA leave by requesting recertification before the six-month period generally required for recertification had passed. The court, however, granted judgment in favor of the employer, finding the request for recertification reasonable since the employee's use of intermittent leave was not consistent with the original certification.[12]

Recording Leave

The FMLA regulations require employers to record both intermittent and reduced schedule leave using the shortest period of time that it uses to account for other forms of leave such as sick, vacation, and personal leave. The period of time used to account for intermittent or reduced schedule leave, however, *cannot be in greater than one-hour increments.*[13] An employer also may not require an employee to take more time off than is necessary to accommodate the need for the intermittent or reduced schedule leave. For example, if an employee needs to be away from work for only two hours a day, the employer may not require the employee to take a half day off.[14]

---

11. On the rules governing recertification, see Chapter 5, pages 75–76.
12. Whittington v. Tyson Foods, Inc., 21 F.4th 997, 1001–02 (8th Cir. 2021).
13. 29 C.F.R. § 825.205(a).
14. *See id.* § 825.203.

Measuring the Amount of Leave Taken

An employee is entitled to twelve weeks of FMLA leave. Therefore, the basis of the entitlement is the workweek.[15] Here are some examples of how leave is calculated on that basis.

- If an employee on continuous FMLA leave who normally works five days a week begins FMLA leave on a Monday and returns three weeks and three days later on a Thursday, that employee will have used three and three-fifths weeks of FMLA leave.
- If a full-time employee who would otherwise work eight-hour days works four-hour days under a reduced leave schedule, she will use half a week of FMLA leave each week.
- An employee who regularly works thirty hours per week but works only twenty hours a week under a reduced leave schedule uses one-third of a week of FMLA leave each week.[16]

Converting Hours to Weeks of Leave

There is generally no need to convert an employee's FMLA entitlement to twelve weeks of leave into hours, even if an employee is on a reduced schedule leave. Employees on a fixed reduced schedule leave will work a set fraction of a workweek every week. If an employee takes an instance of intermittent leave in increments of a full workday, it is easy to know how much FMLA leave the employee has used. In a five-day workweek, one workday will be one-fifth of a week of FMLA leave. A half day would be one-tenth of a week. But the nature of the circumstances that require intermittent leave do not always make for such neat calculations. Often, employees on intermittent leave will take three hours here, five hours there, and on another occasion, a day followed by a partial day. In these situations, it makes more sense to record an employee's FMLA leave in increments of an hour (or less if appropriate).

But the regulations emphasize that when an employer does record FMLA leave in hours, it must be sure that it (or its timekeeping and payroll software) does so *proportionately*.[17] Because leave is based on workweeks, employees who regularly work a 40-hour workweek will be entitled to more *hours* of FMLA leave than those who regularly work a 35-hour workweek. For example, the employee who works a 40-hour workweek will be entitled to 480 hours of FMLA leave (40 hours × 12 weeks). Her counterpart who works a 35-hour workweek will be entitled to only 420 hours of FMLA leave (35 hours × 12 weeks). The conversion into FMLA hours must be based on the number of hours that the employee is regularly scheduled to work.

---

15. *Id.* § 825.205(b).
16. *Id.* § 825.205(b)(1).
17. *Id.*

Fluctuating Workweeks

If an employee's schedule fluctuates from week to week to such an extent that an employer is unable to determine with any certainty how many hours the employee would have worked if they were not on FMLA leave, then the employer should use a weekly average of the hours the employee was *scheduled to work* over the 12 months before the start of the FMLA leave period. The regulations specify that this calculation *must include* any hours for which the employee took leave of any type.[18] The calculation of the number of hours of FMLA leave available to the employee would then proceed as outlined above. For example, if an employee's weekly average turned out to be 46 hours per week, then the employee would be entitled to a total of 552 hours of FMLA leave (46 hours × 12 weeks).

Overtime

The regulations permit employers to count overtime hours that an employee would have been *required* to work as hours of FMLA leave that count against the employee's 12-week entitlement.[19] Here's an example from DOL. A nonexempt employee who would normally be required to work for 48 hours each week (that is, eight hours' overtime), is currently unable to work more than 40 hours because of a serious health condition. That employee would then use eight hours of FMLA leave out of the 48-hour workweek, or ⅙ of a week of FMLA leave. But if overtime is voluntary, the story is different. Voluntary overtime hours that an employee does not work due to an FMLA-qualifying reason may not be counted against the employee's FMLA leave entitlement.[20]

---

18. *Id.* § 825.205(b)(3).
19. *Id.* § 825.205(c).
20. *Id.*

The Difference Between a Serious Health Condition Under the FMLA and a Disability Under the Americans with Disabilities Act

It would be easy to think that the FMLA's "serious health condition" is the same thing as a "disability" under the Americans with Disabilities Act (ADA). But as it turns out, it is not. While both a serious health condition and a disability have the potential to interfere with an employee's attendance and job performance, they are different concepts, and the existence of each has very different consequences for both employers and employees.

Background

The FMLA requires employers to grant eligible employees a total of twelve work-weeks of job-protected, unpaid leave during any twelve-month period because the employee needs to care for a spouse, child, or parent with a *serious health condition*, or because of the employee's own *serious health condition* if the condition makes the employee unable to perform the job (in addition to leave for birth, adoption, or foster placement of a child and military FMLA leave). Thus, the purpose of the FMLA is to give employees a reasonable but limited amount of time in which to take care of their own or their family members' health issues without losing their jobs.

The ADA has an entirely different purpose. Like Title VII of the Civil Rights Act of 1964 and the Age Discrimination in Employment Act, the ADA is an anti-discrimination statute. It prohibits employers from discriminating *on the basis of disability* against a qualified individual in hiring, promotion, and discharge of employees and in all other terms and conditions of employment. Under the ADA, an employer's failure to reasonably accommodate an employee's disability so that the employee may continue to work is itself a form of discrimination.[1]

---

1. *See* 42 U.S.C. § 12112(b)(5).

Serious Health Condition Under the FMLA

The FMLA's definition of a serious health condition is a complicated one.[2] A serious health condition is an illness, injury, impairment, physical condition, or mental condition that involves

- any period of incapacity requiring *an absence from work of more than three full, consecutive calendar days* that also involves one in-person visit to a health care provider within the first seven days of illness and either a second visit within the first thirty days or a regimen of continuing treatment (such as treatment with prescription drugs) under the supervision of a heath-care provider;[3]
- *any* period of incapacity or treatment connected with inpatient care;[4]
- *any* period of incapacity due to pregnancy;[5]
- *any* period of incapacity or treatment due to a *chronic health condition,* such as asthma, diabetes, or epilepsy;[6]
- *any* period of incapacity that is long term or permanent due to a condition for which treatment may not be effective (cancer, for example, or AIDS);[7] or
- *any* absence to receive multiple treatments (and to recover from the treatments) for a condition that would likely result in an incapacity for more than three consecutive days if left untreated (examples of treatments include physical therapy, chemotherapy, and dialysis).[8]

The U.S. Department of Labor's FMLA regulations advise that colds, stomach viruses, the flu, and similar conditions do not qualify as serious health conditions unless they require inpatient care or continuing treatment by a health care provider (one visit and a regimen of care under a doctor's supervision or two visits within thirty days). Bed rest, drinking fluids, exercise, taking over-the-counter medications, and similar activities that can be initiated without a visit to a health care provider do not constitute regimens of continuing treatment for FMLA purposes.[9]

It is worth noting that only one of the circumstances defined as a serious health condition requires a minimal period of incapacity (namely, more than three full,

---

2. *See* 29 C.F.R. § 825.113 (defining *serious health condition*).

3. *Id.* § 825.115.

4. *See id.* § 825.114.

5. *See id.* § 825.120.

6. *See id.* §§ 825.102, .115(c). The FMLA regulations define a chronic health condition as one that continues over an extended period of time, requires treatment by a health care provider at least twice a year, and may cause episodic rather than continuing periods of incapacity, thus requiring leave of periods from an hour to several weeks rather than a continuous period. *See id.*

7. *See id.* § 825.115(d).

8. *Id.* § 825.115(e).

9. *Id.* § 825.113(c).

consecutive calendar days).[10] This covers many acute illnesses and infections as well as medical procedures that require prolonged recovery and that generally result in the employee returning to work at the conclusion of leave. All the other instances of a serious health condition, whether related to inpatient care, pregnancy, chronic health conditions, incurable conditions, or treatments for such conditions, are defined simply as *"any* period of incapacity" or *"any* absence." These criteria cover conditions that are not acute but episodic, or require treatments that are episodic. The conditions that fall into this category are numerous and range from the severe morning sickness that sometimes accompanies pregnancy to indefinite conditions like asthma, arthritis, migraines or diabetes.[11] For these, the FMLA makes a provision for intermittent (recurring) job-protected leave and reduced schedule job-protected leave.[12]

The FMLA was enacted in 1993. In 2008, it was amended to add two additional forms of job-protected leave for the family members of American servicemen: qualifying-exigency leave and military caregiver leave. Military caregiver leave provides job-protected leave for an employee to care for a family member who is a member of the military and who has a service-related serious illness or injury. Although the definition of *serious illness or injury* for the purposes of military caregiver leave is like that of *serious health condition,* the two are not identical. For a discussion of *serious illness or injury,* see Chapter 9.

Disability Under the ADA

The ADA defines *disability* as a "physical or mental impairment that substantially limits one or more major life activities." The ADA provides that this definition is to be construed in favor of broad coverage of individuals.[13]

Impairments

Most medical disorders will qualify as impairments under the ADA. It does not matter how the employee came to have an impairment. For example, lung cancer is an impairment even if the employee was a heavy smoker who continues to smoke after diagnosis. A back injury caused by an automobile accident in which the employee was negligent is still an impairment.

---

10. *See id.* § 825.115(a).
11. *Id.* § 825.115(b)–(e).
12. See Appendix B, *A Guide to Intermittent and Reduced Schedule FMLA Leave.*
13. 42 U.S.C. § 12102(1).

Examples of conditions that would be considered impairments under the ADA include

- alcoholism,
- heart palpitations,
- chest pain,
- back and knee strains,
- hypothyroidism,
- abdominal distress,
- tennis elbow,
- depression,
- panic disorder, and
- erectile dysfunction.

Examples of conditions that would not be considered impairments include

- pregnancy (uncomplicated);
- normal deviations in an individual's height, weight, or strength;
- left-handedness;
- being irresponsible; and
- being overweight.

As the statutory definition makes clear, a person must have more than a simple impairment to be covered by the ADA. An impairment rises to the level of a disability only if it substantially limits an employee's ability to perform a major life activity as compared with most people in the general population.[14] An impairment does not have to prevent or even significantly restrict a person from a major life activity to be considered substantially limiting. "Substantially limits" is something less than "almost completely prevents."[15] And so-called "mitigating measures," like the use of assistive devices such as wheelchairs or of prescription medications, are not to be considered in determining whether an impairment is substantially limiting. If the impairment is substantially limiting without the use of mitigating measures, it qualifies as a disability under the ADA (the sole exception to this rule is the use of ordinary eyeglasses or contact lenses).[16]

Like their treatment under the FMLA, episodic impairments or conditions that are in remission are disabilities if they substantially limit a major life activity when they occur or are active. *Minor* impairments that are expected to last fewer than six months are not disabilities. But an impairment that substantially limits a person in a major life activity for fewer than six months is still a disability.[17]

---

14. 29 C.F.R. § 1630.2(a).
15. *See id.* § 1630.2(j).
16. *See id.* § 1630.2(j)(5)–(6).
17. *Id.* § 1630.2(j)(1)(ix).

Exclusions from ADA coverage

The ADA expressly excludes current drug use from coverage but covers alcoholism.[18]

Major Life Activities

To qualify as a disability under the ADA, an impairment must significantly limit a person's ability to engage in a major life activity. What is a major life activity, anyway? The ADA defines major life activities by example. They include but are by no means limited to

- caring for oneself,
- performing manual tasks,
- walking,
- seeing,
- hearing,
- speaking,
- breathing,
- learning,
- eating,
- thinking,
- reading, and
- working.[19]

Major life activities also include major bodily functions. Impairments of these sorts of functions are not usually visible to an employer:

- functions of the immune system,
- neurological and brain functions,
- normal cellular growth,
- respiratory function,
- circulatory function,
- digestion,
- reproductive functions,
- endocrine functions, and
- bowel functions.[20]

---

18. *Id.* § 1630.3(a).
19. 29 U.S.C. § 12102(2)(A).
20. *Id.* § 12102(2)(B).

Table 1. Some predictable assessments of disability identified by the Equal Opportunity Employment Commission

Assessment	Substantially impaired activity
Autism	Brain function
Bipolar disorder	Brain function
Blindness	Seeing
Cancer	Normal cell growth
Deafness	Hearing
Diabetes	Endocrine function
Major depressive disorder	Brain function
Obsessive-compulsive disorder	Brain function
Partially or completely missing limbs, requiring wheelchair	Musculoskeletal function
Post-traumatic stress disorder	Brain function
Schizophrenia	Brain function

Note: See 29 C.F.R. § 1630.2(j)(3) (providing the EEOC's full list of predictable assessments of disability).

Per Se Disabilities or "Predictable Assessments"

The guiding principle of disability analysis under the ADA is that each employee's impairment and its effect on one or more major life activities must be evaluated individually. Nevertheless, some conditions will almost always result in a finding that persons affected by them are substantially limited in a major life activity and are protected by the ADA. The Equal Employment Opportunity Commission (EEOC) has identified some of those impairments that it considers to result in a "predictable assessment" of disability. Table 1 lists some of them.

Pregnancy as a Disability

Pregnancy is not mentioned in the text of the ADA or in the EEOC's ADA regulations. In the interpretive appendix to the regulations, the EEOC says that "conditions, such as pregnancy, that are not the result of a physiological disorder are also not impairments. However, a pregnancy-related impairment that substantially limits a major life activity is a disability."[21] Thus, an employee who is suffering from pregnancy complications that require her to be on bed rest for ten weeks will

---

21. 29 C.F.R. pt. 1630 app. § 1630.2(g).

be a person with a disability, and an employee's preeclampsia has been found to substantially limit the operation of her circulatory and urinary functions, rendering her a person with a disability. In its 2015 *Enforcement Guidance on Pregnancy Discrimination and Related Issues*, the EEOC gives further examples of the ways in which a complication of pregnancy could result in a substantial impairment that gives rise to a disability:

> pregnancy-related anemia (affecting normal cell growth); pregnancy-related sciatica (affecting musculoskeletal function); pregnancy-related carpal tunnel syndrome (affecting neurological function); gestational diabetes (affecting endocrine function); nausea that can cause severe dehydration (affecting digestive or genitourinary function); abnormal heart rhythms that may require treatment (affecting cardiovascular function); swelling, especially in the legs, due to limited circulation (affecting circulatory function); and depression (affecting brain function).[22]

Note, however, that the courts have been clear that periodic nausea, vomiting, dizziness, severe headaches, and fatigue are not disabilities within the meaning of the ADA because they are part and parcel of a normal pregnancy. Court cases emphasize that morning sickness, stress, nausea, back pain, swelling, and headaches or physiological changes related to a pregnancy are not impairments unless they exceed normal ranges or are attributable to a disorder.[23]

The treatment of pregnancy under the ADA thus differs from its treatment under the FMLA. Under the FMLA, normal incidents of pregnancy such as morning sickness, nausea, and the like that result in incapacity, even incapacity that lasts only several hours, qualify for job-protected leave. Under the ADA, normal side effects of pregnancy are not protected. Only complications and impairments that go beyond those experienced by the general population would entitle an employee to a reasonable accommodation.

The passage of the Pregnant Workers Fairness Act of 2022 fills in some of the gaps in the protection of female workers in the context of pregnancy and reproductive processes, and it may prove to make the treatment of pregnancy under both the FMLA and the ADA irrelevant.[24]

---

22. *Enforcement Guidance on Pregnancy Discrimination and Related Issues*, U.S. Equal Emp. Opportunity Comm'n (June 15, 2015), https://www.eeoc.gov/laws/guidance/pregnancy _guidance.cfm.

23. *See, e.g.*, Gorman v. Wells Mfg. Corp., 340 F.3d 543 (8th Cir. 2003); Gudenkauf v. Stauffer Commc'ns, Inc., 922 F. Supp. 461 (D. Kan. 1996).

24. *See generally* 42 U.S.C. §§ 2000gg to gg-6; 29 C.F.R. pt. 1636; *see also* Diane M. Juffras, *The Pregnant Workers Fairness Act: Is Your Workplace Ready for Pregnancy Accommodations?*, Coates' Canons: NC Loc. Gov't L. (blog), pt. 1 (May 29, 2024), https:// canons.sog.unc.edu/2024/05/the-pregnant-workers-fairness-act-is-your-workplace-ready -for-pregnancy-accommodations-part-1-of-2/, pt. 2 (May 30, 2024), https://canons.sog.unc .edu/2024/05/the-pregnant-workers-fairness-act-is-your-workplace-ready-for-pregnancy -accommodations-part-2-of-2/.

Why the FMLA and the ADA Treat Medical Conditions That Cause Incapacity Differently

The FMLA's purpose is to provide a limited amount of job-protected leave for employees who are not able to work due to a health issue of their own or that of a spouse, child, or parent (as well as to provide job-protected leave for those who wish to stay home with a newborn, newly adopted child, or child newly placed for foster care). The FMLA's focus is separating short-term illnesses that keep an employee out of work for only a few days (and which can usually be handled through the use of sick leave) from those whose effects are longer lasting and require care supervised by a health care provider.

Like the FMLA, the ADA offers protections to employees with medical conditions that leave them unable to work for longer periods than just a few days. But the focus of the ADA is on the effort to find ways to restructure work or provide assistive devices to accommodate employees' medical conditions. What the ADA asks of employers is greater than under the FMLA, and the definition of *disability* under the ADA is therefore more demanding than the definition of *serious health condition* under the FMLA.

Documenting a Serious Health Condition Versus Documenting a Disability

Evaluating a serious health condition under the FMLA is relatively easy. An employer may require employees to provide medical certification of the need for FMLA leave from the employee's health care provider. As discussed in Chapter 5, the FMLA regulations set forth what information an employer is entitled to. It includes

- the approximate date on which the serious health condition began;
- its probable duration;
- a statement or description of appropriate medical facts about the patient's health condition sufficient to show the need for leave (which might include information on symptoms, diagnosis, hospitalization, doctor visits, whether medication has been prescribed, any referrals for evaluation or treatment, or any other course of continuing treatment);
- if the employee is the patient, enough information to establish the employee's inability to perform the job's essential functions, the nature of any other work restrictions, and the likely duration of such inability;
- if a covered family member is the patient, enough information to establish the need for care from the employee, as well as an estimate of the frequency and duration of the leave needed to care for the family member.[25]

---

25. *See* 29 C.F.R. § 825.306(a).

The U.S. Department of Labor, which administers the FMLA, has done employers and health care providers a great favor by developing two forms—one for an employee's own serious health condition and one for the serious health condition of an employee's family member—for employees to give to their health care provider to certify the need for FMLA leave. The forms ask for no more and no less than the law allows.[26]

There is no such approved form for employers to use when seeking medical information to support an employee's request for a reasonable accommodation because of disability. The employer's right to medical information about an employee with a nonobvious disability who has requested accommodation is clearly stated in the EEOC's ADA regulations,[27] the EEOC's enforcement guidance,[28] and decisions from federal appellate courts,[29] but there is no officially provided form to use.

Employers should resist the temptation to use the employee's FMLA medical certification form to confirm the existence of a disability and the need for accommodation. The FMLA's definition of a serious health condition is much broader than that of a disability, and the mere fact that the employee was out on FMLA leave for the same condition does not by itself mean that the condition is a disability for the purposes of the ADA.

Instead, when employees ask for accommodations under the ADA, employers should specifically ask for documentation of the restrictions that the impairment causes. An employer does not have to accept a health care provider's generalized statement that the impairment interferes with the employee's ability to perform the job or a specific job duty. The employer is entitled to know the extent of the interference. The employer should be sure to give the employee's physician a *detailed* description of the employee's actual job duties. Merely printing out the job description is unlikely to elicit the kind of information that the employer needs to evaluate the request for accommodation. Still, an employer cannot ask for more information than is necessary to establish the existence of a disability and the scope of the requested accommodation.[30]

---

26. These may be found in Appendix A, *United States Department of Labor Family and Medical Leave Act Forms.*

27. 29 C.F.R. § 1630.14.

28. EQUAL EMP. OPPORTUNITY COMM'N, QUESTIONS AND ANSWERS: ENFORCEMENT GUIDANCE ON DISABILITY RELATED INQUIRIES AND MEDICAL EXAMINATIONS UNDER THE AMERICANS WITH DISABILITIES ACT, OLC CONTROL NO. EEOC-NVTA-2000-1 (July 27, 2000), https://www.eeoc.gov/laws/guidance/questions-and-answers-enforcement-guidance -disability-related-inquiries-and-medical ("Employers also may obtain medical information about an employee when the employee has requested a reasonable accommodation and his or her disability or need for accommodation is not obvious.").

29. *E.g.,* Atkinson v. SG Ams. Sec., LLC, 693 F. App'x 436 (7th Cir. May 9, 2017); Kennedy v. Superior Printing Co., 216 F.3d 650 (6th Cir. 2000).

30. EQUAL EMP. OPPORTUNITY COMM'N, *supra* note 28 (question 11). *See* EQUAL OPPORTUNITY EMP. COMM'N, EEOC ENFORCEMENT GUIDANCE ON THE AMERICANS WITH DISABILITIES ACT AND PSYCHIATRIC DISABILITIES, No. 915.002, 1997 WL 34622315, at *11 (Mar. 25, 1997).

Choosing the Health Care Provider

Under both statutes, the employee has the right to choose the health care provider who will document the serious health condition or disability, but beyond that, the rules governing medical examination differ. Under the FMLA regulations, an employer may always require the employee to undergo an examination for a second opinion with a health care provider of the *employer's* choice at the employer's cost. (And if the employee's and the employer's health care provider disagree, the employee must obtain a certification from a third provider, again at the employer's cost; the decision of the third provider is binding.) The employee's initial medical certification does not have to be deficient for the employer to have the right to seek a second opinion. It may do so even if the initial certification is complete in all respects.[31]

The rules are a little different under the ADA. The ADA allows an employer to send an employee to a health care provider of the employer's choosing only if the employee has not provided enough information from which to determine that a disability exists, what sort of limitations it causes, and what accommodations might address them. In contrast to the FMLA, the ADA does not permit an employer to send an employee to a health care provider of the employer's own choosing for a second opinion if the employee has provided sufficient information for the employer and employee to discuss accommodations. Indeed, in an enforcement guidance, the EEOC recommends that an employer ask the employee's provider for more information before sending the employee to its own health care professional because, "an employee's health care provider frequently is in the best position to provide information about the employee's limitations."[32]

Under the ADA, as with the FMLA, if an employer requires an employee to go to a health care provider of the employer's choice, the employer must pay all costs associated with the visit.[33]

Conclusion

While the difference between an FMLA serious health condition and an ADA disability may appear subtle, they must not be confused. Confusing the two will likely interfere with an employee's rights under the respective statutes and may lead to litigation. Using the U.S. Department of Labor's medical certification forms will help keep an employer on the FMLA straight and narrow, but complying with its

---

31. 29 C.F.R. § 825.307. For a more complete discussion of second and third opinions in medical certification, see Chapter 5, pages 73–75.

32. EQUAL OPPORTUNITY EMP. COMM'N, *supra* note 28 (question 11).

33. EQUAL OPPORTUNITY EMP. COMM'N, EEOC ENFORCEMENT GUIDANCE ON THE AMERICANS WITH DISABILITIES ACT AND PSYCHIATRIC DISABILITIES, *supra* note 30, at *11.

responsibilities under the ADA requires an employer to be proactive and to draft an individualized request for information about an employee's impairment from that employee's health care provider.

Index

C

D

O

P

Q

R

S